MAUD'S JOURNEY
A LIFE FROM ART

BY MAUD MORGAN

NEW EARTH PUBLICATIONS
Berkeley, California

First edition published in 1995 by

NEW EARTH PUBLICATIONS
1921 Ashby Avenue
Berkeley, CA 94703

Library of Congress Catalog Card Number: 95-069350
ISBN 0-915117-16-9

Printed in the United States of America

COVERS

Front: *My Rain Hat* (1993), Oil on canvas, 30 x 24 in.
Painting photographed by Kathy Chapman
Back: Photograph on back cover is by Jaime Cope

DEDICATION

This book is dedicated
with love and gratitude to my children
Alexis and Victoria
who have unflinchingly nurtured me
through the eight years of its creation.

ACKNOWLEDGMENTS

My appreciation and thanks go out to the many people who made my book possible. To my son Alexis who typed it; to Marie Cantlon who started the process of turning me into a writer; to Herbert Patchel who, from the beginning believed in what I was trying to do and helped me do it; to Kyra Montagu whose solid support was invaluable throughout; to Jill Kneerim for her expert and specific guidance at the end; to Maryel Locke for putting some needed professionalism into my hit or miss methods and for introducing me to Clifton Ross and New Earth Press; to my dealer, Barbara Singer who has always managed to fill the niches which I have left unattended and last but not least to my invaluable graphic designer Kate Canfield.

A maverick, an unbranded calf,

so named after a Texas Pioneer,

Samuel A. Maverick, born 1803,

who neglected to brand his cattle,

hence an unbranded animal,

especially a motherless calf,

formerly customarily claimed

by the first one branding it.

—Webster Collegiate Dictionary,
1946, 5th edition

CONTENTS

GROWING
UP
SLOWLY

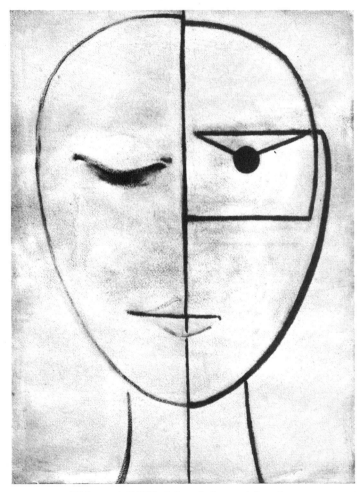

Dichotomy (1956), Ink and charcoal drawing

1. PARIS

Toward the end of childhood I wanted to be a saint; at a certain point in mid-life I wanted to be a whore; in old age I simply want to be myself. In spite of the help, or hindrance, of five psychiatrists, I only achieved this happy state in recent years.

1903 was the year of my birth and the year the Wright brothers finally succeeded in getting the Kittyhawk airborne. True, the plane was aloft for only 12 seconds, but the persistent optimism that brought about that memorable event seems to have rubbed off on me. At least it has given me the spurt to write down some episodes of my life. As Michel de Montaigne wrote, "You can tie up all moral philosophy with a common and private life just as well as with a life of richer stuff. For each man bears the entire form of man's estate."

From the night I attempted to jump off the sleeping porch in childhood to the time of my divorce at age seventy-seven my life's drive was always toward escape, escape from something, but not knowing towards what. As a child I was not able to think beyond the gateway of escape, feeling that once through it, the road would be clear. Of course there was far more to this passage than I realized. At that time I was not thinking beyond escaping from my family, unaware of the more difficult task of escaping from the person I had already become under their tutelage. I was disregarding the well-known prognostication of the Jesuits, "Give me a child until he is seven and he'll be mine for the rest of his life." By seven I was an extremely obedient little girl who had learned her lesson all too well, a lesson necessary to un-learn before I could start to be myself. It's a process which has taken and still is taking a long time.

Although my place of birth was New York City, my real birth, as a painter, was in Paris on a sunny day in April 1927. Spring days there always seem more magical than in any other city. After the dreary days of winter when the city is grey and insidious dampness penetrates the marrow, the vernal sun suddenly appears and all Paris puts on a new dress. The early green of her parks promise a later fullness while the espalier trees still reveal the skeleton of their design. Instinctively one wanders to favorite spots in the Luxembourg gardens, Place de Furstenberg, Place des Vosges, to rediscover the look intended by those who planned and planted so long ago. Lovers rejoice, exposing their joy for passersby to share. Every street café table is occupied as all drink in the city at its sparkling best.

That April day I had a lunch date with a painter friend, Pat Morgan. When I arrived at his place, he let me into a cheerful high-ceilinged space. Only once before had I spent time in a studio. The English painter, Wilfred de Glen, had painted a portrait of me commissioned by my parents. He was a charming man, but I had found the whole experience foreign and boring and hadn't liked the results, although he tried twice. He told me I showed unusual insensitivity to art.

Here the atmosphere was markedly different. Pat greeted me cordially, making me feel at ease while saying, "I can't go out to lunch now because I'm painting a still life of oysters on the half shell and the oysters will dry up and change color. Why don't you paint a picture while you're waiting for me to finish?"

"I don't know how," I said.

"It's simple," he replied as he put brushes into my hand and gave me tubes of color, a canvas, and a palette.

"Just mix blue and yellow and you get green."

He picked up a small pottery vase filled with anemones, plunked it down on a chair and suggested, "Paint that!" before going into the adjacent room.

I squeezed some tubes of color onto the palette as I scrutinized the anemones. Of course they were beautiful. Who can resist the wonderful appeal of their intense colors? But I did not feel comfortable with the background. Pat had put the flowers on a little wooden French provincial chair with a rush seat and two bars across the back. I started to paint but was disturbed by what I saw through the bars, namely the confusion of the studio. I needed some kind of drapery to give a solid background, but couldn't see a piece of cloth anywhere. All of a sudden I realized that I was wearing a two-piece lavender jersey dress of exactly the right color. I took off the skirt, draping it over the back of the chair, and was thrilled. What the lavender background did to and with the anemone colors was exciting. I started to paint and became totally absorbed and unaware of time. When Pat came back and said, "I'm ready. I can go now," I resented the interruption.

"Well I can't. I have no skirt and if I put it on, it will never take the same folds again."

Luckily there was an old raincoat to wrap around me and we went out to lunch. I couldn't wait to finish the meal and get back to my anemones. When I completed the painting, I felt elated and exhausted. I knew I had found my true work. Along with the natural insecurities inherent in any first attempt, there had been an awareness as I put the brush strokes down of rightness or wrongness, almost a pre-knowledge accompanied by surprised excitement and delight in an unfamiliar familiarity. While I feared this might be only a temporary enthusiasm lasting for a year or two, I decided to put it to the proof and kept on painting. My life radically changed direction.

To explain the strong natural affinity for painting that became evident to me that day is difficult. There was little in my family background connected to art. My father's sister painted but I rarely saw her and her works, scattered on the walls of my parents' house, made no lasting impression. In my own childhood only one related incident comes to mind, but I remember it vividly. This was my first act of seeing, really seeing something move from outside to inside, to the body's center, then below to something more visceral, more sexual.

I was probably eight. My cousin Florence, another girl, and I were walking through the fields to the beach in summertime. I stopped to pick a buttercup. We would put them below each other's chins. If a yellow glow reflected from your skin that meant you liked butter. Oddly enough, sometimes there wasn't a reflection.

This day I looked at the flower in my hand, feeling I had never truly seen one before. I saw the petals, between the petals, how the petals curved lower to attach themselves to the core that held them to the stalk. How wiry the stalk was, strong enough to hold them high above the other grasses, yet how thin the petals were with just enough tensile strength to maintain their shape even in a wind. And their color! I experienced yellow inside my mouth, on my skin, in my hands, on my face. I put my nose into the flower. I had a sense of its center and the many little fibers there to attract and tickle the bees and my nose. I was captured and absorbed in the world of "buttercupness". I became the flower. Meanwhile the other Maud was hearing Florence's voice call with increasing impatience. The two girls had moved away from where I was rooted. I kept hearing, "Come on, Maud, come on!" I answered, trying to let them know that I had found a new world. They turned back, reluctantly coming up to me. Florence looked down and said, "Maud, you fool, it's just a buttercup." I walked along with them knowing she was wrong. Those moments of almost being the buttercup gave me an awareness of myself, and something bigger than myself, that I only found again in Paris when I began to paint. This was the initiation.

Such intense participation with the subject became the basis of my life's work. This identification affects the way I bring forms into being, the types of shapes that evolve, their sizes, how they relate to each other, and to the negative spaces around them so that the entire painted surface will work together as a whole. It even affects how the individual brush stroke is drawn. These factors, which create the character of a painting and determine what it says, must unequivocally come from gut level emotion if the painting is to be alive.

Of all the excitements experienced by the artist, the alchemic change from an emotion to a palpable visual object capable of communicating to others is by far the greatest, and occurs when all the elusive "ifs" converge. If you have the right spirit, if your subconscious reaction to what you are about to do is right, if your receptivity is right, if your health is right, if the light is right, if your paints are right – ten thousand "ifs". At that time there comes into the painting something that parallels the sense of watching the painting paint itself. You watch the painting use you as the vehicle by which to come into existence.

You may go home at night after such an experience and be absolutely thunderstruck when you come back to the studio the next morning by what you have done in this state of voluntary-involuntary synchronization. Everyone in the arts knows the feeling when the material flows unassisted without one's conscious control, almost impersonally. Then the skill is to know how far is enough; at what moment, at what exact instant you must intrude yourself into the process as a critical eye. If you do it too soon, you will lose the magic flow. If too late, the painting may be irretrievable.

Hans Hofmann says, "Artistic creation is the metamorphosis of the external physical aspect of the thing into a self-sustaining spiritual reality. On this, and only on this, is creation based."

The magic occurs some place between the original thought and the indefinable process of caring, passionate caring that transforms whatever the intuition is into the final form. This mystery causes the painting to be either a work of art or simply a decorative thing. It happens deep down inside the person, creating the poem, the music, or the painting.

September Still Life (1938), Oil on canvas,
20 x 24 in., Metropolitan Museum, New York

2. CANADA

"Vulnerability is a guardian of integrity"
— *Anne Truitt*

That summer of 1927, I returned to Canada, as I had every year of my life, to La Malbaie, County Charlevoix, Province of Quebec. For me and for everyone in my family, this place has always been the anchor. Now five generations of our American family have sent deep roots into that soil. But our connection goes back even further. At the time of the American Revolution some of my ancestors left the United States for Canada. As a child I felt ashamed that they were Loyalists to England and not fired with enthusiasm for our young country. I've gotten over that. One of my Tory ancestors, Jonathan Sewell, married the daughter of William Smith, then Chief Justice of New York and later Chief Justice of Lower Canada.

My maternal grandfather, George T. Bonner, a Canadian of English descent, married into this part of the family, taking his beautiful bride, Isabel Sewell of Quebec, to live and bring up their family in Staten Island. He made a modest fortune in the New York financial world and in 1903, the year of my birth, bought a large tract of land about one hundred miles northeast of Quebec on the north shore of the St. Lawrence River at La Malbaie. I knew and was intimidated by my grandfather. He was a little man; wiry, energetic and forceful. He loved beautiful women, of which his wife was an exquisite example. She was tall and towered protectively over her husband. I think of her as five foot ten inches or more but that is from a child's memory. I loved her. She wore wonderful black garments trimmed with lace. Her big skirts barely skimmed the ground and rustled as she walked. I can still see the silk moiré pattern that mirrored her graceful motions as she played croquet. Her grey hair was always beautifully combed and piled on the top of her head. She had a long neck that held her head high, showing her clear-cut features which expressed both dignity and love. Isabel bore George Bonner four children, three girls and finally a boy. The child was immediately nicknamed "Boysie" and my grandfather was content. Alas, when Boysie was ten he died of typhoid fever. My grandfather never recovered. He turned to my mother, the eldest of the three girls, and schooled her in the role of a son. Though charming and attractive, Maud was enough like him to make this feasible. She was courageous, capable, hyperactive, intelligent, and entrepreneurial.

When my grandfather bought this large property, known as the Mount Murray Seigniory, he retained the woodlands for himself and gave the Manor House and the farms to Maud. My mother reveled in her position as Seigneur of the Manor and the freedom to use her talents in managing a large enterprise. She received this gift, which became the most important and formative influence in her life, when she was thirty-three and the mother of four, three boys and a six-month old girl.

In 1903 she moved her family into the Manor House for the summer months, a pattern that continued in each of our lives until the end of our teen-age years, and in hers until her death in 1955 at the age of eighty-five.

My father, Francis Higginson Cabot, a wool merchant in New York, spent his short summer holidays with us more as her consort than as her partner. He loved the place, with its cows and the horses he enjoyed driving, but he never learned to speak French in a community where no other language was understood. For us children the four summer months spent at the Manor permeated the whole year, winter time in New York seemed secondary.

Most of these seigniories were the original royal land grants that had been established under the French régime. In order to continue colonization of the vast territory that England took from France when General Wolfe defeated Montcalm at Quebec in 1759, this method continued under British rule. Many Army officers, mostly Scots, remained in Canada, and the favored ones were given large tracts of land.

The La Malbaie property comprised a handsome, large, old stone Manor House, surrounded by a good working farm, extensive woodlands, and lakes. The land, cultivated by about a hundred small tenant farmers, extended fifteen miles along the river and six miles inland. My grandfather bought it for $50,000. The Manor House stood on a bluff overlooking the St. Lawrence. Behind it was a large courtyard surrounded by old barns. It was the center of my mother's friendly association with the French Canadian farmers, the "habitants". She became a legend to her tenants, who loved her. The role of seigneur fit her so perfectly that to miss a summer there would have been inconceivable.

The seigniories operated more or less on a feudal system. The 'censitaires' (tenant farmers) paid a minuscule rent to the seigneur but were obligated to grind their grain in the owner's mill, leaving so many bags as a tithe. I grew up with this system still in operation but during my childhood it evolved into an amicable arrangement. Rents were paid by knitting a pair of socks for my father, bringing in a brace of partridge, doing a day's work on the farm called a "corvée," or simply bringing the many children and a violin for square dancing on a festive New Year's Day visit. Legally eliminated in 1860, in actuality the seigniorial system dwindled along into the 1930s when the government paid my mother a small sum – I think $6000 – for taking over her land. However, throughout her lifetime the tenants still considered and loved my mother as their seigneur.

Each year she trekked up from New York at the close of school with four children, a nurse, several dogs and endless amounts of locally unavailable necessities. It was quite a jaunt. The overnight train from New York to Quebec was the high point. I still thrill at spending the night in a sleeping car enclosed by the stiff heavy green curtains, so harsh to the touch, that create a world of privacy where one can look out the window as the train rushes through the darkness, lessening its speed in passing the occasional small, almost deserted stations where one or two dark figures stroll about under the single station light.

After Quebec the river widens greatly as it moves northeast into the Gulf of St. Lawrence and flows past the large island of Anticosti, which sits akimbo at the river's head before the vast gulf narrows into the neck of the Straits of Belle Isle and on into the Atlantic Ocean. Anticosti is a legendary place to me, one of which I have often dreamed. My grandfather had originally set his heart and hopes on buying this huge island, isolated in the midst of a gigantic body of water, unspoiled and almost unvisited, its seven rivers teaming with salmon and its forests rich in game. My grandfather miscalculated. When Anticosti was offered for sale, he was outbid by only a thousand dollars and the loss infuriated him. He bought Mount Murray Seigniory on the rebound.

Some years we spent the Christmas holidays at the Manor. The journey took us from New York to Quebec by train and by electric trolley to Mountmorency, where we found the sleighs ready and waiting for the two day drive to La Malbaie. How exciting finally to see the cheerful face of Pitre Bouchard, dressed in a fur cap and a bearskin coat cinched by a "ceinture flechée", a wide, many-colored woven woolen belt, standing by his "carriole" (an open sleigh with a back seat for two and a bench-like seat for the driver), his two horses in tandem, ready to go. My cousin Florence and I, dressed in our warmest clothes, often went together. Pitre would tuck us in with heavy moose and bear skin rugs piled one on top of the other: we felt like peas in a pod, closed in with only our faces exposed. As time went on we would be grateful for every extra layer. Gliding smoothly along on the hard packed snow we felt near to the earth, as though we ourselves were part of the on-going motion, so different from the feeling in a carriage. While still in the village we passed others closely in a fleeting moment of intimacy, going in the opposite direction.

Soon we were out in the country where encounters were rare, and we would settle down to the business of keeping ourselves warm until reaching Baie-St-Paul at sundown. Pitre helped by singing songs in French to the accompaniment of the sleigh bells. We joined in on every verse we knew and, as he added more and more verses, we would try to remember them or go over the earlier ones to prolong the enjoy- ment. As our hands began to hurt from the cold, we would talk to each other about ways to combat the problem. The start was to withdraw each icy finger from its glove finger so it could touch the less icy palm and get a little warmth. Our gloves were inside massive knitted mit- tens, making an ungainly boxer's glove protuberance at the end of each

Night Train (1947), Oil on canvas, 28 x 36 in., Museum of Fine Arts, Boston

arm. We played "Peas-Porridge-Hot" giggling as we tried to maneuver our cumbersome hands in order to clap them. The temperature would go down as the sun lowered in mid-afternoon. By the time we reached Baie St-Paul it was twenty-five degrees below zero. When this long-anticipated moment arrived, we struggled out from under the fur rugs, standing for a moment holding onto the sleigh until we were sure our cold feet still functioned, then went into the seemingly overheated inn, that as we warmed up, gradually became a pleasant temperature. The horses would be stabled for the night and the whole family enjoyed an ample French Canadian supper before going to bed. We reached home the following afternoon, where a big two-decker stove heated the hallway of the Manor House to welcome us. Someone had to be on duty day and night during the winter to keep all the stoves stoked in order to prevent the pipes from freezing.

Another winter we took our usual train route from New York to

Quebec, and from there to Rivière Ouelle along the south shore, where we planned to cross the St. Lawrence on the ferry as we sometimes did in summer, rather than make the arduous trip in open sleighs. The ice was unusually heavy that year. When we reached the ferry, the captain said it would be impossible to cross, as his ice breaker was not sufficiently strong. My mother refused to accept this verdict and somehow persuaded him to embark. We were able to leave the shore, but once in the middle of that wide river the boat seemed blocked in by ice on all sides. It was pretty scary. The captain wanted to turn back. Again my mother dissuaded him. By then, whether we could get back to the shore we had left was questionable. We proceeded at an increasingly slower pace till we were almost stationary amidst huge blocks of ice. My mother stood beside the captain, attempting to allay his justified fears. I imagine he said a prayer of thanks as we landed. I know I did.

In summer my mother dressed very much in her own invented fashion, her reddish hair in a braid folded under and tied with a black taffeta bow in the George Washington manner. She wore a short khaki or white linen skirt, a man's jacket, always with a crisp white handkerchief protruding from its pocket and often with a flower from the garden in its lapel, a man's necktie, and flat white tennis shoes, all made to order. Her lovely silk or cashmere shirts were tailored by Wragge, one of New York's best men's shirtmakers. For camping she wore knickerbockers and high laced boots.

My mother, whom we called Mootzie, was not a tall woman but had great presence. Compact, tidy and vibrant, she moved briskly wherever she went, often slamming doors behind her. When I was little, I nicknamed her "Dasher". On being questioned, I said it was because she always rushed about so quickly. This disappointed her, as she had thought I was calling her after one of Santa Claus' reindeer.

She had several very contradictory people inside her little frame. In part she was a conventional Victorian lady, and in part a creative and domineering hellion, with feminine charm and masculine drive. She was highly competitive in all areas and, while taking any liberty she chose for herself, professed to value men above women. She referred to herself and my father as the "well-married couple", but I never felt he had much breathing space. She probably had been so successfully indoctrinated into playing the man's role that she didn't know how to do otherwise. Her surface behavior varied between doctrinaire and friendly, cooperative and delightful, always with tremendous spirit. One wonders if there may have been an underlying anxiety about bringing up a female child. Having a daughter may have posed a threatening challenge to her, as it did to me a generation later.

My earliest memory goes back to the Manor house. This incident haunted me although later I thought I must have invented it. One day in New York, after my mother's death in 1955 when I was fifty-two, I met my mother's friend Mrs Stevens in front of St Patrick's Cathedral on Fifth Avenue. She spoke of what a wonderful woman my mother had been. There was only one area she questioned. Mrs. Stevens had thought that my mother was a little hard on me, "But", she said, "I realize I was wrong, because look how well you've turned out." She then told me the story I had not dared believe, exactly corroborating my memory.

While the Stevens' and my parents were having a pleasant mid-summer lunch in the dining room, I was crying continuously on the porch outside the open window. My father called across the table to my mother, "Maud, I think you should go out and see what's happening, the baby's crying a great deal and she's playing with the boys." My mother answered, "Oh no, she has three brothers and she has to learn how to get on with them. Now is as good a time as any." She would not get up from the table to investigate. What was happening was that we children were all on the edge of the porch and my brothers insisted that I jump off. I was frightened. When I didn't jump, they pushed me off. True, I fell onto the lawn, so to that extent, my mother was justified as I didn't really harm myself. They made me walk up the five big steps and pushed me off again and again and again and again. They said they were going to do this until I stopped crying. I was terrified. As I found out fifty years later, my fearful memory was accurate. I never told Mrs. Stevens what had been going on.

I remember another incident when I was about five. My mother came up to my room to kiss me goodnight before going out to dinner with my father. I said my prayers. She sat on the edge of my bed and asked if I prayed for anything special. "Yes," I said. "Every night I pray that I will be dead before morning." Naturally the poor woman was devastated and showed it. I resolved never again to tell her anything emotionally important to me. I don't think I ever did, which was not really fair to her, or to me.

Growing up as the youngest and only girl with three older brothers in a male oriented family proved to be a complicated affair. I was always keenly aware of my inability to please my mother or fit in with my brothers. I knew I was different, and since I felt they were what they should be, I was somehow inadequate.

However, the north shore of the St. Lawrence River was a pleasant and beautiful place to grow up. These foothills of the Laurentian Mountain chain, where I often camped with my mother, are among the oldest mountains in the world. From the north shore the river is an amazing, ever-changing delight, a mirror-calm surface of pink or silver with occasional darker streaks indicating tide rips where subsurface currents may change in a flash to a sea of choppy, angry, grey waves. Sometimes every tiny white house on the opposite shore, fourteen miles away, would show up. These were times when rain was said to be on the way. Other days the little houses were no more than dots on a distant horizon.

Through all these summers my mother maintained her effective, well-organized dictatorship. Her main support was my youngest brother Quin whom she adored, a love that was reciprocated. From the time he went to boarding school at the unusually young age of ten, until her death, he never failed to write her a letter every Sunday. Why he was sent away so early, I have no idea.

Quin was enough like my mother to be able to work well with her and be an enormous help on the farm. He spoke French like a "habitant" and wanted very much to live out his life there, managing the Canadian property. Unfortunately my parents would not agree. He was a bachelor until he was thirty. They were afraid that living there alone would foster his propensity for alcohol and get the better of him. La Malbaie was extremely isolated in winter then, but I think their decision was instrumental in depriving him of a full life. He became a wonderfully capable workman in many fields, but didn't like living in cities and couldn't tolerate office work. He once had a job on the Radio Tower Building in New York, working outdoors on the scaffolding near the top of that high building. At times I would go and look at him through binoculars, awed by his ability to work in such an exposed, dangerous situation. Once that job finished in 1928 he suggested that he and I take a trip together to Denmark and Norway. We went up the coast to Bergen on a small coastal boat. Sometimes he was upset by my reactions, which he considered eccentric, and would ask impatiently why I couldn't be more normal. But as the trip progressed he became more relaxed, and doubtless I became more "normal". Our natures synchronized again, as they had in childhood, and we had a wonderful time. On returning home he got a good job in Havre de Grace, Maryland. I went down to visit and considered staying on to keep him company. He thought I would get bored and persuaded me not to. So in early spring I went back to Paris. In 1930 Quin married Joy, a woman who hated the life we lived in Canada and farm life in general. Later he worked for many years in Paris under the Marshall Plan. Finally, towards the end of his life, he resolved to return to live in Canada, regardless of his wife's preferences. I last saw him in a hospital bed in Paris. He was working on architectural drawings for installing central heating in the Manor house to make it livable in the winter. Every dimension of the place was still fresh in his mind. He died two days later.

I always idealized Quin. He was a year and a half older than I but about the same height. When we were little we were very much a team, apart from our two older brothers. During the week we were dressed alike in rompers, belted at the waist with elastic at the knee, cotton for summer wear, handspun wool for cooler weather. On Sundays I was usually dressed in a white smock from Liberty's in London, which satisfied my mother's anglophile tastes. But I think it must have pleased her to have us look like twins most of the time. In one letter to my grandfather when I was five I wrote, "Quin is the Master, Maud is his sister." Once when I had done something that displeased him, he hit me, I fell down, and as I stood up I said, "I'm sorry." My mother overheard and became very angry. She said she wouldn't have a daughter who wouldn't defend herself; I should have hit him back. For a long time afterwards she referred to this incident and rubbed it in. I hated it, but I had wanted to please Quin. In retrospect, I appreciate that my mother was simply being insistent in trying to teach me to stand up for my own rights.

When I was seven, my mother took Quin and me to Switzerland for the school year of 1910. I was overjoyed. In Lausanne we were sent to school dressed alike as usual. A boy came up to Quin and said, I've been talking to your brother." "That's not my brother," said Quin. "That's my sister."

"Well, it can't be, he's dressed like a boy."

The argument became heated and finally Quin settled it by hitting the boy. It was the first time I remember someone standing up for me. It seems that I cannot forget it. Also it was probably the first time I was glad to be a girl. That winter in Lausanne was a harmonious time in my life.

Once back home, Quin naturally gravitated towards his older brother George and became one of the boys, leaving his kid sister to fend for herself.

My companion then became Bari, a St. Bernard dog given to me by my mother in Lausanne, a glorious and imaginative present. He was a little puppy when put into an enormous crate and sent on his travels. By the time he reached La Malbaie he was a large dog about thirty inches tall, barely able to fit into his crate. Britain had strict laws prohibiting unregistered animals from touching her shore. As Bari's first ship was due to stop in England, he had to be transferred to another ship which kept circling the British Isles until he could be put on a vessel bound for Canada. Of course once out of his crate he got even larger, until he was fully grown. St. Bernards are trained to find people lost in the snow and resuscitate them by licking their faces until they are strong enough to drink from a small keg of brandy the dog carries around its neck. I used to play endlessly with my beautiful Bari, hiding in the tall grain, pretending to be lost in the snow, waiting for him to come and rescue me, licking my face and hands all over. I adored him. A few years later in the evenings he began to come up from the beach rather than down from the fields, his white chest glistening clean, more beautiful than ever. Then over the next few weeks several sheep were discovered strangled. Bari was caught in the act. I saw in his eyes that he knew his guilt, hidden by his nightly bath in the St. Lawrence before coming home. He couldn't be kept on the farm. There was no help for it. He was shot in the morning. I had lost my best and only friend.

Early on I was put in the position of having to kill chickens. When I was about thirteen my responsibility on the farm was the chicken yard. It had previously been managed by my brother George. He sold it to me for my fortune – not quite three dollars as I remember. I was glad to buy it because I thought it would give me a little more status in the family. The nice part of the job was collecting the eggs in the morning and taking the basket of them up to the kitchen. But I also had to kill and pluck the hens. I'd hold the big knife over the neck of the terrified creature once I'd caught it, but I didn't have the guts to do a good job. One not-quite-strong-enough hack was all I could muster, then the poor thing would escape, flapping its wings and stumbling around the field, its head dangling until it died. I hated this part of the job and I had given up my savings to get it.

My brother George was four years older than I. He had an incredible beauty, charm, and imagination. He was hard for my mother to handle. His love of animals was so innate that as a young boy, he insisted he was a dog. He adopted the traits of a dog, lying on the floor in the middle of the hall, jumping up on people to greet them. He refused to respond to my mother's call unless she whistled for him. This really aggravated her, especially when she had guests. He would sit down in an inconvenient spot and would not move until she whistled. He also loved cats and one summer there were fifty of them living in various barns from which they emerged at meal times at his Pied Piper's call. To watch them rush from every corner of the barnyard to the huge bowls of food he would put out for them on the grass by the kitchen was fascinating. George was much more congenial with our father, with whom he later went into business. I was happy he did so, as our father always seemed so isolated within our family.

My oldest brother, Higgie, short for Higginson, the name carried by his father, always seemed removed from the family. He was an extremely intense, hardworking person who succeeded in making a great deal of money. For me he was like another generation. At an early birthday party of mine I said to my mother, "I don't want any grownups invited." She agreed not to attend. "Oh no," I said, "I don't mean you, I mean Higgie."

My childhood focus on escape varied as the years went by. When I was tiny, the form was vocal. I was the typical good little girl who, when good, was very, very good, but when bad was crazy. For no accountable reason, I would start running around screaming hysterically and pulling things apart. No one could stop me till my time for rebellion was up and I'd again become the good little girl.

While still quite young, about six, my escape hatch became vertical. First I tried to jump off a sleeping porch about twenty-five feet high that I slept on with my brothers. I can remember feeling I would be freer down below. Luckily, in getting out of bed, I aroused Higgie. I had already climbed over the railing and had one foot off the porch when he grabbed me by an arm and my hair. After that I was put alone on another sleeping porch surrounded by chicken wire. Since trying to go down hadn't worked, I tried the opposite direction and was more successful. There was a large, very old spruce tree near the kitchen. I would climb high enough up in it so as not to be seen from the ground and stay there for hours. I often took a book. The books I attempted to read were way beyond my comprehension. I didn't even understand many of the words. I longed to learn but my method was certainly irrational. I'd stay up in that tree till supper time. Someone would come out and call me, then call again and again with increasing irritation. Finally,

I'd come down and be very late for the meal, never telling where I'd been. My pride was that no one ever knew of this hideout. My next tree was much further from the house, way down on the old entrance driveway. This one offered a breeze off the Saint Lawrence, a view and isolation. To my horror, one afternoon when my mother and her crony, Kay, were taking a walk, they found my tree (I was too high up for them to see me) and sat below looking out at the river, saying how wonderful it was to get away from the children. I never went there again.

Next I tried the horizontal: walking away. The first time I got about ten miles from home. Having eaten all the chocolate I'd brought for sustenance, I was tired and had to give in. I called home to be rescued. My second try was with several boys my age. We hopped on a slow-moving freight train going to the pulp mill. Once there, I walked across a narrow walkway just above the dam and fell in. Soaking wet and happy, though defeated again, I called home. That night my mother gave me my first taste of alcohol to warm me up. She started a bad habit.

Sufficiently frustrated by then, I decided to try a different approach, a psychological one. I consciously and successfully developed a vague mannerism in order to avoid questions I didn't want to answer or something I didn't want to do. I remember being sent to the village a mile away to buy a chicken. I walked to the village and back but forgot the chicken; I got a scolding instead of an escape. This deliberately-created negative self image was enhanced by my favorite first cousin, Florence, who in those years when addressing me almost always added the epithet, "You fool!" In all these adventures I was motivated by the belief that if I could get free from my family, I would have a chance to become what I knew I should and wanted to become.

My mother was a superb housekeeper. She saw to it that everything worked and everybody knew precisely what they were supposed to do. We always had delicious food which in summer came fresh from the garden or the farm, mostly vegetables, chicken, and young lamb. Although her own cooking was limited to a camping style level, she had the extraordinary ability to teach others how to become good cooks. Almost anyone, even Ernestine, a "cordon bleu" from France, expanded her cuisine under my mother's tutelage to include Indian and other exotic dishes. House guests looked forward to Saturday morning breakfasts when a delectable salmon pie, warmed by little oil lamps beneath their shining copper support, awaited them. On the side board in the dining room the sturdy, heavily embossed silver jug full of ice water always stood. I've kept this jug, putting it away on a rarely used shelf in my little Cambridge house. When I catch a glimpse of it as I open the cupboard door, the entire picture of life at the Manor becomes vividly present again. I relive the well-systematized régime in which regulations brought about a sense of order along with the restrictions, even a certain serenity. Early each Sunday morning, we drove up the hill to the small, simple Episcopal church of St. Peter's on the Rock, where my mother was warden. She had always filled the flower vases the day before, and would take up the collection if the male warden was not present. She was certainly the most lively parishioner.

Life was still somewhat primitive in the Quebec countryside then– we had no local doctor. There was a man calling himself "Doctor" who had not been to medical school and had only a rudimentary theory of cleanliness. In one crisis, when I was probably nine, I stepped on a needle that entered my instep. Dr. Lapointe was called. He drove up from the village, didn't think of washing his hands after tying up his horse until my mother insisted, cut into the bottom of my foot, couldn't locate the needle, sewed the cut up again, but unintentionally included some of the foot muscles. For close to a year I couldn't put my foot flat on the ground and had to walk on its outer edge, ankle bent over. The needle remained in my body, traveling about in the bloodstream some-what dangerously. I could often feel it poking from the inside. Although sometimes maddeningly close to the surface, it never came out. I suppose it finally disintegrated.

Mootzie had an excellent sense of medicine herself, and was often called as a substitute doctor. She always went and sometimes I accompanied her. By applying simple sanitary measures she appeared to bring about miracles.

Petit Malade (1939), Oil on canvas, 11 x 14 in.

However, there was some local opposition when she tried to start a hospital by bringing a trained nurse down from Quebec to work for a few weeks at a time, lodging with a local family. The resentment took several years to overcome, but she finally won out and the hospital she started flourishes to this day. She had a way of accomplishing what she wanted and usually ended up with others approving what she did.

An important part of her legend had to do with her physical prowess. My mother would go off for weeks at a time on fishing or hunting trips, walking long distances and setting up a homelike camp within a few hours. The guides would make comfortable beds by sticking the tips of short balsam branches, needles facing down, into the ground to give a slightly springy effect when you lay down in the deliciousness of their aroma. Meanwhile, my mother would see to the smaller comforts by nailing a piece of cut wood to a tree with a mirror hung over it for a dressing table, tying up a line for drying clothes, and making sitting places on logs for comfortable eating around the campfire. I camped with her from age fifteen on and always loved the woods, although I was not interested in killing animals. Mother was an avowed big game hunter, proud to have killed a moose and a caribou and always hoping to get a bear.

When I was in first grade we were given the task of writing a letter to one of our parents. Mine was: "Dear Father, Has mother killed anything yet? – Love, Maud." I didn't understand why the teacher looked surprised.

Once my mother took my brother Higgie and three other people in their late teens on a hunting trip. For her principal guide she chose an Indian, Moreau, known for his woodsman's skills but also as a murderer. Two days away from home he came at my mother in the deep woods, knife in hand, threatening to kill her. I can't imagine what she did or what she said, but somehow she talked him out of it. Every summer after that he would come out of the woods, risking his life (he was wanted by the police) to visit her. We all knew he was a murderer and would hang around in the bushes to observe them.

That I should have been a boy was never far from my awareness. My mother would say with no apparent shyness or guilt, "I couldn't believe that I could give birth to a female child." I once overheard her say to a young man, "I am 75 but have never been been able to get accustomed to being a woman." Along with the rest of the litter, she took care of me extremely well, but there was never any question in my mind as to where I stood.

I clearly remember one day years later at my Connecticut boarding school, walking down a long alley of tall shade trees at the time of intensive cramming for college exams and saying to myself, "I'd rather have my brothers like me than pass my college exams." Later, as we all grew older, I ended up being close to both George and Quin and they to me.

The Manor land included a beautiful sandy beach located about a mile and a half from the house, a romantic walk on an old road through cedar and spruce forests. As a family we often walked down in the late afternoon, carrying picnic baskets, to make a fire on a big white rock at the far end large enough to seat any number of us. We children played games and skipped stones as the adults made a fire and cooked supper. I loved these picnics, especially when we walked home through the dark woods, not being sure of our footing and feeling a little scared.

We rarely swam in the river. A quick plunge was more like a head-on encounter with a frightening foe than a pleasurable experience. In the heat of summer the water temperature was under fifty degrees. Imagining the exhilaration that would follow a dip was the only way to persuade oneself to go in. If one did, the reward was a fantastic high.

At the appropriate time my mother decided to explain the facts of life to me. She asked me to come to her bed one Sunday morning. This was unusual. I was not like the many children I know today who jump into the bed of either or both parents at any time of anxiety or stress. I was uncomfortable in her bed, feeling that the stage had been set for something important for which I was not prepared. What little I knew about sex, beyond barnyard knowledge, was about its abnormalities, a knowledge acquired through reading Kraft Ebbing. The father of one of my friends at Miss Chapin's School in New York was a doctor. On rainy afternoons when he wasn't at home, she and I would sneak into the library and look at his medical books on the subject. I didn't want to listen to my mother, nor can I remember how she started out, for I slipped out of her bed and ran upstairs. Probably I was afraid that if I learned more of what was involved in being female, I would be expected to be and do things that I shrank from. I didn't want to know more; I didn't want to grow up.

However, shortly afterwards when I was ten, fate smiled on me and turned my aloneness into its opposite. I was given a bicycle, and with the mobility it provided, I rode into my Queen Bee chapter. Every morning I biked to the nearby golf club where for two summers I reigned as a belle, surrounded by adoring little boys.

I played golf, smoked cornsilk cigarettes and had daily tea with my heaviest beau, Louis. We would arrive at the tea room late, so that we could scurry around after the grown-up tea customers had left and eat up any overlooked cakes. I had my first suit then, a grey tweed skirt and jacket made in the village, an exciting event. Louis had an identical one made with pants. But our romance dimmed somewhat when, practicing swinging a golf club, he hit me in the jaw. While the wound was being stitched up he stood beside me and said, "It was your own fault. You shouldn't have been standing in my way."

Although the Queen Bee period came to an end the following summer, I still had my bicycle and I'd often go off for the whole afternoon, or sometimes for all day with a sandwich. My favorite place was a beautiful, small river with a swimming hole at its height and rushing waterfalls along its lower course. This was the piece of land that my future husband would buy, years hence, on which to build himself a house. Then it was wild, never anyone around, but with many of nature's pleasures at hand. I enjoyed swimming and child-level fishing. After many indolent afternoons of trying, I taught myself how to catch a trout in my hand. It was fun, difficult and exciting. You first locate a quiet pool with moderately still water where fish might appear every now and then. Once there, the fish will often stay for a while, resting peacefully. You lie at the water's edge and extend your hand and arm into the cold water, holding your palm open at a level below which you think a fish will stay. When he comes you must manipulate your hand to be directly under him without his being aware of your movement. For a while you remain still, then starting near his tail, you very gently tickle his stomach, which he loves. In almost human fashion he gives in to actually lying in your palm as you wiggle your fingers. Now there you are, lying on the ground, seducing a live fish in the palm of your hand, holding your breath and moving very, very slowly, so he will not be conscious of it. You must now proceed to move your tickling fingers up his stomach until your thumb and forefinger are within striking distance of his gills, which are in gentle motion. This is the all-or-nothing position. With the greatest possible alacrity you attempt to put a finger into each gill and, if successful, tighten your grip and feel triumphant as you decide whether to pull your prize out of the water and take him home to eat for supper or let him go back to his earlier freedom.

During these formative years I was very alone. The Queen Bee period had been an exciting flash in the pan, a crescendo ending my life as a kid. Now I was plunging into teen-age with minimum equipment to handle it. However, it was during these years that I learned how to make my own fun so that being alone became the norm, a pattern which has never left me.

My mother led a highly organized life at the Manor. Twice a week, Tuesdays and Saturdays, the flower vases were emptied, washed, refilled with fresh water and replaced in their traditional spots. There were at least twenty-five. My mother, dressed in a smock, would go to the garden and fill her beautiful, flat, heavy, birch bark baskets, each about two-by-three-feet wide, with high alder-sapling handles, with mounds of fresh-cut flowers. She would pick huge numbers of whatever flowers were in their prime, bring them back to the house, and arrange them in the various vases. She did it with good taste, her taste, and there was little leeway for an alternative idea. Picking flowers is an agreeable occupation, but since I was obliged to pick and arrange them only as directed, I hated Tuesday and Saturday mornings in the garden. As a teenager I developed an allergy. As soon as I got among the flower beds my eyes would swell up and I would start sneezing. God's intervention! While the allergy got me out of picking the flowers, I still had to pick strawberries and red or white raspberries. These white raspberries, originally from Scotland, were so incredibly good that I didn't mind picking them. Served with thick Jersey cream they made

Mootzie's Tuesday Teas famous. The Manor overflowed with summer guests, young and old, wandering in the garden, playing tennis or chitchatting in the house.

On Friday mornings after breakfast, she and I darned the family clothes. Fortunately this wearying task has disappeared from most womens' lives. Now we have nylon stockings we throw away when a hole appears. Stockings then were more precious, made of cotton, wool or silk to suit the occasion. But all were carefully attended to. This mending ritual at the Manor was rarely, if ever, broken. Once my brothers were entertaining a large group of their fellow members of the Fly Club at Harvard, all attractive, eligible young men. They played tennis and came up to the Manor House afterwards for refreshments: shandygaff (beer and ginger ale) or raspberry vinegar, a specialty of the house. Since it was Friday morning, I was required to be upstairs darning my brothers' socks rather than flirting with their friends on the lawn.

When I was eighteen Mootzie said I needed to kill a moose before coming out in New York society. When I asked why, I was told, "It will give you something to talk about."

Not only did I not like to kill things, I especially hated to kill big things and a moose is eight feet or so at the shoulder. I don't know what it would measure to the highest point of the antler. For hours I had been sitting with my guide near the edge of a small lake – about a dozen feet into the bushes – just far enough to be concealed from sight. One remained silent in the hope of seeing a moose come down to the water to drink. Finally, across the lake I saw the large form of an animal grazing in the bushes, camouflaged by the shrubs between it and the water. I considered, I aimed, I shot. The animal raised its head, a huge head with large ears and jutting out nose, but no antlers. She was a female – a cow moose; a forbidden trophy. I was full of complicated guilt. She rushed back into the forest. I knew I had wounded her and felt terribly about what I had done. However, if I had wounded her badly it would be better to kill her. The guide and I walked hastily around the end of the lake and tried to follow the trail of her blood. After a while we lost her track and paused not knowing which way to go.

Unbelievably, and quite suddenly, an enormous creature thrust its way through the branches, displaying first the leading antler then the head itself with its huge nose, then the other antler. It's astounding to see how skillfully such an animal gets through dense forests, astonishingly gracefully despite its seemingly ungainly body. With startling immediacy, this vast creature stood about sixty yards from me. My guide was with me and shortly my mother arrived with her guide, alerted by my first shot at the cow moose. I took a careful shot, aiming behind the beast's left shoulder, a fatal route to the heart. I was proud to have done exactly what I'd been trained to do, until I watched this great, proud creature fall to its knees uttering horrible loud cries of pain. My guide, assuming that it was all over, rushed towards the fallen beast, somewhat hysterically, calling out, "Mademoiselle a tué son original" (Mademoiselle has killed her moose), at which point the moose staggered up on its feet, emitting horrendous bellows, and advanced towards me, raising one leg as though to strike. Directly behind me I heard my mother's voice saying, "Advance!" which, though terrified, I did, and then "Shoot!" In trying to get out of the path of the advancing moose, the panicked guide put himself directly into my line of fire. My bullet passed through his hat. Now, I was the one who became hysterical. I shot wildly three or four times. With frighteningly loud groans the maimed animal crashed to earth. I watched his great head with its majestic antlers tip over and slump to the ground. Finally, indeed, Mademoiselle had killed her moose. I felt a murderer. My guide, it turned out, had lied about his past experience. This was the first time he had ever guided a hunting trip or seen a moose. He was lucky to be alive.

After the kill there was all the heavy business that follows, skinning the animal, butchering it, and carrying it down the mountain, its great horns and heavy skin to become trophies. It took many hours of hard, and to me, sad work, all four of us helping as we could. That evening as I went to the lake for a swim before going to bed, emotionally exhausted, I looked up and there, just across the water, like an apparition, was another moose, not as large as mine – maybe his brother or son come to seek vengeance. All through the night others came in my dreams. I hope never to kill an animal again.

That winter at an elegant dinner in a Fifth Avenue mansion, I sat next to an enormously attractive, eligible son of one of my mother's friends. He was the "crème de la crème" as well as a recognized big game hunter. Here was the perfect chance to tell my moose story. I froze. I actually could not utter a word to him.

As we both got older, Mootzie came to depend on me increasingly and we grew much closer. I believe that after her death I came to resemble her more than I had when she was alive and I was young.

In those later years we rented out the Manor House during the summers. It was my job to prepare it for the tenants, which I enjoyed doing. I had so much feeling for the house that to make it look nice for each tenant was fun. They always loved the quality and beauty of the place and enjoyed using the stacks of engraved letter paper marked 'Mount Murray Manor'. In 1975 the house was rented to Radio Canada as a setting for a television drama. Through negligence they managed to burn it to the ground. Only the majestic stone walls and towering chimneys were left standing. It was a terrible loss which buried my Canadian childhood in its ashes.

Clearly the whole Canadian experience made an indelible impression on my life. I think it formed in me a deep predilection for nature, not with the botanist's learning, but with the gut's feeling, a deep, undifferentiated sense of belonging, of being part of the wind, rain, and earth; being of their very essence. Although in these early days I had no idea that I would spend the greater part of my life's energies as a painter, I was absorbing the material on which this drive flourished.

3. IN THE CITY

"The important and the unimportant
are the same only at the start"
— *Antonio Porchia*

Although my father was forty-four at my birth, my earliest memories
are of him as an old man, especially in Canada where he always seemed
to be an outsider. He was heavy-set and moved slowly. I worried about
his participation in our super-active life there and felt more comfortable when I saw him reading in the Manor House, as he did for hours,
in his big wing armchair in the window. When I was very young he
used to read to me every evening before my bedtime. I remember *Two
Years Before the Mast* as an endless book that never interested me, but
I loved sitting on his lap and ignoring Richard Dana's words.

We children called him Nappo. He loved me very much. He often
took my side in our very male-oriented family, but he was rarely effective. His efforts to soften his sons' behavior towards me, such as "be
good to your dear sister," were clearly doomed to failure. He bore the
very Bostonian name of Francis Higginson Cabot. I never found out
why he left Boston after one year at Harvard to go to New York. Once
when I asked he said his mother thought he was too much of a tease to
his five sisters. Still it took a great determination to break out of the
Cabot tribe, especially in 1897. I was always grateful to my father for
leaving Boston. Growing up in New York in that period was wonderful.

Our branch of the Cabot family was quite separate from our Boston
cousins. To see them on our occasional visits to Boston was pleasant,
but I never felt a part of the clan. They seemed slightly uncomfortable
with "sophisticated" New Yorkers, as they called us. A gentle person,
my father was unusually handsome with clear, classic features and a
benign expression. His white hair lay smoothly over the top and sides
of his well-shaped head and curled up a little at the ends near his ears,
giving an effect of softness. I remember walking with him in the streets
of Munich in 1932 when passers-by, looking at him, would say "Was
für ein' Schönheit" ("What a beauty"). He smiled when I translated it.

In New York he established a branch of the family wool business in downtown Manhattan and lived in Mrs. Bagbie's boarding house on Staten Island, commuting to the city by ferry. It was there that he met Maud Bonner, eleven years his junior, and married her.

She was the eldest of three sisters living with their parents, George and Isabel Bonner, in a large house on Bard Avenue. My grandfather had amassed a small fortune by the age of forty and took his family to live for year-long periods in Europe before returning to settle on Staten Island. Schooling for the three girls was not a priority.

Maud was a passionate and expert equestrienne who rode to hounds, jumping side saddle, preferring excitable horses and challenging jumps. My father was alarmed by her daring and dangerous feats. Once he had persuaded her to marry him, he begged her not to foxhunt any more. Surprisingly enough she complied, perhaps the only time she gave in to him. At twenty-five she had a twenty-three inch waist around which he could clasp his hands. My parents were married in 1895 and lived in Gramercy Park before moving to a brownstone house on East 75th Street where I was born and grew up. There was a row of identical three story houses, each with a rather steep flight of steps and elaborate cast-iron handrails leading up to the front door. A friendly area, we knew our neighbors and shared the same Irish handyman who put out our garbage cans on the appropriate morning and shoveled snow in winter. My mother's younger sister Isabel lived next door to us. Our houses were connected by fire escapes in the rear, so we children could easily visit each other whenever we wanted. This was particularly nice for me, since my cousin Florence was just my age.

Though we were close friends, first cousins and near neighbors, Florence's life differed drastically from mine. Her mother was beautiful, languid, liberal, informal, intellectual and divorced; also she was a Democrat. Hers was a family of three children, sisters Florence and Milly and one boy, Benny, who rarely was at home. Florence was very close to her mother and able to discuss anything with her, so she was far more aware and mature than I. In almost every way Aunt Isabel was unlike her older sister Maud. I picture her stretched out on her living room sofa in a batik gown, smoking a cigarette held in a long cigarette holder, having an interesting conversation with a guest, often a man, on any range of subjects. She was leisurely, an adjective unknown in our family. She was my godmother and I loved her but never felt free enough to discuss anything with her, probably because I had never formulated my difficulties enough to talk about them with anybody.

My most vivid memory of that early period in New York is of the nursery on the third floor where we children had our rooms. Higgie was at boarding school, George, eleven, and Quin, nine, slept in the back room, and I slept in the front room with my nurse Mazzi, a loving French woman with unusually long dark hair which she habitually wore piled high in a big bun on the top of her head but let down at night. Mazzi was a nurse, not a governess. She was not supposed to teach me anything but simply to take care of me physically, to accompany me when I had to go out, to take care of my clothes, see that I brushed my teeth and such basic essentials. This was comforting. I felt free to love her with no sense of obligation and free to cry with her when I needed to. I find it bizarre that I can't remember in what language we communicated. I presume it was French but don't feel at all sure about this. Probably I thought of her as one of the few friendly, uncritical, and loving areas of my life in which words were not important. I could not express myself easily, particularly to my parents.

My life in the city was simple. Every afternoon Mazzi took me to the Mall in Central Park where we usually encountered other children that I knew and played with. Then back as usual to supper in the nursery at five, alone with Mazzi.

In time I attended Miss Chapin's School on 57th Street. Every morning I walked down Park Avenue with my father and Florence, who was in my class. We walked from 75th to 57th Street, an enjoyable way to start the day. Though people spoke about the increasingly noisy traffic on Park Avenue, the noise or smell of fuel with which we are so familiar today do not remain in my memory. Instead I recollect the walk as purely pleasurable. There was a sense that everybody was going to their proper place, be it school or business, and that there was plenty of time to get there. Beyond being on time for meals and school, haste is not a word I associate with my childhood. One had the time to observe the passers-by, watch the budding trees in spring, and in the fall feel the cold on the knees, bare above wool knee-length stockings. In the beginning school was wonderful. My mother told me later that my teacher Miss Stringfellow said I was the brightest child she'd ever had in third grade. By fourth grade, however, I did not mature like my classmates and a less advanced group was instigated for me. In other areas I became a leader, starting an athletic club of four people. We proudly wore embroidered arm bands of crossed hockey sticks and were the envy of the whole class.

A classmate, Anne Tonetti, whose Italian father was a sculptor, first introduced me to an artist's milieu. Her large family lived in a large and to me mysterious house. You entered through a huge, heavy cast-iron and glass door into a stone corridor as in many European houses, and then went through a small wooden door, up three flights of narrow stairs to Mr. Tonetti's studio, a vast space at least twenty feet high, which was the center of their family life. Many years later, on the top floor of this building, Betty Parsons established herself in a much loved one-room studio where she lived, worked, and entertained her world of artists and patrons.

The first time I was invited to the Tonettis' for supper was a highlight in my life. The menu was spaghetti and artichokes. I had never confronted either before and needed a lot of coaching as to how to eat both. The supper table was laid in the studio which had a twelve foot scaffolding rising like a church tower in its center. Mr. Tonetti had needed the platform to work on his standing figure of an Indian, which had been finished and delivered. As it had been so much trouble to build, he thought it absurd to take the scaffolding down and installed a bathtub at the top level. During dinner one of the younger children climbed up the scaffold steps and happily took a bath in elevated privacy while the rest of us ate supper.

The Tonettis' were a wonderful oasis in my life. I often spent weekends with them at Sneeden's Landing across the Hudson from New

York. Even in winter we'd make the trip across the river in a small open boat. On arrival Anne's delightful mother would put us to work on any project on which she needed help. She was building houses on that steep hillside. What we liked to do the most was make designs around fireplaces by pressing shells and other objects we found into wet cement. This task was fun and occupied all of us children. We created spontaneous and attractive firefront designs in the imaginative houses she constructed. Sneeden's Landing is now one of New York's most sought after suburbs.

When the First World War broke out I was eleven. Our German class at school abruptly stopped and the German teacher, whom we loved, disappeared. We were told that because they were now our enemy, we must have nothing more to do with the Germans. In our accustomed daily walk to school, Mr. Pavensted, a German by birth, would also be walking with his daughter Eleanor to Miss Chapin's School. The two fathers often chatted. In the days after the declaration of war my father greeted Mr. Pavensted in a friendly manner as usual, but explained to me that probably certain people would no longer speak to him. I found this strange, but as the weeks went by I noticed it happening.

When I was fourteen my two older brothers joined the armed forces. With pride I wore a red, white, and blue pin with two blue stars that told the world that my brothers were part of the great war to end all wars and make the world safe for democracy. Had they died in action the blue stars would have been exchanged for gold ones. I was in a small Red Cross group organized for adolescents by a friend of my mother's. We knitted socks for the soldiers (mine must have been a mixed blessing) and made pajamas.

It was important to both my parents that I be kept young and innocent – "unspoiled", they would have called it. "You will have plenty of time to be grown up," I was told. Being kept young and innocent actually meant being in a cocoon, emotionally protected from the world.

At fifteen I had not yet menstruated or matured in any way. My body had reacted physically to the psychological constraints which had been imposed upon it. I had remained a child. Humble on the surface, underneath I felt that I had to get away from my family. I loved, admired, and respected them but was stifled in their midst. I knew I was not like them. To be sent to boarding school became my passionate desire. Finally my plea was acceded to and I was sent to Miss Walker's School in Sinsbury, Connecticut, as a very little girl with glasses and a mop of blonde curls dressed in childish smocks. During my first term there I grew several inches and other parts of my anatomy came into proper proportion. When I came home for vacation my mother had to buy me grown-up American girls clothes. While at Miss Walker's I began for the first time to see myself apart from my family. In my second year one of the younger girls had an intense crush on me. For me, the inadequate one, to be admired by a younger child was extremely hard to understand. It helped me to grow up a little.

I graduated from Miss Walker's in June 1921. By that time of the year my mother had already gone north to her beloved Canada. I was surprised and pleased when my father appeared for Commencement. My graduation did not seem particularly important to me, and I presumed it was even less so to my parents. But obviously my father came to give me moral support. He was not expecting anything but was noticeably delighted when the Improvement Prize was given to me. I also valued the award because as the head of the Student Self-Government I had been able to change the school's guilt-ridden direction, of which I had disapproved ever since entering. Each week we had been obliged to to write down our "sins". "Sins" consisted of disobeying any of over a hundred rules, one of them being "You are not allowed to spit prune pits out the window."

In spite of the responsibilities I had undertaken and successfully carried out at school I was still a child as far as the opposite sex was concerned. I had almost no interest or curiosity in boys. My body cycle had finally become normal at boarding school, but my psyche had not. At eighteen I was to come out in New York society where one was expected to be feminine, beautiful, and seductive – only up to a point of course. A young woman must always play the role of temptress but then be sure to say "No". The whole process completely baffled me. I was bought a wardrobe of new clothes and told that I could no longer smoke, though I'd been smoking for years. A set of precise rules were laid out for encounters with the opposite sex of my age.

My grandfather gave the coming-out party at the Colony Club for his granddaughters, Florence and me. He also bought each of us new dresses for the occasion. Florence and her mother ordered one from a fashionable European designer, Baron de Meyer. It was to be unusual, with a dark bodice and full, light-colored skirt, rather Spanish looking. There was a good deal of excitement about this unconventional choice. My dress was classic white satin, a routine affair. On the evening of the party, we first visited my grandfather at his house across the street at 18 East 75th Street. Florence looked exciting and beautiful but one brief glance was enough for Grandpa to express his strong disapproval of Florence's costume. He didn't like it, said it was totally unsuitable for the occasion, a stupid choice to have made, she could not wear it. Florence burst into floods of tears and was taken home by her mother to put on an old dress she had worn to previous parties. While it was a bad beginning for her, it turned out to be a very pleasant party for me. Since politeness demanded dancing with the hostess, the problem of partners was solved, at least for that night.

I disliked the entire concept of "coming out". It seemed to me like nothing but a marriage market. It is not unique. Something similar takes place in different ways in many countries. In 1921 when Florence and I came out, there was still a good deal of decorum left but it was beginning to crumble at the edges. Vast sums of money began to be poured into more and more lavish entertainments, in the hope of securing a pedigreed husband for a "nouveau riche" girl. Since I was not interested in getting married, the entire structure of this social edifice was for me a hollow shell.

I was a dismal failure. I didn't know anyone in that world. I had never had a period of teenage experimentation to learn how to get on with boys or even to meet any. My father tried to help by telling my brothers they must take care of me at dances. Should I not have a partner at supper, they must keep me company. Certainly the last thing my brothers, or any other young man, wanted was to have to take care of a wallflower kid sister.

Clearly I was not a promising social butterfly. Shy and uncomfortable in this role, without small talk, and with little curiosity about the opposite sex, I was a difficult girl to launch. I wanted to have dancing partners simply because it was so profoundly embarrassing not to. To be left standing, isolated, in the vast area of an empty ballroom as all the dancers chatted vivaciously in pairs, then moved into an adjacent room for supper (a sit-down affair to which one must be invited by a male partner) was annihilating. There was nowhere to go except the ladies room. Sitting out supper there was a grim affair, but getting one-self out onto the ballroom floor with a partner was even grimmer. How to attract a partner? How to avoid panic or tears?

Any interest I portrayed toward my male counterparts was purely a pretense. I wanted no more than to be asked to dance and fervently prayed I would be able to think of something to say if someone acquiesced. Finally, "Good Night Ladies" was played by the band as we all formed a line to say good night and thank our hostess for the lovely party. One of my girlfriends, more spirited than I, once said to the hostess, "Thank you for the terrible party." The tired hostess answered, "You're quite welcome, my dear." These exchanges over, my brothers took me home.

I did have one faithful partner, Jack, a nice but lethargic character who had suffered badly from sleeping sickness. There was also another shining exception. A tall, gorgeously handsome young man from Baltimore whose sartorial elegance was matched by his charming manners and pleasing Southern accent came to pay his respects on various Sundays, just as my mother expected. I liked him but we were not yet good friends. One particular Sunday I was not at home when he called. I returned to find an unusually large and beautiful camellia with a charming note on the hall table. I wrote to thank him. There was no answer. Not long afterwards I learned that he had killed himself. I never found out more about it. It was a terrible shock.

Things dragged along and I remained a misfit for what seemed like an eternity. I couldn't fulfill the role created for me by my mother and felt her displeasure when eligible young men rarely turned up for Sunday teas.

Pushed by my feeling of failure, I decided to get out of this no-win dilemma and signed up as a freshman at Barnard College. My parents had decided I should go to Bryn Mawr the following year, but I resisted, fearing that there would be more of the same protective privilege already stifling me. I believed that at Barnard I would broaden my outlook socially and intellectually. I realized, for example, that the only Jews I knew were members of the Warburg family. I thought that Barnard, a far less elite college at that time, would help me towards my goal. After I signed up I was afraid to tell my mother. One Sunday when three young men appeared for tea, I announced my decision, knowing that if my mother disapproved, which I thought she would, at least she would not show it in their presence.

Barnard turned out to be everything I had hoped for. I met very different young women there, serious about themselves and their studies. But I could not fully escape the uncompleted obligations of being a debutante. I continued going to elaborate dinners and dances, coming home late and attempting to prepare for the next day's classes. I remember my mother waking me up one morning, when I had worked late the night before, saying, "Your eyes look like boiled gooseberries." I'm sure they did.

At the dances, where things were beginning to be a little less grim, I was warned by other debutantes not to mention the fact that I was at Barnard. I probably would lose even the few partners I had. However, the new interest in my life diminished the importance of being socially successful, so I was less tense and began to have a few friends in the social world. One evening about six of us went to a movie and came back to my parents' house for a beer. My parents came home from their evening out and walked into the sitting room where we were gathered.

The Nineteen Twenties (1956), Oil on canvas, 24 x 24 in.

My mother met my friends, disliked them and threw them all out. When they had gone, my guests and I were criticized. I was told that in our family there was a "cheap streak" that I had inherited. I pointed out that one of the boys she had thrown out was the son of one of her bridesmaids. She replied she had never wanted that woman for a bridesmaid. Another of those boys, Eddie Mathews, was the brother of Higgie's future wife, Currie. Another was Ogden Nash.

In no way could I win, at least not then, but my foot was on the first rung of the ladder and the second was in view. Slowly I began to feel more at home with myself both physically and psychically. I sensed that I was beginning to be attractive. I was tall, thin and blonde and becoming less shy. My short hair cut was unusual but becoming more acceptable, having been made fashionable by Amelia Earhart, the "aviatrix", for whom I was sometimes mistaken. I began to realize that I was a person who would find my niche somewhere, though not in the Ritz Ballroom.

I enjoyed my courses and made some friends. My favorite course was in theater, an exhilarating course in writing, acting and producing plays, given by a dynamic and charismatic teacher named Minor Latham. Her students became dedicated to theater. I myself hoped to be able to get into theatrical production after college. New York was a vital theater town and Miss Latham's students made the most of it. We saw every interesting play, successful or not. Eugene O'Neil's "Desire Under the Elms", "Strange Interlude", and "The Great God Brown" were produced then. A little later Pirandello was popular. My cousin Eliot Cabot starred in "Six Characters in Search of an Author". Another friend, Mai Mai Sze, was the beautiful narrator of "Lady Precious Stream", a revival of traditional folk drama from China. Her performance was so exquisite that Eugene O'Neil wanted to write a play for her. She refused, being more interested at that time in painting and Chinese studies. Billy Rose, showman "extraordinaire" of colossal chorus girl productions, surprised the city by introducing Esther Williams, a beautiful young swimmer who appeared with startling simplicity in his gaudy entourage. Standing at the edge of the pool, dressed in what used to be called an "Annette Kelleman", now called a tank suit, she paused briefly before diving in and swimming the length with such extraordinary grace and almost unreal beauty that even the sophisticated New York audience went wild. Miss Latham's indoctrination to theater stayed with me a long time. Through it I became involved in promoting a performance of the monologues of one of my friends, Helen Howe. In order to sell tickets I needed to choose a charity as beneficiary. I decided on Georgia Warm Springs, the newly-found spa of Franklin Roosevelt. It turned out that I was the first person to raise money for this pet charity of his and as such was invited to a private interview with him at his house in New York. Contrary to my brother Higgie, I was a great admirer of F.D.R. Higgie had attended Groton School with Franklin and said that he hadn't been able to balance his own checkbook at school, so how could he run the country? Like many business men of that period, Higgie's feelings were so intensely negative that he gave up his position in New York and moved to a farm in Virginia. I have since heard that Franklin's mother managed her son's personal finances throughout his presidency. Much later, in Andover, I had a short but private meeting with Eleanor from which I emerged captivated by the generous power of her personality.

During two winters when I was at Barnard my brother George and I became very close. He was working in our father's business on Worth Street. Our parents were away on some European tour and we stayed in the family house. We acted like a young married couple, entertained a lot, and generally had a ball. George kidded me about my extravagant housekeeping. I kidded him about the many flirtations he would foster, only to find himself too deeply entangled and in need of my help to extricate himself. This experience made for a solid friendship which held strong through thick and thin in the subsequent years, always there, always close.

The walls of my cocoon were crumbling. The butterfly was in the process of hatching out and I was becoming a "belle," be it a bewildered one, with three or four men wanting to marry me at a given time. I had little sense of who these men were as individuals and rarely understood their jokes, yet I was importantly involved in their lives, and often the cause of suffering, which pained me deeply. I reached the point where I dreaded another proposal.

Attempting to unite the social world of Barnard with the debutante world continued to be difficult. As the president of the junior class I was deeply involved with the junior prom, the most important social function of the four college years. There was a certain status to getting a dance with the class president's beau. Many girls wanted to swap dance dates with their boyfriends and mine. Not having a boy friend, I wondered who I could invite as I continued with increasing apprehension to fill up my dance card for a non-existent partner. In the snobbish world of coming-out parties, I was unable to find one young man willing to come up to 116th Street as my prom date. In desperation, my dance card almost full for a phantom escort, I asked George. Even he said "No." In those days Barnard was not socially acceptable.

By coincidence my parents were about to take a trip to Greece they had talked about for many years to celebrate my father's retirement. They wanted me to come along. In spite of the dilemma of the prom, I wanted to stay in New York and finish my college year, so I refused. My father was bitterly disappointed. Higgie undertook the task of persuading me to change my mind. He pointed out that my father was old and might never have the opportunity of making another trip, that I'd regret the decision all my life, that I was being selfish, and so on. Finally I gave in. I held a special meeting to tell the class I was resigning my job as president and leaving at once because of my father's ill health. So on January 30th, 1924, I sailed for Naples with my parents on the SS Empress of Canada. Several members of my class came to see me off, bearing a beautiful large bouquet to which many of them had contributed. Though relieved that I had escaped the apparently insoluble problem of the junior prom, I felt like a cheat, acutely aware of my failure to reconcile my divergent social worlds.

∽

After retirement my father's main interest continued to be travel. He always wanted me to accompany him and my mother. I was impatient to make a life of my own and I found it hard to be with both my parents at the same time. They were two human beings with disparate, totally opposite, interests. Recently I found a note in my diary from the twenties: "After dinner Dad and I sat on the sofa. His hair was very soft and white and he was very darling. I suddenly loved him terribly and was frightened because he was an old man. I was happy being with Father and wondered why I was so grating with him usually when we were all three together. Alone we got on to perfection."

I remember him more as a presence than as a person and am surprised at how few details I recall beyond his beautiful looks, his gentle and kind nature, his quiet humor, and his gracious Bostonianism. I do not remember conversations with him, though we must have had them. I do not remember engaging in activities with him. I think I deprived myself of a lot. I'm sure he would have welcomed a closer relationship, but I allowed my mother's super-active tempo to take precedence over his calmness. In so doing I missed out on what might have been a much-needed support.

Just as I was happy alone with my father so was I happy alone with my mother. We had a good time together, particularly in the fall of 1926 after my graduation from Barnard, when she took me on a wonderful trip to New Mexico. She felt I should see the West. My father bought our train tickets on the last trip of the Harvey System, which was slower than the Express train and cheaper. This ingenious plan, which was terminated with the introduction of dining cars, added immeasurably to the delight of our trip. There was no food aboard the train, which stopped for meals. Breakfast, lunch and supper were movable feasts, timed by the convenience of stopping places. Lunch might be a quick sandwich in a railroad station in Gallup or Toledo, or an hour and a half full course meal in a hotel in Chicago, where we also had time for a little tour on Lake Shore Drive. Not only was the daily schedule varied, breaking the monotony of the long journey, but we received an interesting impression of the life in each state we passed through, which were then far more differentiated than now.

In New Mexico it was our good fortune to have as guide a friendly cousin, Mary Wheelwright, who had moved there from Boston in her forties at the death of her parents. She broke ties with Massachusetts, selling the various family houses and taking the proceeds to make a new life. By the time Mootzie and I took our trip, Mary was well established and deeply involved in New Mexico life and Navaho culture. She was a generous mentor introducing us to the whole area and to her friends, among whom were Georgia O'Keefe, Mabel Dodge and her Indian husband, Toni Luhan, and best of all, Hassein Klah, a remarkable Navaho medicine man. Together Mary and Klah began to collect everything available to do with the Navaho culture. Their efforts culminated in what is now The Wheelwright Museum in Santa Fe. Due to the close relationship between those two remarkable people, many ritual objects of the Navahos have been saved, as well as some actual sandpaintings preserved intact and many more recorded in beautifully illustrated books. The power of their mutual understanding was far deeper than words. Mary never learned Navaho, Klah never learned English, but they worked in perfect accord. Attending the Navaho dances under Klah's aegis with only one or two other whites present was a tremendous privilege.

Of the many ceremonies I saw in New Mexico, the sandpainting made the greatest impression. Starting from a base of smoothed earth as the tent floor, the image is created with many different brightly colored sands. These are carefully and slowly laid down in abstract patterns known to the one making the image for that particular ceremony, an image handed down unchanged from generation to generation. Every symbol and figure in the design has its precise meaning, usually connected with the points of the compass or the powers of natural phenomena which are represented by symbols or figurations of man or beast against a solid-colored background. This is a lengthy process. The tent is large and the task is great, for in the end the image will fill almost the entire space of the tent floor. Once completed, chants are initiated; songs, rituals, and supplications are made to the gods until the moment when the whole image must be danced away in order to insure its continuing power. At first slowly, then with accelerating speed, you watch the exquisite precision of the drawing become blurred as the dancers' bare feet scatter the different colored sands. Grains fly in all directions as the dance energy mounts until all trace of the painting is obliterated, leaving the smooth earth as bare as it was at the start. The process has been fulfilled, encompassing a formal but passionate beauty of concept, execution and destruction.

This was the first time I had seen abstract art in the making, or reflected about it. This was also the first time I had seen men wearing jewelry, jewelry made from beautiful turquoise and silver or colorful tin cans. In addition, the sandpainting was my introduction to the intrinsic ritual importance of dance, especially male dance as a religious celebration. It was the first time I realized the strength of being able to use a design to express an emotion. I could understand it here in terms of a pattern, developed and improved through generations, to express the feelings of a tribe. But I also began to understand how the same route could be taken by an individual artist.

The trip was typical of my mother's planning. Once she had a vision, she carried it out to perfection. My brother George had gone to the Evans School in Arizona, an unusual institution where the boys became men through a tremendous amount of riding and camping as well as completing the necessary academic demands. My mother had visited him there on an earlier trip. Seeing the West had meant so much to her, she wanted me to have a parallel experience and I have always been grateful. Who could remain unmoved by the ecstasy of riding in the beautiful mountains and deserts of that land, in being part of its vastness? At the San Gabriel Ranch, where we stayed, there was a Mr. Bannister from Denver who took a tremendous shine to my mother, always seeking her out to go riding or on some interesting excursion. At first his attention embarrassed her, then she started to joke about it, referring to him as 'Banny Boy.' Next she became noticeably pleased, and finally quite flirtatious. I thoroughly enjoyed seeing her in this new and uncharacteristic light. She loved it, and so did I.

It was a wrench when our beautiful vacation was over and we had to return to New York. On the trip home we traveled by the "modern" train which got us to our destination more quickly, but far less colorfully, than the old Harvey system.

4. FIRST LOVE

"The existence of pleasure is
the first mystery"
— *John Berger*

Another memorable journey began on the first of February, 1927, when
I sailed with my parents on the SS France to Paris en route to the
Dalmatian coast, where I first encountered that mysterious phenomenon of love at first sight. What causes a person to look across a room,
see another human being, and have his or her life changed, without
volition, without premeditation, without words, even without eye contact? The person is caught in and held captive by a cosmic web for
months, years, or like Dante, for a lifetime.

My first experience in this drama was played with Dr. Goich in
Split, Yugoslavia. Dr. Goich, a dark-haired, slender, thirty-year-old man
of aquiline features whose shoes also ended in long sharp points, was
the first Yugoslav I ever met. The setting was a hotel salon. A central
dance floor was surrounded by small tables and chairs. I was with my
parents. Dr. Goich was at a table on the opposite side of the floor. When
the music started, he walked across, bowed, and asked me to dance.
After a short formal dance, he returned me to my seat and invited my
parents and me to attend the Fencing Society the following afternoon.
After we accepted, he left the room. I did not suspect that Dr. Goich
had already been trapped, but later he told me that every night after
our meeting he walked back and forth beneath my window from midnight till dawn. At dawn he would go back to his house, pick flowers
from his garden and bring them to the hotel to be delivered with my
breakfast tray. We saw something of each other and went to a fancy-
dress ball together, but exchanged no more than a kiss. He knew only
a few words of French, our only common language. He told me he was
bewildered by what was happening to him. He knew I would be leaving
shortly, that he would never see me again, and that he had nothing to
gain. But still he was shattered by this consuming experience.

On my return to New York, the same phenomenon occurred with

Jack who was on the other side of the living room in an apartment where we were both guests. I had not noticed him, nor had we exchanged glances, but by the time he came across the room to speak to me he was already caught in the web. He had fallen deeply in love, a position from which he never deviated from that moment on. Jack, the son of a New Hampshire mill worker, was slightly older than I, an attractive, self-made man, full of charm and Irish whimsy. By the time I met him he had amassed a good deal of money and lived in a rather elaborate apartment with a Japanese servant who did everything for him. His friends were interesting, cosmopolitan New Yorkers. Though I came to care for him, I felt a stranger in his world. Jack was very tender as he tried to indoctrinate me into the elementary exchanges between male and female, which I should have understood in my teens but still did not at twenty-five. I had experienced little and felt nothing. He was a sophisticated man who had had a full life of relationships with women, but from the moment he saw me, as he told me later, he had nothing to do with another woman until our romance ended. He concentrated with great gentleness on trying to bring me to a state of awareness. Finally, he gave me *Lady Chatterly's Lover* in the hopes that it would help me cross a bridge. Reading the D.H. Lawrence book was quite a shock for me. I had buried the awareness of my sexuality at such a depth that I believed that it didn't exist, though unknowingly I was giving out other signals. I did not see myself as part of a couple even in the distant future. Unquestionably Jack was the first to break open my safe, if only by a crack. He suffered in the process, something I only partially understood and for which I did not give him due credit. We became engaged, but I was extremely neurotic about getting married and still fearful of sexual involvement with a man. I would often call him in the middle of the night saying, "I can't possibly do this." And he would always say, "Oh well, don't worry about it. We'll have lunch tomorrow and talk about it. Maybe you'll do it, maybe you won't."

He was skillful in his handling of me. Much as I liked Jack, I was not in love with him and was apprehensive about getting in too deep.

Could it be possible, I wondered, to find someone with whom I could feel sufficiently at ease to be completely myself?

Miraculously, this is exactly what did happen on the top of a Fifth Avenue bus. I met Whitney Cromwell. It was while we were both students, I at Barnard, he at Columbia architectural school. A fellow student introduced us. Sitting there on the left front seat of that bus, I was conscious that I felt completely comfortable in the company of this young man I had just met. The trip from 113th Street to 75th, where I would get off, was short but long enough to change my life. I had met someone who, by his presence, brought me to a standstill, someone who quite suddenly made me question what I was doing with my life. My doubts and confusions were suspended, pushed aside by a person whom I met only a few minutes before. This stocky, not particularly handsome young man made me question the purpose of my life, not by what he said (he was a quiet, unassuming person) but by what he was. And somehow I knew that there was time to answer that question. He possessed a solidity of the psyche. Instinctively I felt his support for my own. With Whitney I didn't feel my habitually estranged self. Silence was not a retreat but a place we shared. We understood each other without speaking. His presence dispersed my doubts about myself. He brought me, who had never been in love, and who doubted that I ever would be, to a full stop. Suddenly I felt at home, and shortly afterwards I began to feel that I was capable of falling in love, that I could be normal, and then that I was in love. That fateful encounter on the bus had been instantaneous, then became permanent.

It pleased me that Whitney was not particularly good-looking. He was a medium blond, about six feet tall with a stocky build and a sensitive face. He was not athletic but strong and highly intelligent. Among other things he loved and knew a great deal about both English and French literatures, a knowledge about which he was totally unpretentious. Fundamentally a shy person of little vanity and great wisdom, he was readily capable of awe, a quality I love because it implies a readiness to accept surprise. He did not push himself to the fore, rather he was just there, always there, solid in judgment, amused, generous and fun.

I saw a great deal of Whitney from then on in New York, and during the following summer when he visited me at the Manor House in Canada. His cousin Esther, who was in love with my brother George, came with him. We had a big wonderful house party. This was the first time I had been with Whitney in a crowd and I loved him more than ever. I can still see him sitting in the moonlight on the porch of the fishing cabin at Lac Gravel, a red cotton handkerchief tied around his neck, singing in his lovely voice:

Remember the night, the night you said "I love you", remember,
Remember you swore by all the stars above you, remember,
Remember you said that you'd be true and asked me to keep on loving you,
You promised that you'd forget me not but you forgot to remember.

One night in New York Whitney told me that he loved me, but could not ask me to marry him because he was homosexual. I was completely shattered, crying much of the time. I only had a vague concept of what homosexuality was and assumed that, were I to marry him, we would not be able to have a child. When I read this in my diary recently, I was appalled and would not have believed my naïveté had I not read the words in my own handwriting. I don't know if my assumption was common for a young girl in my social world at that period. We never thought of seeking advice. We would not have known where to seek it. "We have so little precedent," Whitney would say.

Looking back I see that my ignorance of basic physical facts was fateful, leading me to a path of inaction that drastically affected the rest of my life. Then I only knew I loved Whitney and told him so, he knew he loved me and told me so, and we both knew our feelings were authentic. It seemed natural to expect we would somehow end up together.

When I left New York with my parents for the trip to the Dalmatian coast, Whitney and his friend Pat Morgan were also aboard en route to Paris to study for the Beaux Arts exams. The Beaux Arts was still regarded as the most prestigious architectural school in Europe. After the trip my parents returned to New York while I stayed on in Paris. The shock of Whitney's homosexuality was still very painful to me. Below the surface was an ever present sadness, plus a bewilderment of not knowing which way to turn. The only aspect in which I felt some security was the knowledge that I loved him and was happy to be in the same city so we could see each other easily. I was also glad that that city was Paris.

I was awaiting the arrival of my friend Fanny Colby, with whom I'd planned to take a trip to Ireland. At the last minute she cancelled. Pat had failed the first Beaux Arts exams and had just lost his mother. He was at loose ends. Whitney suggested that I take him to Ireland in Fanny's stead. We went, along with Whitney's older brother, Bobby. On the ferry crossing between England and Ireland, Pat asked me to marry him. I cried as I refused. I just couldn't cope with it. I was in love with Whitney and wanted time alone with him, lots of time away from his mother, from my parents and from Pat. Whitney and I knew we had serious problems to resolve but we also knew we had our love to work with and we were each aware there was a long way to go. After the trip to Ireland I remained in Paris for a while longer, feeling more and more that this was home.

One of the memorable evenings of that spring in Paris occurred on May 21st. I was having dinner with Whitney. During dinner he said, "Lindbergh's supposed to arrive tonight." I asked, "Who's Lindbergh?"

He told me and mentioned when the arrival was expected. "We must go," I said.

We hurried through the rest of our meal and took a taxi to Orly or, rather towards Orly. Long before reaching the airport the traffic was blocked solid. We got out of the taxi and found ourselves in the midst of an excited hubbub of pushing people. At first we could walk by squeezing in the narrow spaces between the cars, but soon these areas became impassable as people crowded in. We felt proud to be Americans. Everyone was talking about Lindbergh's youth. "From his picture in the paper," they said, "he looks like a young kid and he has just crossed the ocean all alone!"

Since most of the cars were taxis, I had the idea of standing on the running board of one and jumping from there to the next without touching the ground. By then the taxis were almost bumper to bumper. Whitney followed me. "This is dangerous," he said, for a taxi would suddenly dart forward if a space, no matter how small, opened up. Some boys were walking on the tops of the cabs.

I can still feel the thrill, still sniff the air of that spring night, heavy with exhaust fumes. The excitement grew, our pace slowed. Now it was almost impossible to move forward. Time was slipping by. We began to realize we weren't going to make it to the landing pad. We weren't going to see the little plane emerge from the clouds to fulfill its mission proudly. Shortly, the word started back like a rumble, getting louder as it got nearer. "Il a atterri! Il a atterri!", ("He has landed"). The miracle had happened, Lindbergh had proved his dream, and we had been close enough to experience the excitement of that historic moment.

Pat and Whitney shared an apartment; they were friends, not lovers, who complemented each other. Pat was artistic, immature, ambivalent, gregarious and timid. Whitney was mature, serious-minded, intellectually curious, and strong. Pat was like a child, Whitney an adult. Pat was handsome, Whitney not. They both had lost their fathers – Pat when he was very young and Whitney as a teenager – and had been brought up by dominating single mothers whom each had learned to handle. They became friends first at Harvard and later at the Columbia School of Architecture, where Whitney re-introduced me to Pat. I had met him two years earlier in Boston and had found him superficial and conceited. When I met him again we got on much better, and often painted together in a friend's studio, which was pleasant. I don't know if he realized that Whitney and I were in love, but if he did, I suspect he suppressed it because of his own interest in me. I never could take him seriously at that level and always thought of him as "Little Pat", a mag-

Green Point Series (1979), Collage and print, 25 x 28 in.

ical child. Increasingly I felt that Whitney was moving away from the homosexuality in his past towards a relationship with me. At that time I was no more than a fledgling woman, unaware of my emotional needs and the necessity of having to fight to express them. What was so new and wonderful was that, for the first time in my life, Whitney was giving me the space and time I needed to grow into my gender. But there was still an enormous, family-inflicted sense of feminine inferiority to overcome. As well as loving me, Whitney trusted my intelligence, which was rare for me then and very precious.

Pat was often with us. Socially we became known as a trio. His presence acted as a welcome shield that helped me divert my thoughts from my sorrow. However, this agreeable "modus vivendi" postponed addressing the real problem that faced Whitney and me. Probably we would have coped more adequately with our relationship had we been alone more often. The more Whitney and I were together, the more we understood and loved each other. However, there was no question but that the three of us had a wonderful time together. I got along easily with each of them and they did not threaten my still undeveloped femininity, perhaps because they, too, were trying to understand their own sexualities. I was the ideal companion for them, and they for me. We fitted perfectly into the Paris of the twenties. Without them, as an American girl alone in Paris, it is doubtful I would have been included in the wonderful world we three knew, nor perhaps would they have without me.

Though I knew very well what I felt for Whitney, I was still not able to translate that feeling into action decisive for our future because I didn't know which way to move. Whitney thought more clearly than I, but he didn't know what to do either. We were both living in suspended ambiguity. On one hand I was elated by my first love, and on the other perplexed by trying to gauge the complications of a relationship with a homosexual man.

I never felt Pat understood me, but that seemed unimportant as I was not romantically interested in him. He was sympathetic, cozy, and good company. Whitney and I saw him as an unselfish, giving person, a good friend to each of us. We three had great fun in that wonderful period, but when it ended, Whitney and I were back where we had started. We needed to get off somewhere together alone.

People were somewhat confused by our trio, not knowing who loved whom, but they accepted and liked all three of us. There was never uncertainty between Whitney and me as to where we stood. When I asked him whether the three of us, being together so much, was unfair to Pat since he also loved me, Whitney simply said, "Pat is in love with every tall blonde American girl he meets" and dismissed the subject.

I knew that my own femininity was retardedly beginning to emerge through Whitney, since only with him could I trust it. I felt and hoped that with the motivation we had, we would sooner or later resolve our problems. Reluctantly I left Paris to return home.

However, it soon turned out that I was more convinced of a positive outcome than he, for not long after my return to New York, Whitney attempted to take his own life. Since I was so involved with him and couldn't marry him, he didn't want to impinge on the rest of my life – so he attempted suicide. Although he turned on the gas, he was not successful. It leaked through to the apartment below, the tenants came up and rushed him to the hospital, unconscious. As Whitney's father had been the head of the New York Stock Exchange, his attempted suicide was reported in the *New York Times*, where I read about it. I sent him a telegram saying,

"STUNG LOVE MAUD"

This strikes me now as hard and unfeeling. What I meant was – "We're in this together, you can't solve it as easily as that." I think he understood. We never mentioned the telegram. We had a different kind of toughness than young people have today. There was a softness with the hardness. Whitney once told a friend of mine that he loved me because I was disillusioned and disinterested.

Meanwhile, Jack, whom I still saw when in New York, was suffering from the strain of unfulfilled desires and of being passionately in love with me and my ambiguity. In May 1928 he finally said he could stand it no longer, telling me to either marry him or leave town. I returned to Paris. Shortly afterwards he followed me, and found me picking up my mail at Morgan's Bank in Place Vendome. Jack and Whitney never met, but Jack soon became aware of the validity of my interest in Whitney. He abandoned his long and arduous pursuit and returned home. As he said to a friend, "I've done a wonderful job with Maud for the benefit of some other man." I stayed on in Paris.

∼

The central setting for my Paris life was Ivy Troutman's apartment on Rue de Lille. Whitney and Pat introduced me to her. Ivy was an American who had run away from her home in New Jersey at age fourteen to join the Southern and Marlow Shakespeare Company.

Waldo Pierce, the well-known American painter, described by my aunt as looking like Wotan, had met her in the theater and became her husband. He left Ivy when she couldn't bear him a child. After Waldo left, Ivy, dressed in scarlet, gave herself a divorce party. She continued to live in the beautiful apartment they had shared where she minored in art but majored in people. Her apartment had two large rooms. One had been Waldo's studio, which she always kept as such, allowing Pat and later me to work there. Ivy usually sketched when we went on excursions to the environs, but would rarely dabble with paints in Paris. Essentially she just loved the ambience of living in a studio. Hers was a charming, friendly and traditional French apartment. She brought a sense of beauty to her surroundings that expressed her personality. There was a tremendous openness and panache about everything she touched.

Ivy was a handsome, well-proportioned woman of medium height with classic features, vigorous wavy dark hair and a fanciful imagination. By the way she habitually put perfume behind her ear lobes, one felt her awareness of her own beauty even if she was not, as she used to say, in her "salade" days. Her delighted laugh, her pleasure in the unexpected, her ability to, rather theatrically, turn a detail into an event, all were done with great bravura. She flowed rather than walked, more like a river than a dancer, trailing a scarf or swishing a full-cut skirt to enhance the effect. She created an opening for friendship into which one could enter if one chose. She loved being at the center and shone in the world she created of unusual people who pleased her. Hers was an attractive, happy milieu, a great starting or ending place for finding one's niche in Paris life.

Ivy loved to give parties, and in 1928 she gave two unusual ones. Only "beautiful people", men and women of outstanding looks, were invited to the first. Noguchi, the now famous Japanese sculptor, young and very handsome then and only beginning to be known, was there, and another Oriental beauty, Mai Mai Sze. She was the slender, strikingly beautiful daughter of the Chinese ambassador, first to the Court of St. James and later to Washington.

To the second party, Ivy invited the "wonderful people". There were some crossovers, of course, who were both beautiful and wonderful. But only a handful of insiders knew the basic requirements for the invitations. Both parties were vivacious, highly individualistic, intelligent, fun, full of laughs – a "succès fou."

This was the surface Ivy. Beneath the fun was a practical, kind, extremely generous person, a survivor who managed ingeniously on diminishing returns. Ivy never had any extra money, but for a while she did have enough for her wonderful sun-filled apartment with its large windows and high ceilings, and for Mariette in the kitchen. After a time Mariette vanished but Ivy kept things up. Accompanied by her miniature white poodle, "Fifi," she often received guests while having breakfast in bed. She was someone to whom the comment of the "Mad Woman of Chaillot" applied: "False pearls, if worn long enough, become real." Whether her pearls were false or not, she wore them with élan. Ivy was the core of Paris for many of us at that time. Without the use of her apartment as a studio and as a center for an interesting social life, I might never have stumbled on my life's work.

I often worked at Ivy's and was still heady with my discovery of the world of painting. I tried a few more adventurous subjects than the anemones. I painted Mariette in the kitchen, which came out surprisingly well. Next I tried a canvas of Pat and me painting – my first experience of looking at the subject in a mirror. This was not at all successful. Then I tried my first nude. For some reason I was the only one working in Ivy's studio that day. The model lay down on the sofa, a traditional copy of Louis XVI, upholstered in tan velvet with rounded ends. I managed to block in the background and the sofa itself enough to begin. I got the model more or less placed, then painted the skin tones in shadow, unadulterated black, doing the best I could to get something resembling flesh tones for the skin in highlight. At that point Ernest Hemingway walked through the room to call on Ivy. He stopped, greeted me, and looked at the canvas. "That's very good," he said with surprise in his voice, and walked on through. As this was probably about my fourth oil painting ever, I was amazed. "Wonderful," I thought,

"If he says it's good, I'm going to go ahead and make it better, I'll make these stark black shadows more real."

I believed I was achieving this when Ernest walked back through, looked at the canvas and said, "Now you've ruined the whole thing," and left. Total bewilderment set in and some despair. I had not the faintest idea why he had said the painting was good in the first place or bad in the second. To find answers to those questions took me a long time.

After that first small batch of paintings done in Paris, all of which I still have, there is a gap, although I kept painting. That following summer at La Malbaie I only painted landscapes. Perhaps I kept the early Paris work and not the early Canadian simply because in Paris there was receptivity to it while in Canada there was not. I needed encouragement. I needed Paris. Fortunately I was able to be there for prolonged visits during 1927, 1928, and 1929. Increasingly I felt I belonged.

What a wonderful era it was to be young and to be in Paris! It felt like the center of the world. These periods there laid the foundation stones of my attitude toward my work, toward accepting the necessity of art in my life and toward recognizing the difficulty of sustaining that work no matter what the circumstances. Painting is a lonely profession. Day after day isolated in the studio alone is routine. One must be able to maintain an ego strong enough to support continuation and yet open enough to welcome the unexpected. The solitude was not a problem for me. It had been the "modus vivendi" of my Canadian youth and it stood me in good stead. The European approach to art that I absorbed in Paris gave a different flavor to all the subsequent years.

Both Whitney and Pat were deeply involved in their work at the Beaux Arts. Luckily, I was able to share in this by also studying with their mathematics teacher, Monsieur Mayence, who lived in a fifth floor walk-up attic and was a delightful old man whose whole life was mathematics. He taught me solid geometry, which I loved. I had wanted to major in mathematics at Barnard but couldn't get a recommendation to do so from my elementary math teacher there.

He said that since I was not interested in science, I, as a woman, would have no use for mathematics. Now I more than made up for that loss with a wonderful old man in a Paris attic. I was pleased by my routine. Alternating between studying math and working in Ivy's studio was an ideal pattern. Through Ivy I met many new friends. Sandy Calder was a good friend of hers and became my good friend also. Sandy was always fun to be with, dressed in his perennial red shirt and tie and always with his contagious laugh and wonderful common sense. We saw the Hemingways, and met the Joyces, James and Nora.

As I sit here this evening in Cambridge writing this chapter in long hand, my thoughts go back to an afternoon in 1928, to a café somewhere in Paris with Ernest, Pat and Whitney. The day was slightly drizzly. We had walked along one of those small, nondescript cross streets in the area of St. Sulpice, a street you have to go through to get somewhere else. The only café on the block, on the left, was Chinese. We went in. There were little round tables and wire chairs, an impersonal Oriental place. I sat opposite Ernest. We ordered drinks and he started to talk. We were there a long time. Ernest talked steadily to Whitney, telling him how he wrote, what some of the pit-falls were and the pleasures. I can recall his wonderful concern for Whitney, a concern for someone for whom it was worth making the effort to register certain important facts.

Ernest liked Whitney and wanted to help him decide whether to go on with architecture or switch to writing, his hobby. He said how for him long hand was a better tempo because it gave you more time and the words were more personal that way – at least for him that was true. He said he did an enormous amount of rewriting – four or five times, often more. There are the sections that you know right away are good. They just come. And then there are the others. The ones that have to be written and rewritten. "Use the most direct simple words and don't put in anything extra. Make it tight. Do the whole thing at a first sitting, or at least a whole section of it. Write it as it comes. Much later do the rewriting. When you're describing something be sure to position yourself precisely in the landscape.

Each day is different than the day before. A lot of things have to be right in your own frame – then it flows – otherwise rewrite it until it does."

When we came out, the weather was still drizzly. Ernest had to leave us. We three were very quiet. "Imagine," Whitney said, "having one of the best living writers talk to you, a beginner, like that for two hours."

I had met Ernest Hemingway earlier that year in New York. Waldo Pierce, Ivy's ex-husband, had wanted us to meet. When Waldo and I arrived at the Park Avenue apartment of his friends the Stratters, Ernest was already there. Our hostess came down a winding staircase dressed in a red velvet tea gown. We had a pleasant time, a few drinks, and left. Going down in the elevator, Ernest put on his hat, into which were hooked some fishing flies. Quite irrationally I took exception to this, claiming that though fine for a fishing trip, they were pretentious for the Big City. I had read very little of Ernest's work at the time and didn't realize I was trespassing on sacred terrain. Ernest asked me what I knew about fishing. "Not much," I said, "But I've gone trout fishing all my life and salmon fishing once." When we parted company, he said he hoped we'd meet soon again in Paris. My first impression of Ernest was of a big, stocky man, not too talkative at first meeting, speaking in short sentences with a sort of subdued shyness. Only later in Key West did I realize how good looking he was. Four years later, at a very tense moment, he was to remind me of our first meeting.

When I first knew Ernest in Paris he asked me to come with him while he bought himself a new suit. For some reason I didn't want to go, but agreed to meet him later for lunch. We went to one of his favorite bistros along with several of his men friends. The small place had a steamy atmosphere, good food, and sawdust on the floor. As we were leaving Ernest took his hat down from the coat rack. I looked into its very grubby interior. The leather band was sweat-stained and filthy. Quite suddenly I took it from him, ripped out the leather band, and threw it onto the sawdust. I surprised myself as much as everyone else by this impulsive action. Was it just an off-beat flirtatious come-on or what? I think he loved it.

I saw a lot of Ernest and Pauline, his second wife. She was unusual, with a very personal, slightly kooky sense of humor I found irresistible. Her unmarried sister, Ginny, had the same qualities, very funny ladies both of them, diverting and delightful. They came from Pigot, Arkansas.

The previous winter Pat had visited the Hemingways in Key West and had been invited there again, as were Whitney and I. I accepted, planning to go down to Florida from New York in February.

Now there were two wonderful invitations from the Hemingways – one for early July to Pamplona, for the St. Fermin fiesta in the company of other friends, and the second to Key West the following winter.

I thought I could not accept the one for Pamplona because I had promised my mother to be back in Canada for my father's 70th birthday, June 28th. It was hard to refuse the invitation, especially since, as an added attraction (as though one were needed), Harpo Marx was to be one of the group. Pat, fortunately, was able to accept. He went and ran with the bulls in the streets in the early morning. Ernest admired Pat's athletic skills, mostly tennis and squash. In fact, when their child was born that next year, Ernest named him after Pat. On being asked why, Ernest answered, "Because you would have made a wonderful Jai-alai player."

Whitney wanted to take me to the Quat'z Arts Ball, which he had never attended, and I wanted to go. The party had the reputation of being as far out as a party could be; every kind of sex going on quite openly. The day before the event Whitney and I were having a drink with Ernest and Pauline. Ernest took Whitney aside and advised him strongly not to take me to the ball. He felt the shock could be traumatic as I was far too innocent. Whitney heeded Ernest's suggestion. We were both disappointed. In retrospect I think Ernest was right. He was protecting me and was certainly right about my innocence.

One day I was taken out to lunch by Bridget Patmore, a member of the Bloomsbury set. I had been introduced to Bridget by her son Derek, a friend of mine who was living in New York. The other guests turned out to be Vita Sackville-West and Harold Nicolson. Clearly they didn't understand why Bridget had introduced an unknown American girl into their intimate group. Their chit-chat was vivacious with occasional polite asides to me. At some point during the meal, Vita became curious and patronizingly asked me, "And what do you do in Paris, my dear?"

"Oh," I said, "I go to museums and the theater and occasionally I paint and see friends."

She wanted more. "Well, for instance, what are you going to do this evening?"

"I'm going to see the Joyces," I said.

"Oh, I didn't know there was a ceremony for Joyce this evening."

"No. It's not a ceremony, just a small dinner of six."

"Really," she said, her curiosity mounting, "Who are the six?"

"Some friends of mine," I said, naming Whitney, Pat and Ivy, whom I was sure she wouldn't know. There was an astonished interval and then a long drawn-out "Well, well." I think they were glad when I left.

The dinner with the Joyces took place in Pat and Whitney's beautiful high-ceilinged apartment on Isle St. Louis, which they had been lucky enough to sublet from Madame Sert. Large windows looked out onto the Seine. Joyce was quite blind then. I sat next to him at dinner and helped him put food on his plate as he couldn't see well enough to serve himself from the dish passed to him by the maid. After dinner he went to the piano and sang Irish and Italian songs with his eyes closed or semi-closed, playing softly. He had a high, clear, perfectly pitched voice. Every vibration reached one's solar plexus, not loud but clean and pure, like a pointed shaft.

Paris was alive with marvels. The Cirque Médrano was a revelation. I had always loved the Barnum and Bailey circus as a child, but in Paris the circus was a very different matter, a small one-ring affair where one could concentrate on everything going on and feel a part of it. And what was going on was the ingenious showmanship of the Fratellini Brothers, the greatest clowns in the world, loved by everybody. This was the basic source material for the inimitable wire pieces Sandy was making that later became "Calder's Circus" and is now in the lobby of the Whitney Museum in New York.

The six-day bicycle races were a new wonderment to me. Ernest loved these and I went with him and Waldo one night to the Velodrome d'Hiver. Thinking back, I can hear again that whirring sound of the tires on the wood as they passed at lightning speed; the crash-helmeted rider, almost a part of his machine, bending low over the handle bars, legs turning the sprockets like flashes, climbing high on the banked corner – his body appearing momentarily horizontal, then plunging down to rise again at the next corner. It was literally breathtaking.

Diaghilev's Ballet Russe was another joy. To be at the openings was thrilling. The most vivid ballet was "La Chatte" which I saw in 1927. Balanchine was the choreographer. The sets and costumes were designed by the Russian constructivist brothers, Naum Gabo and Anton Pevsner.

A young man, played by Serge Lifar, falls in love with a cat. He begs Aphrodite to change the cat into someone who can return his love. The goddess complies and turns the cat into a beautiful girl, danced by Alice Nikitina. They make love. But the goddess is not content to leave this idyllic situation alone, and she toys with them by sending a mouse running across the nuptial chamber. The girl sees the mouse and jumps up to follow it. Then Aphrodite turns the girl back into a cat. The young man is left desolate. What Gabo and Pevsner created in "La Chatte" with wire and plastic was modern magic, a liquid geometry within an architecture where costumes and sets were often indistinguishable. The transparent flat shapes edged or traversed by wires floated across the stage sometimes independently, sometimes interacting with each other or with the dancers as they moved far apart or so close together that the tension of their not meeting made you draw in your breath. The two dancers approach, each extending a hand with thumb and first finger shaping an uncompleted loop; they draw near; the gaps in their fingers intersect but their fingers never meet to close the link. This ballet had the beauty of the solid geometry I was studying with Monsieur Mayence, and of cubist painting.

Nightlife was a habit in Paris. Le Boeuf sur le Toit and Le Grand Ecart were our favorite spots. There the deep, soul-searching love talks of our youth unfolded against the smoothly exciting jazz of Coleman

Hawkins. Even now his rhythms are so much a part of me that when I recently attended a small jazz group here in Cambridge with a particularly inspiring trumpet player, I was instantly and unexpectedly taken back to Paris in 1928-29. Then I found out that the trumpet player, Thomas Lindsey, had for many years played with Coleman Hawkins.

Many Russian émigrés, a wonderful group of people who had been fortunate enough to escape from the Russian Revolution, sang for their livelihood in Paris night clubs. We often went to an after-hours café where they would congregate and relax when the night clubs closed. We loved these warm friendly Russians who added an enriching element to our lives.

As we drove home to the Left Bank in the small hours one morning, the taxi careening around the corner of the Rue de Seine, I remember Whitney saying, "Jeunesse, jeunesse, Paris, Paris. I can think of no other tradition to which I would more willingly subscribe." I totally agreed with him. Paris gave all of us an indefinable, very interior feeling of how to live. Everybody seemed to feel that to be there, in Paris, at that moment of their lives was just right for them, though many of us, of course, were going through our various kinds of wringers.

I find it difficult to realize that my whole magical Paris experience covered only three years, and those intermittently. The effect was lasting. Living in Paris then was like coming home after a long voyage, home to a place only sensed earlier, a place filled with new pleasures, new images, new colors and values, and the acceptance of unrealized sensibilities within myself that, in being honored by others, gained validity for me. Another portal was opening. Joseph Campbell, the mythologist, used the phrase, "Follow your bliss." In Paris and the world that expanded from it, I found where my bliss lay. Paris made the choices a lot wider and the differences greater than in the world I had known before. It's taken me a long lifetime to be able to celebrate them.

5. TRAVEL

"Set out from any point. They are all alike.
They lead to a point of departure."
— *Antonio Porchia*

The year after graduating from Barnard I decided to visit the Soviet Union. Having majored in contemporary history, I had come to believe that Communism offered the best hope of liberty for the human race and wanted to see for myself; Whitney was eager to accompany me. I applied for our visas but months dragged on with no response or any evidence that one would come. Still I wanted to proceed. Whitney was in Paris, where I joined him, and together we planned to work our way towards Russia geographically, hoping luck would be on our side. We got as far as Berlin where we joined up with Pat again; he was there with Sandy Calder who was then showing his work at the Neumann Nierendorf Gallery, as was Chantal Quenneville, a French painter friend.

Life in Berlin then was a strange mixture. The flashing hardness of glamorous, luxury stores failed to conceal the growing economic despair. Inflation, already high, was to rise disastrously in the following years, laying the groundwork for the appeal of Hitler's message to a youthful generation suffering from lack of opportunity. The women walking along Berlin's immaculate streets appeared hard and determined. As Americans we were conscious of the ever-present "Verboten" signs, keeping the parks and avenues looking so well-tended and their citizens so well-controlled. At first this made one feel constrained, but later one accepted, appreciated and soon preferred their way as opposed to our slovenly habits of littering scrap papers anywhere.

Sasha Stone, a Russian photographer whom we came to know, took us to see "Die Dreigroschenoper", a musical production based on "The Beggar's Opera" first produced in London in 1728 and written by the Englishman John Gay. It became the greatest theatrical success of that century, save for the interval of Victorian and Edwardian times when it was thought improper. Its popularity was due to the catchy, impertinent tunes and the fascinating inversion of morals, with bad behavior shown as acceptable. The opera's originality lay in its cast of characters, who were based on real inhabitants of London's under-world. Bertolt Brecht's modernized version, which we saw, used the same characters with similar sardonic music written by Kurt Weill. His opera was as popular in 1928 as Gay's was in 1728. In 1929 it was by far the most important cultural event in all of Germany. Its radical influ-ence was felt throughout Europe and eventually reached the United States, where there was a successful presentation after various failures. The powerful force in the German presentation was not achieved in America. Once initiated, we attended the opera every evening, despite the fact that none of us spoke German. The dynamism on the stage made language of secondary importance. With her high, haunting voice, Lotte Lenya could manipulate one's emotions from a feeling of complete ruthlessness to deeply experienced tenderness. Supported by the music of Kurt Weill, Brecht's songs became graven in our mem-ories. Of course we bought all the available records, and for many years this music was the leitmotif of our lives.

Sasha Stone also took us with him on a newspaper photographic assignment to the cherry blossom festival at Werden, just outside Berlin, a glorious Bacchanalian celebration for the coming of Spring, featuring the delicious, intoxicating, freshly-made May wine. We took part in everything, including riding on the gigantic Ferris wheel with its seats suspended by chains. Sasha took a photograph I still have which appeared on the cover of the *Hamburger Illustrierte* of June 8, 1929. Pat, Chantal and I are in mid-air, clasping the chains of our free-flying seats. Another, an enlarged head of me, appeared on a subsequent cover with the caption "eine typische deutishe Mädchen" ("a typical German girl"). What a glorious orgy! Streets cleared of cars, crowds of people with cherry blossoms tucked behind their ears or in their jacket lapels laughing, singing, beautifully intoxicated with life. Box cars with straw on the floor waited to bring the drunks back to Berlin after dark. The day was a Dionysian festival where everyone was inebriated but no one was unpleasantly drunk, at least not in daylight hours. We were among the strollers, swaying along, arms around each others' shoulders. When a large black limousine attempted to get through the resentful crowd, we reluctantly moved to one side. As the car passed I looked in at the important looking men in business suits. To my horror I was virtually face to face with Mr. Pierre Jay, a close friend of my parents and the director of U.S.-German monetary affairs. I feared the worst, at least a letter to my parents criticizing my behavior. But quite the opposite happened. The next day a message arrived at the unpretentious pension where we were staying, inviting me to tea. Whitney and I went and met there a friend of my brothers, Bob Litell, a reporter on the *New York Sun* who was en route to Russia. I asked if he could help get us visas. He said he would send them from Moscow and take rooms for us in his hotel. This was magical. Even my mother's wish would be complied with. I had told her that I wanted to go to Russia with Whitney. "How wonderful, darling," she had said. "Of course, you must have a chaperone." I knew that getting to Russia would be difficult enough in itself and decided to forget her conjunction. Now both ends would be satisfied.

Berlin was an exciting place to be while waiting for the visas. It was a wide open city at night. One skyscraper many floors high had a night club on each floor, varying from Hoola-Hoola to striptease. One night four of us, two men and two women, went to the night club area. The first joint we went to refused us entrance. We tried the next with the same result and so it went all the way down that long block. Men and women together weren't admitted anywhere. At the very end of the street we were allowed into a large dance hall which for whatever reason was decorated entirely with American flags. To distinguish the sexes of the patrons was a conundrum. About half the men were in evening dresses and several women in men's clothes. I don't think any of us had ever been to such a place before. We sat there having drinks and watching. None of us danced.

It was not too long before our visas came through and Whitney and I left for Russia. At least to the visitor, Moscow is not a lovable city. Apart from the magnificent Red Square and some spectacular mosques, it is a plebeian city, in total contrast to St. Petersburg, then

Leningrad and now again St. Petersburg, with its majestic open squares enclosed by beautiful yellow edifices. But Moscow is a working city. A lot goes on there.

It would be hard to repeat the trip Whitney and I took to the Soviet Union because in our two-or three-week visit we never saw another tourist. The government was issuing visas only to a few very important people including journalists. We were there by the luck of having met Bob Litell in Berlin. Language was a problem. French and German helped. Only Kitty, among those we met, spoke English. On our first days we went to several factories, where we were greeted with resentment. When asked who we were and what we did, we replied that we were students. "You cannot be," workers said angrily, "or you would be back at home studying."

I had read about Soviet divorce laws and wanted to see how they worked. If a couple wanted a divorce they sent in a postcard to the divorce office stating their reason. This card was acknowledged by another postcard, which the couple then brought to the divorce bureau. We spent several hours in that bureau observing the line of would-be divorcées. Once they got up to the desk they handed in their card and were checked off the list. I marvelled at the simplicity of the affair compared to our cumbersome legalities, but in spite of the ease of the procedure the couples didn't look very happy. I thought about this and several other observations made since arrival and began to question if what I had read or imagined to be true before coming really was so. Were the Soviet people really as free as the books reported? That evening, as Whitney and I were enjoying a vodka in a forlorn hotel dining room, I had a sudden conviction based on what we had seen. "I was wrong," I said, "Communism is not the liberation of the individual as I have thought, but his enslavement."

In New York, a Russian-American woman had given me an introduction to her friend Kitty Puchevitch in Moscow. Kitty invited us to her one-room apartment, where we sat on the bed and talked. She considered herself lucky to have the room to herself and received us with great excitement. She said she had been dreaming about me and believed that Krishnamurti had sent me to her. I knew something about theosophy. I'd read Krishnamurti and had had many discussions about him with my friend and cousin Eliot Cabot in New York, who was deeply involved with his philosophy. We saw Kitty on and off during our time in Moscow. She was an attractive, charismatic, middle-aged woman who had been a well known actress before the Revolution. At that time her husband left Russia, but she decided to stay on and cast her lot with the new regime. She was now working as a journalist. Kitty became extremely attached to me and counseled me to rush into life, even at the expense of making mistakes, because I had a heart open to all. Clearly I was filling an important role in her life.

When the time came to leave for the airport, she arrived at the train station with a huge bunch of lilacs which she put into my arms. One of her friends said, "That represents a week's worth of lunches." Kitty handed me a list of books and asked me to send them to her from Paris. I looked at the list carefully. Many of them were books on theosophy, all of them in some way religious. I asked her if she were truly serious about this and expressed a fear that there would be reprisals. She insisted. I asked again. Again she was insistent, so I agreed. I sent the books from Paris. They were returned after several weeks, each torn in two. I tried again with the same result. The third time there was no response. Much later I received a brief letter from Siberia, whose meaning had to be deciphered between the lines. My worst fear had been realized.

Fortunately by one subterranean means or another, I was able to keep in touch for several years through a German sailor who would come to my parents' house in New York after dark to pick up money for her. I never knew who he or any of the other strange characters were who acted as intermediaries. Once a present arrived from Kitty, a little birch bark container with a fitted cover and a white linen table scarf embroidered in red and blue. I painted a picture of the table scarf in her memory and still keep the scarf itself on a chair in my living room. After a long time there was a letter in which she wrote that she had been given butter that week in reward for good behavior.

After that nothing. Even now I feel pain for what that valiant spirit must have suffered.

Our most extraordinary day in Moscow was the one spent with Dr. Makarianko. Bob Litell had set up an interview and took us along. During the Revolution and the hard times that followed, many children were abandoned when parents were unable to feed them. As their numbers increased, these children formed bands and lived by stealing in the city and by what they could find to eat in the woods. Like animals, these wild children became dangerous. Dr. Makarianko took on the problem. In a little country place near Moscow, he set out to tame them, putting out food regularly in certain places in the woods. After a while the food began to be picked up at night. Slowly, he brought the bait closer and closer to his cottage. Eventually many children quit the forest and joined him. He fed and sheltered them for ten years and was teaching them shoemaking as a trade. Hearing Dr. Makarienko talk about his adventure was an unforgettable privilege. Sitting at the long wooden eating table surrounded by these children, mostly young adults by now, some of them married, was like taking part in Russian history. This man's dedication, passion, and compassion remain an ideal for me. Later these young people felled trees on which to lay railroad tracks between their village and Moscow. Their experience has become a Soviet legend immortalized by a thrilling film of the first train to go through.

All too soon the time came to leave Russia. Bob was taking a boat trip down the Volga and invited us to come along, but I had promised my mother to be back in Canada for my father's 70th birthday. Again a wonderful invitation had to be refused. Our departure was memorable. Whitney and I arrived at the airport in the early morning and went through customs. Our bags were opened, pockets checked, and all our money taken away. Then we waited. A tiny four-seater plane was revved up and taken up by a pilot as we watched, but it soon came down again. The pilot suggested we have a cup of tea as he needed to test the plane further. Eventually, after quite a wait, we boarded. Whitney and I sat in the two front passenger seats, one on each side of the aisle. There was a noticeable crack in the window in front of us. When airborne the whistling sound coming through the crack was so loud we couldn't talk. Whitney yelled across at me, "It's fun to sing". We both did, belting out at the top of our lungs, "I can't give you anything but love, Baby," Kurt Weill's "Surabaya," and many others, each of us independently giving tongue. We made stops in Estonia, Latvia, and Lithuania before changing to a larger plane for Paris. The stops all held pleasant surprises. When we deplaned in Estonia, a woman gave me a large bunch of lilacs. We had to talk in sign language. She made it clear that she was delighted to see us and happy that we were in love. She thought we looked alike and kissed us both. In Latvia we were invited to the house of a woman who lived at the edge of the airfield. She gave us cups of tea infused with strawberry jam. In Lithuania another woman gave me a bunch of artificial flowers, probably a household treasure. We were strangers and probably the first Americans they had ever seen. We did not need language to communicate, our love was self-evident. Whitney and I shared a golden experience that radiated to everyone we met. This was the only protracted period we had alone together.

To leave Whitney in Paris was painful, but I felt duty-bound to keep the promise to my mother and was able to get immediate passage to Montreal. I managed, by hook and crook, to get to La Malbaie on the day of my father's birthday, appearing in evening dress at his birthday dinner. When describing my wonderful time in Russia, one of the guests asked me why I hadn't stayed longer. My mother joined our conversation. "Yes, darling," she said. "Why didn't you?" Knowing that my honesty had cost me a trip to Pamplona with Ernest Hemingway and a trip on the Volga with Whitney, I could not answer her query.

In retrospect, I find it unconscionable that I cut short this trip in order to be a good girl and keep my promise to my mother, rather than stay with Whitney. This was the first of two such actions in 1929. The second was in the fall, when I agreed to go with my parents on a seven-month trip around the world. They accepted my condition: after the trip I would have my total independence. Whitney felt my decision was misguided but he did not try to dissuade me, saying rather, "It's right if you think it's right." Unfortunately, the Atlantic Ocean separated us

Nautique (1974), Drawing in process X, 23 x 26⅛ in.

at the time I was deciding and, as usual, I was being pressured strongly by my parents to take the trip. Whitney and I were both under great tension about our future. I felt we needed time before attempting to live together. I had thought that the length of my trip, seven months, would be just about the right time span. I remember Whitney saying, "Our relationship, which has less solidity than any other, is by far the realest thing I have. I cross oceans saying, 'God, oh God'."

My parents' trip was to start on November 1, 1929, leaving by ship from Marseilles. Meanwhile Whitney, disillusioned by the rigidity of the Beaux Arts academy, decided to drop out to pursue his other love, writing. Pat, having failed his exams, was happy to spend several months in Tunis with him, Whitney writing and Pat painting. As their ship was to sail from Marseilles the same day as ours, the five of us traveled together from Paris to Marseilles where we had a brief but delightful time sightseeing at the Chateau d'If, sketching, eating delicious Marseillaise food, and enjoying the rich local accent. I was pleased that my parents were getting to know my close friends, especially at my father's obvious pleasure in Whitney's company, but I was heavy-hearted at leaving Whitney. One glimpse of the SS Morea docked in the Marseilles harbor, a dreary, dark brown and black ship ready to sail the following day made me realize that my thinking had been wrong. Seven months seemed like an eon. Already I was looking forward to my return. I knew I needed to be alone with Whitney.

The farewell on the SS Morea was poignant. Whitney and Pat came on board. We just had time for a brief drink in the bar when the ominous toot sounded, indicating it was time for visitors to debark. I kissed them both goodbye, then Whitney again. The ship slowly pulled away from the pier and soon they were no longer visible. I went to my cabin with a stone in my heart.

Each evening after dinner there was dancing on deck. The first night I was asked to dance by an attractive man about my age. I welcomed the opportunity to distract myself. We danced for a long time. We danced well together, very close. It felt good. The next day, stretched out in deck chairs, we talked. He had observed me kissing Whitney goodbye and wanted to know more about me. He talked about himself: he was an Englishman searching for his dream woman. He had looked widely but unsuccessfully in England, then in America, where he thought he had found her. They had married and he was now a young father, but the marriage, alas, had already become routine. Then, too late, he found me, unmarried, available, the fulfillment, he thought, of everything he had longed for. Again it had been love at first sight, and he said he would have to pay heavily. He was extremely upset, miserable and crying. Once again I found myself in the unenviable position of being at the root of all this pain. I liked this man and was physically drawn to him which only made things worse.

On rereading my diary I find that throughout this period of travel various men were telling me two things: that I knew less about life and sex than a fifteen year-old girl, and that I was very passionate. I think both comments were probably accurate, though I was less sure about the passion because I was still in a strait jacket. How could they have known when I myself felt like a blank cartridge? This may partially explain why so many men became deeply involved with me, a seemingly available but inaccessible virgin of twenty-six, and also why I sometimes confused these relationships simply by not being sexually aware.

It was the first time I had ever kept a diary regularly. On November 3rd, 1929, I wrote, "I looked out the porthole of my cabin for half an hour. My head and shoulders just go out. It seems so soft and warm out there. The horizon is near and lower than in northern waters. There is something intimate about the sea here, it is tempting." I thought about jumping in, more for pleasure than from depression. It was seductive, like the feeling I had when I tried to jump off the sleeping porch at a very young age. I was mesmerized by the sea but then became apprehensive lest I should actually take the leap.

The boat trip lasted 18 days. There was leisure time to reflect in loneliness and sadness. Besides deck tennis, reading and dancing, I also painted watercolor self-portraits that interested me enough to keep through seven months of travel. I was beginning to take myself seriously as a painter, even though I didn't realize it then.

Recently, in going through old work for my Massachusetts College of Art retrospective show in Boston called "An Autobiography," I found these portraits and included two of them. I had misgivings, for they were among the first half-dozen water colors I had ever done. I was very pleased when one sold to a New York art dealer and the other to the Boston Public Library. Later, when I looked down into the library case that displayed this and another portrait bought at the same time, I felt a true thrill, a surprise at how good the older piece was and amazement at having produced it so early in my career.

6. WHITNEY

"I have never ceased to search for
what I somehow was born knowing"
— *Anne Truitt*

In Calcutta, two months into the trip, I received a cable from Tunis. Whitney had died on January 3rd, 1930. At the very end, Pat told me later, he came out of a deep coma and asked, "Why didn't you tell me Maud had died?" Though both Whitney and Pat were in love with me and had been living together in an isolated situation, my name had never been mentioned before that moment. Until I learned Whitney had died of pneumonia, I feared his death might have been self-inflicted. To know otherwise was a relief, but I still had many questions. Did he really believe I was planning to be with him after my trip and hoping we would be together for the rest of my life? What did his final comment mean? Since we were each other's life force, when he believed me dead, did he know his life was over? I knew I felt unequivocally that I had lost mine.

The cable arrived on January 7th. The next day a trip had been planned to Darjeeling, ascending Tiger Hill to see the sunrise over Mount Everest. We started at 3 AM. The night was bitter cold. My parents and I, were carried in dandis through the dense darkness. Above, the sky sparkled with brilliant stars. The dandi, a chair supported on two very long poles, is carried on the shoulders of bearers, in this case, Bhutanis. Their Chinese looking faces, so different from the somber Indian ones, were cheery. All through the cold night they chanted as they walked while I, sitting in the chair, was trying to keep my hands warm with a hot water bottle. After two hours of this wondrous, detached, mysterious night, the birds started to wake up, twittering and chirping. One sensed that dawn would come soon. We continued up farther and farther, a heavier and heavier burden for the bearers. But still no warming sun. The long, sorrowful journey continued, precious time for me to be alone with Whitney. As I adjusted to the rhythm of the bearers' strides, listening to the soothing sound of their chanting,

I recognized that I was in a place to which I would never return, suspended between my life when I had known and been part of Whitney, and the life I would have from now on without him. I was a sentient human being, but an isolated one. I was no where and no one. As we approached the top of Tiger Hill, we came into heavy, cold, damp, fog. But twice, as we looked in the direction of Everest, the clouds suddenly dispersed for a few moments and the beautiful, gleaming white, irregular peaks of Mt. Kitchinjunga magically appeared just 50 miles away. They disappeared to once again reappear and disappear. After that all one saw was the hulk of a great, dark brown, mountain in the foreground, dotted with little white villages in layers. In what was still the early morning, I walked the eight miles back to Darjeeling and just once saw Mt. Everest, a white button a hundred-thirty-five miles off. The walk gave me more needed time alone.

With Whitney alive I was a special person of real worth to myself. In losing him I felt I had lost caste. I was just an ordinary girl and the potential for my life that he nourished, no longer existed. I became middle-aged overnight. Having finally, and for the first time, found the core of myself through him, his death was my death. I gave up the burgeoning control of my own life and no longer cared what happened. I knew that I would never find that rapport with another human being. In spite of his efforts to the contrary, he has dominated my life. I have never emerged from the shadow of Whitney's death. I believe some people are only able to love once in a lifetime, I am one of them.

From my diary January 1930:

"When you were alive you wouldn't let me say that I could never forget you. Now after your death I know it to be true. No one will ever be to me what you have been and are. In all my life you are the only person I have ever earnestly missed so you are the only person who has made me feel a desire to be at a certain place at a certain time. You are the only person in terms of whom I have thought of myself. When I look in the mirror I see you. We're one person. I am mixed up as to which is which. You are the only person to whom I talked as to myself, you are the only person who made me alive and complete. You are the only person who made me think. You are the only person who made me really suffer. Darling you are the only person. We are one – it's the airplane game. And your kisses – intense, intense, intense. Not a man's kiss, not a boy's kiss, your kiss, different than anything I shall ever know, quite apart and more wonderful. I feel so far removed from everything in the world except you, and you are no longer in it."

Whitney always believed in my painting. He was impressed not, as I was, at how much I enjoyed the work, but at how good I was right from the start. He never saw anything but the very beginnings, still, his confidence helped me in this area as in all others. During the short time I knew him I began to see myself, standing apart on my own feet, though still insecurely. The time was too short to have that new belief in myself take root and grow. I needed his support. There was never any question but that we were equals, very open with each other. He said, "We are just like a 'petit ménage'," (a young married couple). Once I had said to him, "We love each other because we are so different." He answered, "We love each other because we are identically alike." We were both right. As to feelings, sensitivity, and human values, certainly we were very similar, but where the intellect was concerned, he far outshone me, opening my eyes to the very best of contemporary writing in French and English and directing my reading with dexterity and economy. I looked to him as a mentor.

Only with Whitney had I been my own person. He truly loved me for who I was and he knew who I was better than I did. With him, I became myself to a greater extent than at any time before or afterwards, until my divorce in 1980 when at long last I was able to take my life back into my own hands and let it blossom. Before Whitney and after his death I had no concept of taking responsibility for the direction of my life. I simply reacted to what happened around me. This was partially triggered by the indifference caused by the loss of the only person who I felt understood me, and partially by an unrecognized long-standing fear. I had been afraid of my grandfather and was afraid of my mother and later of my husband. The fear was not superficial, but at a deep level beyond my reach, which became more powerful the more I tried to disregard it. Could the very strength of that dark side have given me the needed power for reversal? Possibly. Now people often say, "You don't seem to be afraid of anything."

The ancient Greeks had a word for this, "enantiodromia," which means that when an emotion reaches a point of intensity beyond which it is incapable of going, it changes in kind, reversing itself into its opposite. This is related to the alchemist's belief that what poisons you is that which also heals. Back in 1954 I made a painting on this subject called "Shafts," which deals with a related kind of 'volte face', (a turnabout), based on the idea in a sermon of Howard Thurman's, chaplain at Boston University, that the painful, sharp spears of frustration can be transformed into their opposites, benign shafts of light. This large horizontal painting belongs to the Congregational Church in Auburndale, Massachusetts. On the left I put dark, angry, angular shapes of magentas and browns that lose their aggressiveness towards the center of green growth, from which a bird form flies towards the brilliant, pale, clear yellow sky at the right. Against the sky a gigantic, vigorous iris plant stands out, the spears of its strong leaves becoming shafts of light that triumphantly announce transformation. At its dedication, Eugene Meyer, the clergyman, had the painting placed on an easel beside him in the pulpit and took the artwork as a text for his sermon.

Not until 1948 in my Graves Hall studio in Andover was I able to paint a memorial to Whitney. The image appeared to me quite suddenly one evening. The next day I started the work, just painting the strong large abstract form which I had in my mind. I painted it lying flat, something I had never done before, or since, with the masonite raised only a few feet off the ground on a model stand. I was excited, using colors that were new to me: an olive grayish green with pink and a little red.

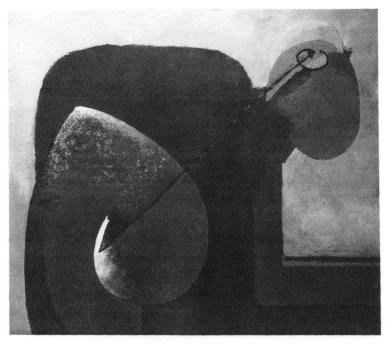

Denkmal (1948), Oil on canvas, 37 x 44 in.

The work went smoothly and quickly with minimal changes along the way. What I would now call a medium size piece, 36" x 43", was large for me at that time. I call it "Denkmal" – German for "memorial" or "monument". Few people were interested in the painting. That summer Phillips Academy was having the interior of our house repainted. When Pat and I left for Canada on vacation, I stacked my work against one wall. "Denkmal" happened to be on top leaning against the others, uncovered. The work on the house was not quite finished when we returned from vacation. The painters were still there. One of them took me aside, pointed to "Denkmal" and asked me if I had painted it.

"Yes," I replied.

"Well," he said, "I've eaten my lunch in front of that painting every day all summer and it's affected me very much."

I asked him in what way.

"I've started painting myself, and it's wonderful."

I told him how pleased I was and asked him what the painting meant to him.

"It's obvious," he said, "it's a broken heart."

I was speechless. He was the first person who had understood.

That it took so long before such a painting for Whitney emerged is strange. Of course, one is not in command of such things, each occasion bears its own subconscious timing. I have done several other memorial pieces, a large collage in memory of Anwar Sadat, an oil painting for Martin Luther King. In 1968 I was in my studio working on a 5'9"x 3'7" canvas when I heard the news of Martin Luther King's murder on the radio. After the first stunned reaction of horror, I knew I wanted to make a painting for him. I didn't even take the canvas on which I had been working off the easel. I just painted on top of what was there. I painted it all that day and the next. I am proud of that painting, it says everything I wanted to say.

My painting for Whitney, "Denkmal," was opposite in timing to the King painting but similar in execution. When the image finally came to me, the work painted itself in two days without a hitch, although it had taken eighteen years before coming to the surface.

Had I stayed with Whitney that autumn of 1929, establishing right then the fact that I wanted to live out the rest of my life with him, and to do so immediately, would he have died? His final comment will always make me question. At his death a friend wrote me, "I wonder how many people knew what strength and wisdom he showed, what a 'right' person he was."

BRANCHING OUT

Striped Shirt (1979), Oil on canvas, 49½ x 34 ½ in.

7. MARRIAGE

"In a good marriage we become custodians
of each other's solitude"
— *Goethe*

My marriage to Pat Morgan took place in a lawyer's office on a snowy
winter day in New York in 1931. I didn't feel that my belief in the
Episcopal Church was sufficient to validate a marriage ceremony. Being
married in a lawyer's office made the occasion seem less formidable
and less binding than a promise before God. I wanted to minimize the
importance of the occasion. I was not interested in getting married. My
bridegroom looked like a teenager.

In July 1930, after my return from the around-the-world trip, just
seven months after Whitney's death, Pat came to visit me in Canada.
Whitney and I had hoped to live together after that trip, which would
have been hard on Pat, but fate protected him and here we were now,
face-to-face and no Whitney. Pat had emptied out their beautiful apartment on Quai de Bourbon, where we had all had such wonderful times,
and said good-bye to Paris for what turned out to be the next twenty-
seven years. He came with bags of French sailor's striped shirts and
red Brittany sailor pants – considered rather extreme in America at that
period. All were in need of repair. In the end I grudgingly fixed them. Pat
was like that, he would just wait around till someone did what he wanted
and needed to have done. At that time my closest allegiance was to
Hooza, the Lhasa terrier given to me in Peking by Billie Christian
because she exactly matched my beige fur coat. In Malbaie a friend had
said to Pat, "If you want to win Maud, you better win over Hooza first."

One sunny, windy day Pat and I went for a walk to the beach with
Hooza. We both needed to talk about Whitney and the recent past. In
a field near the St. Lawrence we slumped down into a declivity to escape
the wind. We were there for hours. Symbolically we never got out.

Since receiving the cable on January 7th in Calcutta telling me of
his death, I hadn't been able to speak about Whitney to anyone. I
needed to hear as many details about him as possible from Pat, I wanted

to talk of nothing but Whitney. I can't remember if I told Pat that Whitney and I had planned to live together. I think not, but I did mention Whitney's homosexuality and Pat said he knew nothing about it. I found this extremely disturbing. Was Pat lying to me? Was it possible that he had lived for two years in an apartment with someone and not known? Or had he known, not wanted to know and wishfully forgotten? Had he, a virgin, known and been jealous? I was uncomfortable, suspicious and apprehensive. It was the first time I mistrusted him. Pat said a wise thing that day to which I agreed. "We must not, in order to keep Whitney's memory alive, form a relationship around it," he said. I am reminded of one of Whitney's favorite songs, the last line of which is, "But you forgot to remember." In this case the "you" was plural.

In Paris, Whitney and I had thought of Pat as a childlike spirit, which was the way he thought of himself: companionable, easy to get on with, and good company. He had great empathy with children, animals, and especially plants. His own childhood mystical connection to life was still very much alive in those years. He was an engaging person with winning ways and ingratiating manners, as well as a vain person aware of his own charm and accustomed to making himself "persona grata". A middle-sized man with a good figure. He was slightly heavy in the hips with extremely good-looking legs that he took great pleasure in showing off. Summer was his best season. While working in the garden he liked to dress in shorts, preferably short-shorts, without a shirt or with a shirt open to the belt. He had a beautiful face with an aquiline nose, he looked like a daguerreotype of a young man of the previous generation.

At the end of a long real estate search, I found a suitable place at a reasonable price in a new building on East 44th Street which resembled the old, so-called railroad flats; namely a long and narrow apartment with windows only on one end looking onto the street. As I lay in bed at the far end, I longed for another window near me to give the sense of light flowing through the room. An idea began to germinate that crystallized a few years later after I had left New York. It became a painting called "Corner Picture". It was a long, narrow horizontal made up of two sections of unequal lengths, assembled in a right angle position. My goal was to imply a window by introducing images of clouds, wind, and most importantly, air, light and space. I had never seen a painting of this shape and I became excited about the concept. It proved tricky and interesting to work on, for, while the actual canvas turned the corner, the image it portrayed must appear to be a continuous one of extending space. I liked the result and later sent it to New York for one of my shows. As I went into the gallery on hanging day, I met the truckman who had just delivered his load. "We had a little trouble," he said. "One of the paintings must have shifted en route because it was crooked when we got here, but we straightened it out and there's no harm done." I rushed upstairs. Indeed they had straightened it out, breaking it apart at the corner joint, severing the two panels of the painting as well as the frame. What a nightmare! We managed to hang it anyway, in two pieces, forcing each into the corner and pushing the frayed ends of the ripped canvas into the crack.

The night I moved into my new apartment I had a dinner date with Pat who also had found a space. Unknown to each of us, his space was in the same building as mine, just two floors below. This was companionable but not good. I needed to grieve for Whitney in my own way and in my own time. All too naturally Pat invaded my life. I saw something of earlier friends, but Pat's presence was predominant. He was very lonely, as indeed I was. He badly needed someone to depend on, although what I needed was to learn to depend on myself and perhaps find professional help, which would have been a far-out idea for me then. I was like a puppet being operated by its strings.

Pat was in love with me. Marrying me seemed to solve most of his problems. He had no family he cared about, no money, and no profession beyond painting, at which he had not been financially successful. For him to pursue this marriage was natural. For me it was a step taken without considering the consequences, without having given myself time to grieve the loss of the man I loved, or for reconsidering what I wanted to do with my life without him. I am not proud of this action, which was neither fair to myself nor to Pat. If after a year or so with

Early charcoal drawing (1933), 28 x 24½ in.

time to think and possibly find help, I had wanted to marry Pat, that would have been a different matter. The decision would have been a healthy rather than a neurotic one. The connection with Whitney, the good times we three had had together, was the basis of my connection to Pat, the very connection we had agreed we would not misuse. I was not able to make my needs clear to myself nor to him since I had not yet formed them. I felt strongly that I would never be in love again. I got along well with Pat but I was not in love with him. Still, I allowed him to make my choice. Whitney never died for either of us.

I was still a virgin, thoughtlessly so. Pat wanted marriage, which meant nothing to me, and I let him lead me to it. There was a nice friend of his, a slightly older married woman, Elly, with whom he talked about wanting to marry me. Since she knew us both to be rather timid virgins, she sensed we would have trouble and told Pat that the best thing would be for me to go to an obstetrician to have my hymen broken. I'd never been to an obstetrician or heard of a hymen, but if Elly thought I should have this done and Pat agreed, then probably I should. As I write now I realize how childishly innocent and totally alone I was. I could not possibly have mentioned such a thing to my mother and didn't know any other older woman or doctor I could have approached. I had a few girl friends, but they were not close and I would have been far too shy to ask them about it. So I went to the obstetrician. At her first touch of my genitals, I leapt back as though I had been electrocuted. She had to strap me down but she accomplished what she was supposed to. Four months later Pat and I were married and set out to visit the Hemingways in Key West via the Arthur Whitneys in Charleston. At our wedding party Pat's then-best friend, John C., said to me, "So you decided to marry Pat. Well, someone has to take care of him." I found this nasty. I hadn't thought of our wedding like that, but then I really hadn't thought of it at all. I was moving like a sleepwalker.

Among the congratulatory wedding telegrams was one I kept.

"NEWS WONDERFUL STOP BEST LOVE TO YOU BOTH STOP PAULINE CAUGHT A SEVEN FOOT SAILFISH STOP ARM BETTER STOP DONT STAY TOO LONG CHARLESTON STOP YOU AND MAUD CERTAINLY BOTH SPLENDID CHOOSERS – PAULINE ERNEST."

Pat and I arrived in Key West as a just-married couple with my beloved Hooza in tow. We took a little house at the corner of Pine and Florida Streets where we stayed, taking many of our meals with the Hemingways nearby. Delicious meals prepared by Henriette, their Parisian "bonne-a-tout-faire" who took care of the baby and the grown-ups. Poor homesick Henriette. She wandered around Key West saying, "Partout la mer, partout la mer," ("Everywhere the sea"). They couldn't get back to Paris soon enough to suit her.

Some days after our arrival we went deep-sea fishing. I sat in the stern with the unaccustomed holster to hold the butt end of the rod strapped around my waist. I practiced reeling in and out to get the feel of the pull. I was struck by how hard it was to reel in even the unloaded line. I tried three times with Ernest's best and favorite rod. I let the line out a fourth time when WHAMBO, a heavy strike. The fish ran the line out fast. Ernest was standing next to me, instructing me when to let out line, when to pull it in, until the fish finally tired. Then the time came to start reeling in. I was giving it all I had. As the fish got near the stern of the boat, the rod started to bend, then bend more and more into an arc. Keeping the rod raised up away from the boat's edge was increasingly difficult. At this point Ernest said, "I've given you my best rod and I suppose you know that if the rod touches the boat it will snap." He paused. I was tightening my stomach muscles as much as I could and praying that my arm muscles would hold out, when Ernest continued, "I've never forgotten what you said in the elevator in New York." By now the rod was not more than six inches from the edge of the boat. I gave one final contraction, like the last birth pain. It worked. The line was now close enough for the boatmen to reach out and haul the catch in. There was a lot of excited pulling and tugging with appropriate vocal accompaniment to get the big fish on board. This monster was intimidating to anyone accustomed to think of a thirteen inch trout as a big fish. Now I only had to get out of the way and watch the men work. Once on board and off the hook, the fish was measured. Later on shore it was weighed. The colossus came within a few ounces of the record kingfish caught in Florida that year. I had passed the test. Ernest grabbed me, hugged me, congratulated me, and said I must have been lying when I told him that I came from New York. A girl like me could only come from the Midwest. Everyone was jubilant.

Ernest had planned a ten day fishing trip to the Dry Tortugas. We started our six hour boat trip on time. Good weather was important as we were carrying all the gear, bedding and food for eight people. The larger boat was pulling a huge square wooden frame with a wire mesh bottom. Into this the live fish were to be put as we caught them. We planned to drag the frame back to Key West, sell the fish and pay for the trip. Pat and I, Ernest and Pauline, and two others were in Bra's smaller boat. Bra, a fascinating character as well as a superior boatman, was scrawny, thin, small-boned, with skin tanned into leather. His eyes always seemed to look beyond you, out to sea, except when they focused directly, burning at you. I think, though I have no proof, that Bra was Ernest's inspiration for *The Old Man and the Sea*. The favorite story of that year was Bra's exchange with Ernest, on his arrival from Paris: "How are things this year, Bra?"

"Well, Ernest, they're not good. In fact, they're bad. People have died who've never died before."

We left the Key West harbor and headed south. Although the weather was propitious, I was not feeling well. I'd been in bed for several days previously, not knowing what was wrong. Pauline had come to see me and been very consoling. When I didn't feel better she said, "Maybe you're pregnant." I found this very disturbing. As we left the harbor, I had a miserable stomach ache. I wanted to throw up but couldn't. Ernest was standing in the boat beside me. "Put your finger down your throat," he said. "Make yourself throw up." I tried. "You're not doing it right. Here, open your mouth." He thrust his finger down my throat. It worked. I threw up and immediately felt better. I was embarrassed by the incident, but relieved physically and mentally. After all, we were off on a camping trip, and on a camping trip you do for yourself or another what has to be done. Ernest had been perfectly matter-of-fact about it. He rinsed off his hands in the ocean and paid no further attention to me. I felt carefree for the rest of that whole fabulous trip.

We were a large party, two friends of Ernest's from Key West, Charles and John, Ernest's sister Carol, nicknamed Beefy, Max Perkins, Ernest's publisher, dressed in Abercrombie & Fitch clothes, nicknamed (behind his back) Maxie Deadpan, Pat, me, Ernest and Pauline. The fishing went well and our box was beginning to get full. We fished and read, swam and talked, drank and slept.

The Dry Tortugas is a large old abandoned fort. Despite the name, there is a fresh water spring on the tiny island. The half-roofed fort was our all-purpose quarters. We lived on the dock. Everyone was happy except Pauline, who was pregnant and felt sick. By luck a Coast Guard boat stopped by and was able to take her, Beefy, Max Perkins and John back to Key West. The rest of us, Ernest, Charles, Bra, Pat and me, were to leave the following day, dragging the completely full fish box behind us. We went to sleep early to be ready for an early morning start. That night a heavy north wind blew up. On waking to a brilliant day, we were horrified to see that during the night the fish box had broken free from its moorings and been carried out to sea. Ernest made the decision that Bra must go back to Key West immediately, have another fish box built, and return with it, food and liquor. With luck and a good wind he should be back in four or five days. The four of us would wait it out and when Bra returned we'd fish hard and try to fill up the new box.

At first our time was rather pleasant, certainly restful. We had no boat, no place to go, not much to do except to read, swim and fish through a hole in the floor for our supper. There was a look-out tower on the dock and by the second day Ernest with binoculars in hand was charging up and down the steps every few hours to see if he could spy Bra in his returning boat. Ernest became very fidgety. Food was running low. We were still catching jackfish through the hole in the dock, but the coffee was almost gone and the grapefruit juice was finished. Without the juice peoples' insides were not functioning normally and tempers flared.

Very importantly, the last gin bottle was empty. When it got dark, after we'd eaten our miserable little jackfish for supper, we lay down on our sleeping bags and talked. The light was not strong enough for reading. Ernest usually led the conversation, guessing when we would run out of food and have to start on each other. Who would we choose first? Which part would be the most tender? Would it be better roasted or boiled? I wish I had a tape of those lurid conversations. Of course, these were pre-tape recorder days. The talk would go on till we all fell asleep.

On the fifth day a small yacht anchored off the island. Ernest was excited. He delegated me to get to the people on the boat and bring back a pound of coffee and a quart of gin. I put on my bathing suit and made for the beach closest to the yacht. As I approached, I saw a nice-looking young man about my age swimming there. We swam together for a bit, then he asked me if I'd like to come out to his father's yacht.

Once on board, his mother invited me to have a drink with her, her husband, their son and his bride. I accepted willingly. After much chatting over several drinks, the young woman asked me what I was doing alone on a desert island. "I'm on a fishing trip," I said. "With my husband and Ernest Hemingway." She repeated the name in a vague, faraway manner and said, "Oh yes, I started a book of his once."

When I got back to our dock with my pound of coffee and quart of gin, feeling rather proud of myself, I hid the gin momentarily in a bush and appeared with the coffee. Ernest was furious. He accepted the coffee without much grace. "You can never count on a woman," he said, "and a woman on her honeymoon! I was a fool to send you. You've been gone for two hours or more." Then he wanted to know exactly what had happened, what had been said. I hedged. He pushed me. He didn't want descriptions, he said, he wanted conversation. He wanted to know what they'd said when I told them I was with Ernest Hemingway. The truth came out in spite of my efforts. Poor Ernest. He was so let down. When I produced the hidden gin things changed markedly. We finished the bottle that night feeling we'd had a good evening.

Bra returned finally, having been held up by adverse winds. After we filled up the fish box again we headed for Key West. I was happy to get back to our little house with leisure time to paint. I made some watercolors which were quite inept. I easily accepted that this was not my medium. I was deeply drawn to oil painting. Partly the smell entices, the smell of the paint itself added to the smell of the turpentine. But the application of the paint is also seductive, whether from a heavily-loaded sweep of a wide brush or the meticulous precision of a tiny one. It's all there, along with the marvelous fluidity for easy change, as one watches the transformation take place when the bristles of the brush follow their course, a course often unknown to the painter until it actually comes into being. I painted several oils, the most ambitious and successful of which is a painting of one of the lovely old Key West houses fronted by palm trees. I believe Ernest bought the house after we left. While we were there the Hemingways had a little clapboard house like ours.

In 1987, going through material in the studio in Canada, I found tacked up, face to the wall, a canvas that had been there unnoticed for fifty-five years. I took it down overjoyed to find the Key West house again. I was surprised at the quality of the painting. It is far more knowledgeable and structured than were my other paintings of the period. I had also been further encouraged by Ernest's enthusiasm. He let me know that, although I was just beginning, he thought I was already a better painter than Pat, which was hard for me to believe. This conversation with him suddenly comes back to me and I remember that when he was being complimentary he always called me 'beau' (masculine for 'beautiful') and not 'belle'.

I had the Key West painting cleaned immediately and put into my current exhibition, appropriately called "Surprises from a Lost Portfolio", at Barbara Singer's gallery in Cambridge. I am happy to say that it is now loved by its present owner, Jane, and no longer tacked up facing the wall.

Our wonderful trip to Key West was nearing an end. We were due back in New York for my cousin Florence's wedding. Bobby Cromwell, Whitney's brother with whom Pat and I had taken a trip to Ireland four years previously, had given us a lavish wedding present, a yellow Model A Ford convertible. Ernest and Pauline gave us the extra tire in a shiny metal rim that attached to the running board. Ernest didn't like this gift, he would rather have brought us back something nice from Spain, but we obviously needed a spare tire so he and Pauline filled the gap. Those Model A Ford convertibles were sporty little cars for two, augmented by a rumble seat. The lid of what would normally be a luggage compartment lifted up backwards to form the back rest for two rear passengers. To climb up and into that rear seat always spelled adventure and romance, isolated from the driver and alone with the wind, the pleasure increased as the speed augmented. Pat had never driven a car but on the day for departure he got in behind the wheel. I told him what to do and we took off on the trip from Key West to New York. There was one nervous moment at the start when he was so pleased to be driving successfully that he attempted to pass the car in front of us, not seeing that another car was coming toward us in our lane. My scream narrowly averted an accident, but everything went well from then on. He learned quickly. We neared Palm Beach driving on a parallel road. The city looked like a great wedding cake. I was curious and anxious to turn off and drive through, presuming that I would never be there again. Pat was at the wheel and refused. I was surprised at his unwillingness to fulfill such a simple request, which might have taken an hour at most. Though my life was not greatly diminished by not seeing Palm Beach, I was angry at the time and a red flag of caution went up, telling me that Pat planned to have things only as he wanted them.

After our return from Key West and attending Florence's wedding in New York, we drove to La Malbaie to stay with Mootzie. She offered to give me a piece of land of our own choosing on which to build a house. Pat jumped at the idea. Near the Manor House was an undulating field backed on two sides by a high hill, thick with birch and spruce growth, a good protection from the cold north wind. On the other sides was flat arable land with a stream running through it. It was a lovely piece of property. Once when the moon was full, Pat dammed up the brook with a few boards, saying that if enough water collected to reflect the moon during the night, we could have a lake there. It did and we chose that spot. There was a great deal of interest and fun connected to the whole enterprise, but I soon realized something was wrong in our marriage and my health began to deteriorate. I became weak with severe back pain, able to be out of bed for only a few hours a day. My mother took me to see Dr. H., an orthopedic doctor in Montreal, who pronounced my back condition permanent and incurable. He prescribed a brace from my neck to my sacroiliac, saying that, unfortunately, I would have to wear one for the rest of my life. I was carefully measured and a rather heavy metal structure lined with an inch of felt padding was created. My mother agreed the situation was unfortunate, but being her practical self, observed that since I would be wearing the brace next to my skin, it would need to be cleaned. She ordered a duplicate. As Pat and I were anticipating going to Munich in the winter to study with Hans Hofmann, I asked Dr. H. to recommend an orthopedic doctor there. He gave me the name of a Herr

Doktor Geheimrat, and with that in hand, one brace on my back and one under my mother's arm, we went back to La Malbaie.

Our house in the field with the brook had already been started, but I seemed unable to concentrate or care about the plans. I would say, "Now we are going in the front door," but couldn't imagine anything beyond that. Pat planned the house. I was sick for a year and a half. Before my head knew it, my body told me I had married the wrong man. I needed time alone to realize what Whitney's death had done to my whole sense of being. But I wasn't going to get any.

Though I was still frail, we left La Malbaie for Munich that fall, planning to study with Hans Hofmann. We sailed from Montreal in mid-October. Reluctantly I left Hooza behind with my parents. She was an important part of my life and this would be the first time I had been without her. We crossed the ocean on a nice old fashioned steamer. One bright morning around eleven, getting up to dress for lunch, I put my head out the open porthole to smell the air and feel the freshness of the sea on my cheeks. I always loved doing that. One experiences the essence of the sea so much better from the cabin porthole than from the deck higher up. I was holding up my metal brace, not anxious to put on the heavy, uncomfortable thing. I looked more closely. The brace didn't look as wide in my grasp as it felt on my back. I approached the porthole again and put my head out once more. If I could put my head out and sense the freedom, could I go further? I held up the brace and measured; an almost exact fit. I balanced the brace for a moment on the porthole's edge, then let go. I was exhilarated. After one moment's hesitation, I reached for its mate to follow suit. Joyfully I realized this was the first step towards altering my thinking, if not my body.

Most of what I learned about Munich was in hospitals and from doctors. I went to see Herr Geheimrat. After a brief examination he said, that although I was recently married, I must leave my husband for several months at least. This was surprising and perceptive. At a deep level I knew he was right and anticipated time alone. He recommended a sanitarium in the mountains, a Seelkurort. I went there immediately by way of a tiny train that kept climbing higher and higher. When we finally arrived, it was snowing. There was an open horse-drawn sleigh ready to take me still higher. I loved being driven through the dark night to an unknown Schloss. We arrived at an enchanting old castle made over into a sanitarium. The furnishings were delightfully Bavarian, wonderful old pieces. I walked into the dining room where there were many long tables of men and women, halfway through dinner. I sat down. With only two verses of the Lorelei in my German vocabulary, I was able to carry on a lively, if limited, conversation. My neighbor asked me to have some beers with him after dinner, which was pleasant. I thought I would like being there. In the middle of the night I felt sick, and by morning had a fever high enough to alarm the staff. They telephoned Pat in Munich to come and get me. By the time he arrived I was out of it and have no recollection of the trip back nor of seeing a doctor the next day. But I still remember that enchanting Schloss.

I entered a hospital in Munich where lovely German nuns in white took care of me. I practiced the little German I knew and tried to pick up more. It seemed I had osteomyelitis and after a while had an operation on my jaw. We had not informed my mother of any of this, but Pat received a telegram saying,

"DID MAUD GET THROUGH THE OPERATION ALL RIGHT? ARRIVING (SUCH AND SUCH A DATE)".

My mother at her psychic best. I had small operations all through the year. The infection would be cut out of one place and move to another. Fortunately, and probably because of my doctor's skill, it never got beyond the jaw, but I lost almost all my teeth in the process. I had several other operations on my jaw when I got back to America.

I was put on a three-item diet – no cooking necessary – first, yogurt, which I had never tasted before; second, Märzen beer, a very heavy black beer originally created when Munich was under siege. (The people attribute the nourishing quality of that beer to saving their population) And third, caviar – beautiful Russian black caviar, not too expensive at that time, which I ate with a spoon and enormous relish. My doctor said he would not consider me cured until I weighed 155 pounds. My normal weight then was about 118. Eleven months later I achieved his required weight and he was delighted with my size. "Sie sehen wie eine Bavaria aus," my doctor said as he dismissed me. Indeed I did look like a statue of Bavaria.

Pat knew instinctively how to take care of people and took wonderful care of me that year when I was so frail and had to spend most of my time in bed. I was appreciative but not surprised. This was the Pat I had always known, tender and thoughtful. He took care of me because he loved me and because I was now his. To start married life this way was hard for him but it also lessened the immediacy of having to face the basic, radical differences in our personalities, ambitions and sexual needs. Those could wait till later. During that year I was a fragile person who needed to be looked after, which Pat did beautifully and, I think, enjoyed doing. My psychic and personality needs had to be subservient to health demands. We existed side-by-side in harmony. I have many tender and loving notes from Pat then and from the period that followed, which are painful to read now. I had not emotionally recovered from Whitney's death just ten months before and so Pat's loving concern was welcome.

We lived in a charming place on Franz-Josef Strasse, part of a private apartment where we had a large bedroom, tiny living room and use of the kitchen. During most of our time in Munich I stayed in our apartment, or took little walks in the Tiergarten when the weather was clement. I wasn't strong enough to go to the Hofmann class but saw the drawings Pat brought home and sometimes heard Hofmann's theories discussed on the rare occasions when students came to our apartment. His theories were hard to grasp, as I learned later when I finally did study with him in New York. In Munich he was even harder to understand – his English was not strong and liberally mixed with French, German and, surprisingly, Turkish. He had many Turkish students and had picked up phrases of their language to help his criticisms. I was not considered strong enough even to have German lessons. Occasionally we went to see a Leni Riefenstahl movie. She was a great star then but one whose reputation was about to be tarnished by her upcoming film on Hitler, "The Triumph of the Will," for which she was widely criticized. However, the brilliant camera work of the following film on the Olympic Games put her back into a top spot again. Being in Munich was lovely, well or ill.

When Pat wasn't at Hofmann's school, he hounded the bookstores. Due to inflation, excellent books could be had for half their value – especially art books. He bought many on the folk art in different areas of Germany. These influenced us considerably in the building details of our Canadian house and planted the seeds of the folk art movement that grew up around us when we returned there.

He also hunted down hardware supply stores and bought all the hardware for the house, whose shell was waiting to be completed. The doors open by pushing down a handle rather than turning a knob. These non-American accoutrements have been a constant pleasant reminder of Europe. We incorporated so many German accessories into Chouette that the French Canadians were convinced Pat was German.

A joke was going the rounds in Munich about Hitler. He had recently attempted and failed in a putsch, a local coup d'état. When his followers were routed, he couldn't be found. Fraulein Hampfstengel, an ample lady was sitting on the sofa in her well-to-do house. Under that sofa and under that lady's skirts, they discovered Hitler.

Her brother Putzi Hampfstengel was a close associate of Hitler in those early days, which explains why the Fuhrer ran for shelter there. I had met Putzi, a Harvard graduate, the year before in Paris. I asked if he was working in the family business. The Hampfstengels made the best color reproductions of art in the world at that time.

"Yes," he said, "but mainly I am working for someone you have never heard of who will change the world."

"Who's that?" I asked with some skepticism.

"Adolf Hitler," he said.

Indeed I had not yet heard of him.

That spring Pat and I heard Hitler give a speech in a great open air arena in Munich. There had been parades and other prolonged diversions before his arrival, then a small plane circled low around and around the stadium. A loudspeaker told us that the Fuhrer would be late because an attempt had been made on his life. As the plane circled, the announcing voice got louder and louder, and the shouting crowd joined in, in high crescendo. Then he came onto the podium – what showmanship! He had the whole arena in his hand while he lectured in that screaming voice. The speech was scary, hysterical.

The landlady from whom we rented our rooms was short of cash and needed to sell her piano. No buyers. One day she announced we were going to celebrate and have goat and wine for dinner. She'd sold the piano for the price she wanted. We were delighted for her. There was only one string attached, she said. She had to promise to vote for Hitler. "But that can do no harm, a weakling like him who hides under a woman's skirts." Nevertheless, gradually, in different places and ways, his power was beginning to be felt.

One of our ambitions in Munich was to find a mate for Hooza. Pat claimed I loved her too much not to continue to own one of her lineage. This posed a problem, since we had never seen another dog like her. One evening when there were only a few days left before our departure, we saw, to our overjoyed amazement, a dog in the street which seemed as though it might be the same breed, though of a very different coloration.

We followed the dog home and asked the owner if he would sell it. He agreed and we fixed a price. At that moment his daughter came in, heard the arrangement, and burst into floods of tears. Her father relented and, after a prolonged talk, told us they had bought the dog in Králu°v Dvu°r bei Beroun, Czechoslovakia. He believed there was still one puppy in the litter for sale. Pat started out the next day with a rucksack on his back. After a good many hours and five changes of trains, he reached the town, which was built around a cement factory. He went to the largest house where he saw a puppy in the yard. The owners were absent and the gardener spoke only Czech. Pat could not understand him, so, uncertain what to do, he paid the man a suitable price, put the puppy in his rucksack and came back to Munich. We left for Canada the next day.

8. THE FIRST YEARS

"The surprise may only come when we look
back and see whence we have come"
— *Jerome Bruner*

For three and a half colorful years before we had children, we lived at Chouette year 'round, surrounded by friends in the summer, isolated in the winter when we concentrated on painting and raising Lhasa terriers. In winter our life was without much intellectual companionship. About twice during those winter months Père Boivin, the incumbent priest of the neighboring parish, a charming, cultivated, frail man, would hazard the cold of a three-quarter-hour drive in an open carriole (sleigh) to come to us for dinner. That was gala. Otherwise there was as much social life as we needed with the delightful, warm French Canadian farmers around us. Winter was their big season when there was no farm work and a little money in the pocketbook earned from the summer tourists. Their parties were marvellous fun. Always good food, drink, and jokes, the earthier the better, and dancing to the violin. The guests were the entertainment and everyone had to supply some diversion. Pat and I would sometimes do a Charleston – to wild applause and amazement. There was no radio or television then, so our Charleston, compared to their square dances, seemed as exotic to them as a dance of Fiji Islanders. And after such an evening we would walk home in the bitterly cold, starry night.

As long as Pat's and my interests were the same, things went along pleasantly. We both cared about building our house and were absorbed in that process. We called it "Chouette", the French word for screech owl, or an adjective meaning "stunning" or "excellent." Before going to Munich we had spotted the house when we were on a picnic fifteen miles from home and bought it for $175, an empty two-storied fieldstone house of handsome proportions, built lovingly by a mason and his four sons, also masons. Once built, these good people couldn't afford to live in it because of the cost of heating.

Then our adventure started. We labeled the cornerstones, took careful measurements and had the house torn down. The stones were put piecemeal onto a schooner and sailed 15 miles down the St. Lawrence River to be deposited in the field my mother had given me, where the house was to be reconstructed. The original walls were two feet thick. By diminishing that thickness to eighteen inches we gained enough stone to add on a small kitchen wing. The stone shell of the house was all completed before we left for Munich. During the year we were away my mother had the kitchen and bathrooms put in so on our return we were able to move in, going up to the bedroom on a ladder before we had a staircase.

We occupied ourselves within the house, making it easy to supervise the work and be nearby to answer urgent questions from carpenters. From his mother Pat had inherited some Louis XVI short, swinging barroom doors decorated with paintings of the Comedia del Arte figures. We decided to build them into the dining room walls. They looked inappropriate and lost. Either there were too many or too few. We decided there were too few. Pat started painting additional ones in the same style, depicting other Comedia del Arte characters copied from books. He continued until all the walls were covered with four-foot-by-four-foot squares, while I painted narrow, decorative panels to go above and below them. This came out very well and made an enchanting room, a harmonious potpourri of authentic French antiques, simulated French antiques, Italian country furniture and heavy exposed French Canadian hand-hewn spruce beams from the original house. The net effect recalls an Austrian Stuben.

Chouette became a magical place. Pink-washed buildings surround the courtyard, one side of which is the house itself. In the court's center a gigantic elm tree grows out of an elevated pentagon of earth, formed by a low cement wall, perfect to sit on when making the day's plans. Opposite the house is a thirty-foot slatted building for firewood, needed when we spent winters there, and a twenty-foot ice house. Before artificial refrigeration was common we sold ice cut from our small lake to the local hospital and the train between La Malbaie and Quebec. The huge square blocks of ice were packed in snow in the icehouse and would occasionally provide the material for a summer snowball fight. Next to the icehouse is the garage, with the studio above it. The farmer's house and a barn at a slight distance away are also constructed out of used materials. The barn housed Poulette, the old grey mare, Caillette, the dappled cow, some chickens, pigs and sometimes pigeons.

Hélène was our wonderful cook through those first years, and on into the summers when Pat was teaching at Andover. She was a handsome, stylish woman with quick, often earthy humor. The first encounter with Hélène when we were looking for a cook was memorable. She arrived with her husband, Joseph, by taxi from the village dressed in an elegant black winter coat and a silver fox fur. Pat and I were coming in, bedraggled, from a walk in the woods, carrying baskets of sphagnum moss for his garden and surrounded by barking Lhasa terriers. Before the taxi driver introduced us, I heard him say to Hélène, "C'est ça, ton bourgeois." (So, that's what your new boss looks like.) In spite of the shock our appearance must have given them, they accepted the job. Hélène cried every day for a month and, when she was not cooking, had lengthy telephone conversations with her relatives about her unhappiness at Chouette and with us. Her sorrows finally ended and she came to accept and love us as we did her. We soon came to depend on her more than she did on us.

We were both painting happily in the same studio then, criticizing each other's work or sometimes both working from the same still-life. I was somewhat in a position of being Pat's pupil, as he had been studying painting since childhood but he only once gave me a lesson: twenty minutes on how to paint a head. After that I relied on my own observation.

In the early winter mornings Joseph would light the stove and we would be up in the studio all day, coming back to the house only for a brief lunch of string beans, often baked with cheese and apple sauce. Both products we had grown and preserved during the summer. The studio days were short because by 3:00 PM the light began to fail. We would then go skiing through the beautiful twilight 'till dark – around 4:30, come back in to wash brushes, comb dogs and change for supper. We never drank during those winters. It was a beautiful, serene time.

Though most of our artist friends in New York had strongly advised against this kind of isolation for beginning painters, we both improved noticeably and probably worked more assiduously than we would have in the city with its multiple diversions. The harmony we had in our art at that time extended for the first eight years of our marriage, both at Chouette and in New York.

When we first arrived back at La Malbaie from Munich, my mother's farmer looked at our new puppy, Mingki, and said in that knowledgeable way that farmers have, "He's no good. You won't be able to breed from him, he's much too young." Soon he was put to the test. Hooza came into heat. I read every dog book I could put my hands on. Nothing happened, though we did what the books advised. I sent a desperate telegram to my mother in New York, "Are there aphrodisiacs for dogs?" She valiantly hunted something down, but the time was too short. This was the last day Hooza would be fertile. The autumn day was clear and cold. We lit a fire in the fireplace, shut the two dogs in the living room, put "Tristan and Isolde" on the phonograph full volume, closed the door, and went for a long walk. IT WORKED! In due time Hooza had two puppies, Lisl, a female, and Fleuri, a male. They were inseparable. Later when it was time for Lisl to be bred, we gave her to another male we had acquired by then. Fleuri had a nervous break-down. On a walk we heard him screaming. We rushed towards the sound, thinking he must have had an accident, maybe gotten a branch in his eye. Instead we found him standing in an open place, screeching. We were unable to calm him. In fact he suffered a drastic change of temperament. From having been an amiable dog, he became vicious and tried to bite everyone except Pat and me. We were told he was dangerous and would have to be put down. Luckily we had acquired another female by then who came into heat. We mated her with Fleuri. He immediately became quieter, but still not his old self. Lisl, his beloved sister, had her puppies, and Fleuri lay beside her during her entire period of nursing them.

Of course Hooza was always with me in Canada as elsewhere. During the time that we lived there all year round, the dogs were a big part of our life. With Hooza first as mother, then grandmother, and so on, we had four, six, eight, ten and, at one time, counting the three litters of puppies in various baskets, thirty Lhasa terriers in the house. Luckily that didn't last too long. But there were often six regulars.

Our dining-room windows, like most of the windows in Chouette, have deep, eighteen-inch reveals. Below each window, and there are four, is a rush-seated, window-width, Italian bench. Through dinner two dogs sat on each bench and on each window sill above them two others, all dutifully waiting for the end of the meal when each jumped off the bench and got a little treat. There wasn't always a full house, but it was always beguiling to watch them as we ate, and a good in-house discipline for the dogs.

Pat taught me a lot about traditional interior design and architecture during that period. It interested me, but I was apprehensive about settling so permanently on the land my mother had given me, which rooted me more deeply back into the family from which I had finally earned my independence and wanted to be separated. A cottage in a field where we might come for brief vacations with minimal responsibility and still not completely break family ties would have been more to my taste. I soon came to realize that what I thought had been understood before marriage, namely, that we would respect each other's autonomy as artists and that I would not be expected to work in a garden, were not promises that Pat intended to keep. Quite to the contrary, everything that we did, he felt we must both do. Togetherness was his oft-repeated slogan in spite of the divergence of our personalities, our aims and sexual needs. I began to feel caged in and reacted psychosomatically, becoming less and less able to state my preferences. Pat planned the house and place exactly as he wanted it and did a superb job. That there were anxieties below the surface became increasingly clear. Much as I cared for Chouette which was rapidly becoming Pat's chef d'oeuvre, I still clung to painting as my main concern and passionate interest.

We had our first fight the second summer after Munich about the correct way to cook string beans! It was the only honest fight that we ever had, one in which we were each dealing blows at the other straight from the shoulder. From then on, to my dismay, differences were handled with deviousness and one-upmanship. This one was a bitter, straight-out fight and I was frightened by Pat's angry and unrelenting persistence, which caused me to again feel I had married the wrong man. I wanted to divorce him. In fact, the problems I saw on that occasion were the very ones that eventually wrecked our marriage. We were then in the midst of building our wonderful new house which we both cared about. The argument seemed so absurd I talked myself out of it.

Early on my mother had tried to teach me to fight back, but I had never learned to do so effectively and didn't realize for many years to come that just fighting back blindly with anger was not the answer. The blinders I had put on harmed me more than they did Pat. I think he was desperately afraid of losing control over me and fearful of a power that I didn't know I had. What I did know was I had to learn to protect myself in order to survive. I thought of nature's ways; a tree which learns to grow around a rock in its path or to traverse a stone wall through a miniscule passage, or even to split the constructed walls of a building to eventually knock it down, as I saw in the jungle at Ankor Wat. Or of the seed, the tiny seed placed in the ground, way down in the darkness of the earth, which must make its way up to the light. Even given its inherent energy toward growth, how does it know which way is up? How does it know enough to retain its own true nature, defying lack of rain and sun? How does it survive?

In 1948 I tried to address this question in a painting called "Chthonic", a work about the intrinsic urge of a seed searching for access to light. Though it was not a large painting (31"x 29"), I had a great deal of trouble trying to resolve the simple shapes into forms that would express my rather complex idea. I worked on it for several months, changing the original shape only minimally but trying to get the texture to describe what I wanted to convey – "earth". Finally I gave up. The idea was both too solid in the texture of the earth itself, and too ephemeral in the urge of the seed. It was more than I could handle. That afternoon Oliver Evans, a southern poet visiting my mother, came to call. "Where is that wonderful painting of Earth?" he asked. "I've abandoned it," I said. "I poured a can of white enamel house paint on it this morning." "Shame on you," he said, "I'm leaving." After he had gone I rushed down to the trash barrel, retrieved the work and took it back up to the studio along with a gallon of turpentine. I spent the rest of the afternoon trying to remove the white paint. Finally I got enough off so that the original forms began to reappear roughly under the haze of white. The next morning I went to work again. Several weeks later I finally did manage to finish it. By then an affectionate pride had grown up between us. The painting had put me through the wringer, and we had both emerged intact. That winter in my show at the Betty Parsons Gallery in New York the painting hung opposite the elevator door. At the opening I greeted a friend emerging from the lift who said, pointing across the room, "What is that wonderful painting of Earth?" My heart sang. Under it I had typed some lines from Edith Sitwell's poem "The Beekeeper": "Thick earthiness, half sun, half clod, plant alive from the root, still blind with earth and all the weight of Death and Birth."

In early winter of 1935 I became pregnant and had what I thought was a miscarriage. Since there was no reliable doctor in La Malbaie, I called my obstetrician in New York describing my symptoms. He said he couldn't be sure if I had lost the baby or not. I should stay in bed until I could see a doctor and observe meanwhile if my abdomen swelled. As it was winter this meant waiting till spring, when the roads would be clear and a doctor could drive down from Quebec. Meanwhile my abdomen did swell. I spent the three months in bed believing I was carrying a child, but when spring came and brought a doctor, I learned that the swelling of my abdomen had come from lying in bed doing nothing and indeed I had lost the baby three months earlier. Stopping painting just then had been particularly hard, because I was working towards my first show at the Frank Rehn Gallery, but the enforced time alone, seeing Pat only briefly for lunch and supper, proved to be very much of a learning and maturing period for me. I read Joyce's *Ulysses* at leisure and loved it. After that we decided not to spend the winters in Canada. It was a lonely period for me in bed all day but Hélène was a solace. By then she and Joseph had adapted their lives to ours and were taking wonderful care of us as they did for the following forty years. She was thrilled when we all thought I was pregnant.

Looking back on those early years there was much pain but there was also much positive activity. Chouette became the hub of an active folk art group. Pat and I shared this interest, which sprang up quite naturally when it was known that two artists were living in La Malbaie all year around. People who had done some painting independently started coming to our house on Sunday mornings after Mass, bringing along their work. This turned into one of the most creative groups in folk painting and sculpture of any primitive art that we knew. Besides a yearly local summer show, we organized shows at the Quebec and Montreal museums and at the Marian Willard Gallery in New York. This was a sell-out and brought an offer for a show in Paris which was flattering but never took place.

The French Canadian primitive painting and the breeding of Lhasa terriers, were of mutual interest to both Pat and me. Bookkeeping was necessary for each. Neither of us wanted to do the work. There was more to this than I realized. We began selling dogs world-wide, even to England with her strict immigration rules for animals. This required a lot of correspondence and record keeping as did the French Canadian paintings – lists of the artists, their works, to whom they were sold, exhibitions, etc. This became my job. The job of direct contact with the artist and criticism of his work fell to Pat. He first exercised his skills as a teacher at La Malbaie.

I often wrote to Dr. Martin, then head of the Montreal museum, regarding a show of the primitive works there. The charm of his many letters changed the business of being a bookkeeper from a burden to a pleasure. Dr. Martin and I were definitely becoming friends through our correspondence. Pat sensed this and resented it. When we finally met in Montreal, Pat spoke with him apart, probably saying that I was frail and needed protection from overwork, or something similar. But whatever he said caused Dr. Martin never to address another letter to me. Every letter afterwards came addressed to Pat. It was clearly a

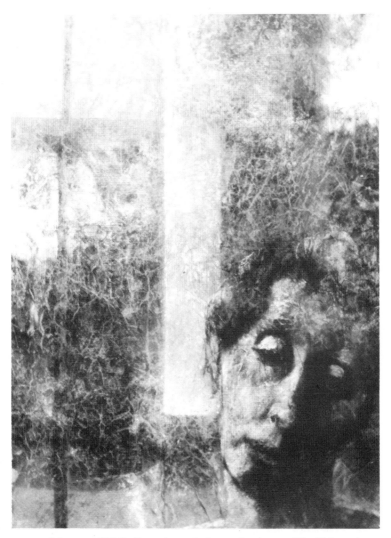

Schmertz (1956), Gouache and charcoal on paper, 29 x 22 in.

deliberate strategy that cut very deep. Pat couldn't allow me the pleasure of a gratifying experience. I thought back to the fight about the string beans and the ingrained and devious nastiness that was hard to forgive. I did not recognize it at the time as a lack of security in himself. However, I cared enough about our endeavors to continue the bookkeeping but without enjoyment.

It had always been a great sadness to Hélène that she and Joseph had never been able to have children, so when in the early summer of 1936 Pat and I arrived from New York with our newborn son Alexis in a basket, there was tremendous rejoicing. It took only a short time for our couple to slip into the roles of second parents. I can still picture Joseph sitting in the kitchen rocking chair with the baby cuddled up in his lap while Hélène was cooking supper. It seemed like the fulfillment of a long-time dream for each of them. It was in February, five years later, that our daughter Victoria was born, and the following summer we went back to Chouette as a family of four. Again spirits were very high. Joseph and Hélène were a source of uncomplicated, unconditional devotion for both Lex and Vicky, giving them what Pat and I as a couple were unable to. In this Hélène was backed up by Hippolyte, our tiny, part-Indian farmer who much later claimed, and with some justice, that it was he who had brought up our children along with two of his own. And so it came about that when at Chouette, Lex and Vicky had in effect two sets of parents who loved them in their different ways. It's not that Pat and I were not around but that we were over-preoccupied by our other projects: Pat in his garden and me in the studio. Basically I believe that we were both frightened at being parents and felt that we should straighten out our relationship together before we could be a good mother or a good father. I realize in retrospect that we were not able to give our children the love they needed, and although the dealings of each of us was always very affectionate with each of them, it left unheeded many of the issues which are all-important in childhood. These however, due to the unusual situation that developed in the Chouette household, were usually amply cared for and I think the children never felt a lack of attention when they were there. Meanwhile, Pat and I each struggled to establish our own terrain and personae. I viewed the situation with anxiety since it was becoming increasingly difficult to talk together about the questions that seemed to me to be all-important while Pat was determined to keep the upper hand at any cost. I think we both realized the blessing it was for the children to have so many loving adults around them at Chouette, and we relaxed into the situation without giving it much thought. However, returning to the dormitory life of Andover each autumn was always a shock. We both became preoccupied by the different, demanding problems of the school year, leaving an aching void for the children.

At Chouette things seemed simple by comparison. Lex and Vic played with Hippolyte's two sons of like ages. All four were often commandeered by Hippolyte to keep him company. He let them ride on the top of the hayload or go along with him when he sold potatoes or apples door-to-door in the village from the four-wheeled wagon pulled by Poulette. These trips often ended with a stop at the little store to buy peanuts for the children. The peanuts came in sturdy little plastic bags of 5-or 10-cent sizes. The peanuts were quickly eaten and the bags saved and treasured as tender for rainy day games. Hippolyte was an adorable, sociable man of wonderful humor and great wisdom with skin the color of leather. He was universally loved. I imagine there must have been a lot of gossip exchanged with each potato sold. On rainy days he would gather his children and ours in the workshop, give them each a hammer and set them to straightening crooked nails which had been extracted from old constructions and saved in Players tin cans to be used again. Simple lessons make a lasting impression. During the children's childhood there is no question that our life at Chouette was a self-nourishing nugget with Hélène and Hippolyte as its heartbeat. When Hippolyte died I felt that I no longer wanted to return to Chouette. The place was never the same without him.

My brother George lived nearby with his wife Maggy and two children the ages of ours. They seemed somewhat remote, however, as their lives were played out in a world of tennis lessons at the golf club and social picnics. Now that they have all grown up, George's daughter Bonner is the most loved of all our cousins.

One glorious, early morning in full summer I left Chouette around five o'clock to walk up the hill to the chapel. It was early enough for the heavy morning dew to soak my jeans up to the knees going through the tall grass. The fields and hills looked fresh and pure, which they often don't later in the day. Nature was beautiful but I was not. I had slept badly and was miserably unhappy. I thought that going to the little stone chapel I loved might help me. My father's ashes and later those of my mother and brother Quin were buried there. My mother had always wanted her own chapel, and I was surprised and delighted when in 1926 she decided to build one and to let me choose the location. I picked a spot which is about a mile and a half above the Manor House at the top of what is called the Upper Farms. We built it from field stones which we picked up in the fields and had a mason put together. Its tiny windows are about 15 inches square, its wooden benches, enough to seat a dozen people, are made of well-worn barn flooring at least a hundred years old. There is a tiny belfry, housing a bronze bell made in Paris and dedicated to St. Joan of Arc that tolls pleasantly. I have always loved this place. That morning I went there for refuge and comfort. As I sat on a little bench outside the chapel watching the morning come over the beautiful valley of the Murray River, I couldn't stop crying. I was very unhappy in my marriage and couldn't see a right way to stop all the pain for me and for our family. But there up on the mountain by the chapel, all alone, I could cry as much as I needed and I needed to cry a lot. I was ruminating on where support could be found. Then I thought of Mootzie and her friend Agnes, both fortresses of strength, both deeply religious women, both Episcopalians. Mootzie had given me a sound foundation in the Episcopalian Church for which I was grateful but I had always had trouble saying, "I am a miserable sinner, there is no health in me." It seems so without hope. But my sense of God, the supreme spirit, has always been, and still is, strong. It has involved me from time to time in one or another of the myriad structures created for worship. As I sat on that bench near the chapel, I thought about the Russian Orthodox Church in Paris I used to attend frequently when I was studying at the Sorbonne in 1924-25 on my junior year abroad. I particularly remember the Easter Sunday service, one week later than our calendar Easter, with its joyful ending with "Christ is risen" on every lip and an embrace for and from whomever you encounter walking around the church after the service. There one truly felt the joy that Christ had indeed risen. For that moment at least, hope had been reborn.

I also recalled my reaching out to Roman Catholicism when I was in Paris, inspired by Ste. Thérèse de Lisieux and the writings of Simone Weil. That was a closer connection than Russian Orthodox because of the heavily Catholic French-Canadian experience of my childhood. In fact, when Alexis was born, Pat and I had hoped he could be baptized into the Catholic church. We spoke to Père Boivin but realized that his unwillingness to do this unless one of us became Catholic was sensible. Neither of us wished to convert. Now I look back on that gesture of ours as being faint-hearted, as wanting a result without being willing to go the full way. In Paris in 1924 I had read *La Cathédrale* of Huysmans, which impressed me so greatly that I decided to join the church. I went to a small town which seemed an appropriate place to proceed on my path. I took a room in a private house by the little river across from a monastery. Every day of that week I talked to a sympathetic priest who was indoctrinating me. I planned to stay there until I was accepted into the church. Then Friday came around. That evening after supper with Madame, I went up to my room, which faced the monastery. It was a warm night and the window was open. I was sitting there thinking about my decision when I began to hear weird cries, sustained, blood-curdling and very disturbing. At breakfast the next morning, after a restless night, I asked Madame what had happened. "Oh, that," she said offhandedly, "was just the regular Friday night flagellations." I felt sick and went back to Paris that afternoon. Afterwards I had no hope of help from the Catholic church and realized that I would have to seek within myself, which I knew would take tremendous courage and faith on my part, both qualities in which I felt I was singularly lacking.

Sitting there in tears on the little bench looking up the valley, I began to be aware that I was not alone. I halted my breathing. There was a presentiment that something was near and warm. I waited in suspended excitement, very alert, not wanting to break the spell. Then I heard heavy breathing close by and soon felt an extremely coarse tongue licking my cheek. How unbelievable! Another living creature had come to my help. I semi-turned and saw a young white heifer's head close to mine, her tongue sticking out about to lick my cheek again. Willingly I let her continue. I felt blessed by the encounter. It seemed that she had been sent to me as a virginal symbol by a benign spirit. Gratitude invaded my whole being. Somehow the contact of that rough tongue on my cheek had stirred in me a life larger than the tormented one I had carried up the hill that morning. She had brought me harmony. After a while I patted her and she moved off.

Later as I walked back down to Chouette, I realized that that heifer was important to my life and that I must incorporate her into it. I arranged to buy her and bring her to Chouette. When she arrived I tried to lead her across the road to the field but she refused to budge. This worried me. Finally the two men who had brought her dragged her across the road, pulling her by the rope around her neck as she braced herself against them, pulling back and stiffening each of her four legs. Once in the field, she seemed to make the most of the lush pasture so I put aside my anxieties. Later that fall I was in Boston and went to the Artisans, the delightful store run by Mr. Mack, Clara Wainwright's father, where I thought I might find something for my heifer. To my surprise and joy as I entered, I saw a heavy necklace hanging on a hook by the door. It appeared that Mr. Mack, when in India where cows are sacred, had purchased some cow necklaces for his shop. I chose the most beautiful and looked forward to adorning my white heifer when I returned to Chouette the following summer. She wore it proudly, I thought, but still remained an outsider, a singleton, always grazing alone, just like me. She was not accepted by the other cows and people made unflattering remarks about how out-of-place she looked, the only white cow among the beautiful herd of Jerseys.

It was now her second summer and Hippolyte said that if she were to remain a part of the farm, she must be productive and have a calf. Emotionally I was against it. I wanted her to continue to be what she had been for me at our first meeting, a magical symbol of virginal purity. Were she to have a calf, I thought she would lose these symbolic traits. However, Hippolyte's point was valid and I agreed with apprehension. Something was amiss; I thought back on the bad omen of her not wanting to cross the road into the pasture on her arrival. There was also another bad omen. One day while walking in the woods near the pasture, I found her necklace looped over a fence post. I could only feel that she must have tired of her finery and somehow managed to rub it off against the post. Presumably someone found it and looped it there for retrieval By now I was also recognizing that the magic she held for me resided more in the memory of the experience of our first encounter on the bench by the chapel than in her current presence in the field. Perhaps I should not have tried to extend that first experience, to pin it down and make it mine. Probably I should have just taken the event for what it was, a beautiful affirmation of the oneness of the universe, all of us together, people, animals, plants, air, and rocks. My smooth skin may have felt pleasant to her rough tongue, much as her rough tongue had awakened me to renewed life, but that was not a reason to change her life to suit my needs, rather than leaving her to peacefully live out her own.

Inevitably her time came and she had her calf. I agreed with the general consensus of opinion of the nearby farmers that she had given birth to the ugliest calf any of them had ever seen and that, again like me, she had very little milk. The calf died after a few hours and the heifer was pronounced useless as a breeding animal and sent to the butcher.

If there is any moral to this tale, I'm sure I don't know what it is beyond, "Let magic follow magic's way." I only know that I still treasure her necklace along with a nostalgic sadness. Later I learned that one must not try to possess "joy as it flies."

During that period Walt Disney was making his ethnic films and was anxious to produce one of French Canada. His scouts found our house and in 1961 he decided to make the movie "Big Red" there. Huge trucks came over from Hollywood, the drivers arriving frightened by the narrow roads and steep hills. But as Walt Disney told me, the crew was happier on location there than ever before. Walter Pidgeon, looking rather like Ronald Reagan, was the Hollywood star, but the real star was the unknown French Canadian boy Gilles Payant. It's a story about a dog. The Hollywood people were delightful though not knowledgeable about farm life. It was a good laugh for Hippolyte when at a certain point in the film it was important to have the cow put her head over the fence and say "moo". The director indicted as much to Pat who told Hippolyte. Caillette was like a pet in our family so she came over when he called and, not understanding what was wanted, put her head over the fence and said "moo". It did not occur to the Hollywood group that it was unusual for a cow to follow the instructions of a film director. Her "moo" was the best thing in the film.

In front of our house is a small portico for boots, tools, baskets and garden things. Over its door is a delightful carving of two little owls (chouettes) sitting in the woods. It was carved to fit that triangular spot by one of the local artists. He cut it all out with a small hatchet, never using a chisel. It's a lovely piece of folk art. For some reason the lighting was not right for the film makers so they duplicated the whole portico and set it up on the other side of the house. By using rubber cement they made an exact replica of the owl carving. I had been away for a few days and when I drove back into my driveway I found my house turned back to front.

9. NEW YORK

"New York, New York, it's a helluva town, the
Bronx is up and the Battery's down"
— *Betty Comden and Adolf Greene*

Previously when we came down from Canada during the winter months, we stayed with my parents on 75th Street. It was important to be in New York to keep in touch with the art world, to have a bout of studying with Hans Hofmann, to go to the theater, to see people and have a good time, which we did. We loved the solitude of our winter life in Canada, but a break from it was also good.

Now, after the miscarriage, it seemed better to stay near a reliable doctor. We moved to an apartment in the Hotel des Artistes on West 61st Street, just opposite Central Park where Pat walked our four Lhasa terriers twice a day. I became pregnant again, and on July 6, 1936, after three more months in bed, Alexis was born, healthy and happy. Since I did not have the requisite number of paintings promised, Pat took over my exhibition time slot at Frank Rehn's Gallery. I was apprehensive when at the opening I heard Pat saying, "It's wonderful with Maud and me, there is no jealousy." I wondered if that were true, would he mention it so often? Fortunately, I was able to get a show at another gallery for the following year.

My father, then an old man, was disappointed that I had married an artist. His heart had been set on my marrying a diplomat. He loved to travel and I think he saw himself as a guest in embassies around the world. To make his last days happy I was determined to show him that since I intended to be an artist I was going to be a good one. This meant getting a gallery, having a show and doing well. Somehow a book called *Think and Grow Rich* fell into my hands. I read it through several times and followed its instructions: "Decide what you want to do; the time you will allow for doing it; how you will do it; and how much money you want to make. Review this list at least three times a day." This I did. My list was: I want a gallery show. I will concentrate on this for a year. I will sell to the Metropolitan Museum at some point in the near future.

And I want to make $2000. Here I frightened myself. I had never sold a picture for more than $25 and was ashamed to have put down this large amount. I was far too embarrassed to tell my husband about my project. But, it all came true.

That 1938 show at Julian Levy's 57th Street gallery was an exciting and strange one. His was a perfect setting for me. Julian was involved in the avant-garde, introducing surrealism to America, showing Frieda Kahlos' and Dali's work, among others. Later he became better known for his keen interest in photography. The gallery was new, young and enterprising – almost the reverse of the Frank Rehn Gallery. By losing Rehn, who focused completely on American painting, I had become connected to a gallery of far more scope and one better-suited to my work. From my show there, I sold paintings to both the Whitney and Metropolitan museums in the first week, and during the second week a painting was bought and donated to the Museum of Modern Art. The best reward was that my father was surprised and overjoyed. He died shortly after the Levy show.

Now I had to pay the price for quick success. I was completely confused. Basically I didn't understand why the museums had bought my work. I was proud of my paintings and had hoped to sell a few pieces at Julian's and perhaps in five or ten years to sell to the Metropolitan, but here my ambitions had all been satisfied in the first ten days of my first show. I was extremely disoriented. I tried going back to art school, but I was still getting a lot of publicity so the other students recognized me. I felt shy and left the school.

I believe the confusion of my early success came about because I had been painting by myself and not showing my work to others. I was not accustomed to criticism, good or bad, and I was totally unprepared emotionally for such an overwhelmingly positive response. I didn't know how to handle it. I felt the way I had in Paris when Ernest Hemingway had first complimented me on my painting and then said that I'd spoiled it. I had not understood his comment then, nor this parallel situation ten years later. When I see this early work now, I am amazed. I find it good, fresh, strong, and original.

Recently I found an *Art News* review of that 1938 show written by Rosamond Frost, one of their established critics. She wrote, "a show of real quality at the Julien Levy Gallery where the paintings of Maud Morgan prove the artist to be not only a rarely sensitive observer but a thoroughly proficient craftsman who handles her medium with no trace of preoccupation at the technical problems attendant upon her fertile imagination. The freedom of her brushing and the pureness of her color seem to flow directly from tube to canvas."

Rereading this now, and seen in the light of a review of a first show in a good art magazine, a beginner's show, I am not surprised at my having been thrown off keel by it and of having been overwhelmed by the success of the exhibition. Pat must have read this review but I don't remember any ruffling of feathers at that time. I was the one having a hard time adjusting.

1936 to 1940 were wonderful years for us in New York. We were popular and socially active in many worlds – artists, museum people, socialites and family. Alexis spent his first four years in our delightful apartment over a shoe store next to Carnegie Hall. There was a large roof off the apartment where Lex spent his outdoor hours in a crib. He was healthy and adorable. Next door to us was the artists' models club. These gorgeous young women would crowd around him lovingly, an enchanting way to start a life.

Openings at the Museum of Modern Art were everything openings should be. Everyone was at their best, at least half were friends, and the excitement was palpable. Everything was new and fun and MOMA was the center under the direction of its outstanding and distinguished director Alfred Barr.

I enjoyed crazy clothes and would buy wonderful birds twittering on wire stems in Chinatown and wear them in my hair to an opening, or, other times, I would wear far-out, outré hats which I sometimes found reduced at R.H. Macy's, hats with gigantic flowers or all-over feathers. I still have a brilliant yellow cock-a-do one in which I painted a self-portrait. One spring, when I was fussily trimming a blue straw hat, Sandy Calder observed my not-too-successful efforts.

"Take those flowers off," he said as he picked up pliers and made me a beautiful wire daisy about ten inches long.

I thought it looked wonderful on the blue hat, an opinion not shared by my fashion-minded friends. After I tired of the hat I had the daisy made into a pin. I still wear it with pleasure, remembering Sandy, that great, big, warm, laughing, loveable bear, always dressed in his red shirt and tie.

Pat and I were attending Hans Hofmann's school then. It was a first for me since I had not been well enough to go to his classes when we were in Munich. Pat already knew the ropes. Hofmann's ideas were not easy to grasp. He was introducing us to the European theories of Picasso and Matisse with whom he had been friends while in Paris. This was a far cry from the teaching going on at that time in the New York Art Student's League. Hofmann's teaching was extremely dynamic. He made you feel that the volumes of the model's body were in motion, or about to be. He drew them that way and tried to instruct us to do so also. Hofmann was a superb teacher and excellent draughtsman. Everything I know about space I learned from him.

There was one particular occasion which stays in my memory. That day Hofmann came into class for the weekly criticism, walked to my chair, sat down and scrutinized the drawing I had been slaving over all week. Carefully he removed the four thumbtacks which held my sheet of paper to its board and asked for four more. Once he had my drawing in his hands he tore it down the middle. My heart went into my boots. He pinned the left half back onto my board, then the right, lowering it about a quarter of an inch below the left. At that point he drew one powerful sweep of a line rejoining the two halves of the figure. He had by that quarter of an inch difference in height added the intangible element of motion to the figure. I never forgot that lesson.

Most of Hofmann's students loved and respected him as a master. When he came to America his reputation as a brilliant teacher was established quickly. In California, New York and Provincetown his schools flourished. But his reputation as a painter languished. He had an extremely difficult time achieving recognition for his own work. His students were concerned about this problem. I vividly remember dreading having to tell him I was to have a one-woman exhibition of paintings at Betty Parsons Gallery. The task was especially painful since my show was to be at exactly the gallery where he should be showing (and fortunately did some years later). He was generous about it, went to see my show and wrote me a complimentary letter, commenting on my beautiful colors.

But I was not confident about my draughtsmanship and Pat's opinion of my skills in that area was even lower than mine. Painting was a different matter. There, from the start, I felt at home. I knew what I wanted to do and how I hoped to achieve it. I loved experimenting. Innovative ideas came easily and often problems were resolved with unusual and good results. I didn't want to study painting with anybody, even Hofmann. But I knew my drawing was weak and I was eager to improve. What I learned about drawing and space from Hofmann was constructive, because I could incorporate it immediately into the structure of my paintings.

Louise Nevelson was with us in the Hofmann class. She was a noticeable member. She wore spectacular hats or head creations which she made herself; piled up shapes, sweeping brims, massive volumes. She looked magnificent, these constructions topping her already imposing physique. We were all friendly in the school although she was not keen about the classes. Years later at one of her exhibitions I had a chance to introduce my son Lex to her. He was anxious to meet her and we managed to find a quiet corner where we could talk. During our conversation a young man came up and interrupted. Louise's disapproving look elicited the comment from him, "But I know you." Turning to him, she said, "Have you slept with me?" "Well, no." came his embarrassed answer. "Then you don't know me," she said as she turned her back on him to resume her conversation with us.

Down on 10th Street, the Whitney Museum, an outgrowth of the Whitney Studio Club, flourished. Started by Gertrude Vanderbuilt Whitney, a remarkable, courageous, wealthy socialite sculptor who, assisted by Juliana Force, a self-made woman from Hoboken, first as secretary and later as dynamic director of the museum, staked out new terrain for American art. These two powerful women ideally complemented each other and brought about a wide recognition and acceptance of American painting and sculpture. Juliana became one of New York's leading figures in the art world. Her parties on the top floor of the museum, which was her private apartment, were legendary. She had great flare and was feisty, with quicksilver moods and great understanding of artists and their difficulties. She was extremely generous, made lightning judgments and loved to buy pictures. Gregarious and enterprising, she was always the center of action. Gertrude Vanderbuilt Whitney was firmly behind her, giving freely of her largesse. The daughter of a man said to be the richest man in America, Gertrude had the vision to recognize that she must find her own path in life and through her love of art became one of the greatest benefactors of American art in the country.

One day when I was unusually tired a friend called inviting us for cocktails. I just wasn't up to it. She pleaded. Salvador Dali was coming. He had recently arrived in New York and didn't speak English. She had no other guests who could speak Spanish or French. The party was a small spur-of-the-moment one – we must come. We gave in.

Our friend lived in a third floor walk-up, one of those typical, delightful, small apartments carved out of the old New York brownstone houses. At the top of the stairs she opened the door and introduced us to Dali, who was standing beside her.

"I am going to faint," was the first thing I said to him.

He saw this was true and led me to a small back room where there was a day bed. I collapsed onto it. He sat on a chair close beside me, occasionally putting his hand on my brow. He started to talk about his childhood. How deeply frustrated he had been. He adored his father, wanted and needed to get special attention and love from him. The father was an important, busy man always surrounded by people. The son would plot ways to be alone with him, but never successfully. Just as he thought he was about to gain his attention, the telephone would ring and the father would plunge into a vivacious conversation, laughing and talking enthusiastically, forgetting his son. He'd hang up, they'd start talking and the same thing would repeat itself endlessly. "I gave up," Dali said, "and that's what all the telephones are doing in my paintings." By then I was feeling better and we joined the others.

Shortly afterwards Dali was hired to decorate a window at Bonwit Teller's on Fifth Avenue. A violent argument developed with the floor manager. Dali was furious at anyone trying to interfere with his work. He smashed the plate glass window and jumped through it, landing amidst shattered glass on the sidewalk. By chance Pat and I were walking up Fifth Avenue at the time and saw the shattered glass and Dali surrounded by the police. He saw us at the edge of the crowd and waved as they took him off. He had with one great gesture settled the argument with the floor manager, made himself a New York celebrity, and virtually introduced surrealism to America.

I rarely went to a party without an unusual bouquet pinned to my shoulder, often exotic orchids combined with something unexpected, to suit what I was wearing. Pat knew and cared about flowers. He usually had these bouquets made up at Max Schling, a florist on Fifth Avenue near the Plaza Hotel. Mr. Schling was a short, slender, alert, charming and sensitive man who was in love with flowers. I remember one day he carefully explained the sex life of the orchid to us, holding a specimen delicately in one hand while tenderly lifting the petals with the other to reveal its inner construction, its secrets, inviting us into the whole reproductive sequence with precise scientific words – an intimate and erotic experience. Then he turned to me and said, "I love you but it doesn't concern you." He was speaking to the core of my being, to that place deeper than I could usually reach but which I intuitively understood and where I felt at home.

The Great Depression formed the backdrop for many of these glamorous events. This economic disaster changed the face of the city. Suddenly men looking cold and unhappy were standing on street corners all over town, selling apples for five cents each. Headlines every day told of another financier who had jumped out of his office window. There were many individual tragedies, families ruined overnight, people's lives changed for ever. As in most great cities, dark and light events stood in stark contrast like a chiaroscuro painting. My family was fortunate in not having its financial life disrupted.

One of our friends in New York was George E. He was sweet, fat, funny, very bright and a long-time alcoholic who very much wanted me to paint his portrait. I resisted, I didn't want to paint anyone's portrait. But George insisted, and in the end, I agreed to give it a try. He started coming to the studio to pose, enchanted with the project. We began pretty well on the first day. The second day, my sitter had changed. He'd had a heavy night of drinking and his whole face was different, bags beneath the bloodshot eyes, the face rounder and fatter, the expression, morose. The third day he was back to his old self. I realized that this was how it was going to be, on and off, off and on. I decided to split the face down the middle. That way each day I could work on the side appropriate to how he had spent the previous evening. I was intrigued by the process and finished the painting. It was a great success, he was crazy about it. It was the first time I had divided a head down the middle. George's drinking increased and not long afterwards killed him. Six months after his death I was having an exhibition in New York and was short one painting. Since I'd liked my portrait of George, I called his mother and asked if I could borrow it for the show. She told me the first thing she had done after George's death had been to burn the painting. A strange compliment. Evidently my split face had captured too much of the man. It was odd that I was not more aware of a similar split in my own life.

One evening at a New York dinner party I sat beside a psychiatrist who was curious about me. Willingly I told him who I was, how I had developed, and why I didn't have anything to fear. He was skeptical, but asked for more background. My thesis was that, having been so unhappy during the first twenty-five years of my life, my dues had been paid. I was insulated against further pain. He raised an eyebrow. I was presenting myself as a happy, young, married woman with a clear slate ahead. Here, across the diner table sat my handsome, charming, intelligent husband who was in love with me. But the psychiatrist must

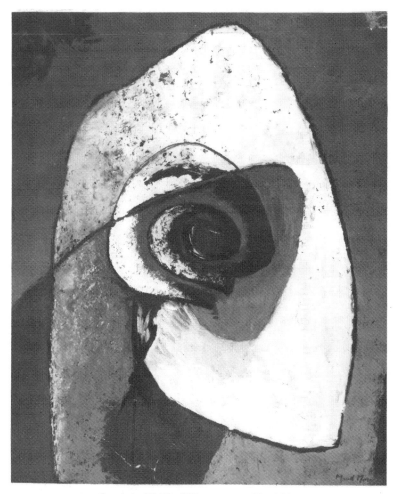

Involute (1947), Oil on canvas, 29 x 24 in.

have guessed that all was not as well as the portrait I was depicting. I needed to be loved for the maverick I was. Pat loved the surface maverick, that was easy to take, even an asset. Beyond that he didn't and couldn't go. He was afraid of the unknown, the unexpected, the surprise. He didn't want growth or change, which were my goals. He sensed danger in me.

Betty Parsons, who was my friend and became my dealer, was one of the pivotal figures who ushered in the new art that eventually came to be known as abstract expressionism. This art, monumental, free, abstract, and highly personal, could only have emerged in America. Most of the major artists who created abstract expressionism showed in Betty's gallery: Jackson Pollock, Robert Motherwell, Mark Rothko, Barnett Newman and others. I was fortunate enough to be one of those others, right in the eye of the whole extraordinary force. All of the artists in the gallery were unknown then and many were ridiculed, but Betty stood fast, and finally, valiantly, made her point. The art she had fostered became the most important art in the Western world at that epoch.

The group was an intimate one then. At the opening of my second exhibition, Betty called to ask if I could hang my own show with the help of the janitor as she wanted to listen to Edith Sitwell, who was reading her poetry that afternoon. I willingly agreed. On my arrival at the gallery, there was no janitor to be found. I even had a hard time locating hammer and nails. The opening was scheduled for late that same afternoon. I was alarmed and a little panicky as I didn't see how I could get the paintings up in time. However I started, coping as well as I could with the step ladder needed for the larger pieces. Part way through this difficult process the elevator door opened and a pleasant-looking, heavy-set man walked in and looked around. "This show looks terrible," he said. I agreed and explained the situation. He listened, took off his jacket and said, "Let's take it all down and start over." We did, and made a good-looking exhibition out of the confusion. That man was Barney Newman, one of the most outstanding abstract expressionist artists of the time.

New York continued to be wonderful. Socially and artistically Pat and I got on smoothly and affectionately there, if no more successfully sexually. We were more like teammates than lovers. It was a rare period during which we reacted towards each other directly and with equality. In New York we were friends. Later in Andover we became rivals and sometimes enemies.

In 1939, Bart Hayes offered Pat an art instructorship at Phillips Academy in Andover, Massachusetts. It was Pat's first job offer and he was loathe to take it. Neither of us wanted to leave New York, but the job fit seemed perfect for him and I thought he should take it. He had already shown himself to be an excellent teacher in the little class he held in our New York studio. I saw it as an appropriate opportunity for his future and was afraid that he might not get another offer and sure that he would never job hunt. He did not want to work for anybody but took the job.

It seems strange to me now that I never evaluated what leaving New York would mean to my own career. I left an ideal spot, firmly placed with the most avant-garde gallery in the city and with a good track record behind me. Once away from New York I was no longer "in". I kept showing, but I had lost the strength of my contacts and couldn't be there enough to stay abreast of current happenings or produce sufficient work to build up publicity or a reputation.

Before we left New York Pat and I went to visit Kirk Askew, who was the director of Durlacher Brothers where I had shown my work following the exhibition at Julian Levy's. Kirk had been a student of Paul Sachs at Harvard, one of many who went from those classes to direct museums and galleries all over America. Kirk and his wife Constance held open house Saturday nights in their lovely New York house. Many of his former classmates from different cities and museums as well as other people in the arts would attend. These were wonderful evenings. There I first met John McAndrew, for so long the influential head of the art department at Wellesley College, Perry Rathbone, later the director of the Boston Museum of Fine Arts, and countless others. Kirk was a good friend. We told him that we were leaving New York and that Pat was going to become a teacher. Kirk's reaction was interesting and accurate. He thought Pat would be an excellent teacher and that teaching would be good for him for a while. "But the time will come when you must stop. You won't know when that time is but Maud will and you must listen to her and quit then or you will be seduced by adoring students and be ruined."

Pat agreed. We both knew Kirk had spoken wisely.

To fantasize about what might have happened to our lives if we had remained in New York is futile. But I can and do remember our time there as a rare, lovely period of work, pleasure and a mutual understanding which we never achieved again.

10. PAT IN ANDOVER

"The courage of the knife but not of the blood"
— *Nietzsche*

By far the most difficult part of writing this book has been dealing with my husband, Patrick. What a mixture of tender and tough, gentle and vicious, helpful and hindering, spiritual and worldly. He is a conundrum to capture in words, just as he was to deal with in life. I am obliged to write about him as though he were two people, which indeed he was.

While in New York I had been enthusiastic about Pat's accepting the position at Phillips Academy Andover, but when we went to be interviewed in the spring of 1940, on entering our room at the Andover Inn, I threw myself down on the bed in floods of inexplicable tears. Obviously there was foreboding about the future beyond my knowing. I could not have imagined how this move would radically change our lives from then on, together and individually.

No job could have been better tailored to Pat's various talents and interests than art instructor and he certainly carried the role off beautifully. The position gave him leeway to use his many and varied talents, most of which worked extremely well in the teacher-student relationship. Pat was not disturbed by being surrounded by many students and was able to do his own painting in their midst. This teaching as a sense of 'working together' was enormously effective. Students valued seeing an artist not only teaching but working along with them.

On the surface I seemed to be the perfect wife for him, but on the surface only. He loved me, we shared artistic interests, we enjoyed similar types of people, I was undemanding and malleable. I had a large family that he could adopt at a time when he didn't like his own and wanted one. I had a little money when we married, but there was clearly more down the road which I would willingly use to support our family. All these things, plus two wonderful children would seem to fulfill the entitlements Pat thought were his due, but they were not enough. The right wife should have remained frail and acquiescent, as he had known me, except for the happy time in Paris when he, Whitney, and I were a trio, a time in which the love between Whitney and me had been the defining factor. After that when we saw each other "tête-à-tête," I was grieving Whitney's death and later questioning why I had become involved with Pat. As my natural energy regained its strength after Munich and as I began gradually to see myself as an independent person again, he became alarmed. This was no longer the wife he had married. He was often critical, complaining angrily that I had changed, that I was getting tough, something he had not spoken of in New York.

But not until the first day of my arrival in Andover in October 1940, when the job had become a reality and I was a new faculty wife, did I realize that Pat blamed me for pressuring him to accept the position. His behavior changed so radically that I had difficulty understanding his new persona. I had stayed on in New York to pack up our apartment and see that our possessions were put on the moving van. I took a midnight train to Boston and another train to Andover, arriving at our empty, rented, house exactly as the van got there. I was pregnant and tired. Pat directed the placing of the big pieces of bedroom and living room furniture and took off to teach his class. As he left he told me he had invited four people for dinner that night. They had been kind to him, he said, before I arrived and he wanted to repay them. I said we would have to take them to the Inn. He became angry, flatly refused and left.

The house was not equipped. There was no salt, no pepper, no car, I didn't know where or how far away there was a shop. I was desperate. Finally I asked directions from a passerby and walked towards town, about a mile and a half away. I was extremely depressed and surprised at Pat's anger and inconsiderate demands, which seemed to have come out of the blue. Only later did I realize that I could have legitimately claimed fatigue and gone to bed, letting him cope with his own dinner party, but that would have created a very bad impression on our first night together in a new job. At the store I bought the minimum necessities, as I was already big with Vicky and it was a long walk home.

When I returned to our Abbot Street house, the telephone was ringing. Someone said, "I am Cookie. Pat insists we all come to dinner tonight and we think that's a terrible imposition since you just arrived this morning, and we're not going to do it. We'll just come for drinks and snacks and go out to a restaurant to eat." He hung up.

I didn't have drinks. I didn't have snacks. I sat down trying to evaluate the situation. I rested a bit and started back down to town to get what I needed. The evening passed pleasantly enough but I was under a heavy cloud of apprehension. The next morning Pat went off to school unwilling to discuss the events of the previous evening. Could this be the man about whom I had written in my diary five years earlier, "Pat's personality is unique in the world, he continues quietly towards his undefined yet always very definite goal, touching much, being touched by little, sorting instantly without analysis what is fruitful and what unfruitful for him, giving always instinctively without thought, a real Christian." Now I began to wonder.

Although he had successfully taught small classes in our studio in New York, the students had all been friends. This was different and he was very nervous about it. I felt for him. Having one big class after another showing up relentlessly was a frightening prospect. I tried to help out in the beginning and would drop in unexpectedly, comment on the students' work, make a suggestion, or talk about art a little, anything to give a slight break. I think Pat appreciated this. However his classes went so well that it was not long before he was given an assistant, so I stopped dropping in.

On December 7, 1941, the outside world exploded into our lives when the Japanese attacked Pearl Harbor. We listened in stunned silence as the words came over the radio. Only the night before we had met a high-ranking naval officer who had expounded during dinner on the impregnability of the United States to foreign invasion. War seemed unthinkable. But then, as is always the case, despite shattering events or deep personal sorrow, daily life continues, albeit as though in a dream. The school maintained its routine.

Pat became a superlative teacher, both in studio and art history.

According to one of his first students, "He was wonderful in the studio, very civilized, treating everyone the same way whether they had signs of talent or not. He made everyone feel quite adult and opened our eyes to lots of things, not just painting."

He also started a weekly film society, unusual at that time, that exposed the students to exceptional and international films which they later discussed and analyzed.

I only heard Pat give a few lectures but they were memorable: inventive and knowledgeable, well-structured but free-flowing on the surface. Appropriate slang words were used with great discrimination, skill and humor. The people who studied with Pat when he was in his prime, or those who heard his many lectures were fortunate. His talks were almost like a dance that ended in a pirouette as the final bell rang. His sense of timing was superb. Even today, middle-aged men some-times stop me, saying, "I just want to tell you that Pat changed my life." I think he loved his teaching, though he disclaimed it and somehow continued to make me the enemy for having forced his hand.

After our stormy first evening, there were several uneventful months in our personal life. Things went along adequately. We were well received as a new faculty couple and the novelty of school life held both our interests.

A little before Vicky's birth I went to Brookline to stay with my brother George and his wife, Maggy, where my mother joined me from New York. The hospital was near their house and being with them relieved me of worry about the possibility of Pat's being away when I needed to be driven to the hospital. Once at the hospital and the first early pains over, there was a long uneventful wait. I was given some castor oil, told to get up, get dressed and go for a walk to induce labor. On the walk I met my friend Bill Cummings, director of the Skowhegan School of Art. He asked me to come to a nearby bar where we could dance. I said unfortunately I had to refuse because I was on my way to the hospital to have a baby. The unusual maternity coat I had designed clearly was a success.

I was in excellent physical condition, having worked with Mabel

Todd in New York, a remarkable physical therapist who had prepared me for natural childbirth, still an unusual practice at that period, and I was very excited by the prospect. I explained all this to my new obstetrician in Boston. He promised not to give me a knock-out shot unless absolutely necessary. The delivery of my first baby had been very easy – only three hours of labor. I expected that the second would be similar. But I had been given a medication in New York and was not aware of the moment of birth, now I was eagerly anticipating being conscious throughout the whole procedure. However, when the time came, the doctor was out at dinner so they held up the delivery process and finally, when I wasn't looking, the nurse gave me a knock-out shot in the rear, I suspect more for her well-being than for mine. I have never forgiven Dr. Irving for depriving me of that avidly-anticipated experience, which I think might have been truly significant for me due to my feminine insecurity. I wonder now if it might even have made a difference in my having milk. It was an easy birth and I presume that I would have gotten through natural childbirth adequately. This was only the first of my bad experiences with Boston doctors and hospitals. However, in spite of the disappointment in my doctor, I was thrilled by Vicky's birth on February 10, 1941.

Pat arrived from Andover, was told he had a daughter, looked through a glass wall at a crumpled little thing in a crib, and came in to see me. This whole episode seemed to me artificial and frigid and made me feel as though I were an actress in a drama of which I did not know the plot. I had come out of the medication when a nurse appeared with a baby in her arms and introduced me – I use the word advisedly – to my child. She was a cunning little creature who looked strikingly like Queen Victoria, for whom we then named her. Hospitals in the early 1940s did not allow infants to spend much time in their mother's rooms fearing germs. They were usually brought in to nurse and almost immediately taken back to the glass-walled infants dormitory. Contrary to the concern, love, and interest Pat had shown in New York at Lex's birth, now he was very preoccupied with his teaching, came to the hospital only occasionally for short visits, and seemed very remote. I cried bitterly after he had gone but was relieved each time when he left.

I believe I saw Vicky four or five times in the hospital after her birth. Unfortunately again I had no milk. I smoked and drank a lot in those days and don't know if that was the cause although it was not considered harmful then. After those early visits I didn't see my baby again. I was given no information beyond the fact that everything was all right. I simply couldn't see my child. They said I was a neurotic mother and wanted to give me a sedative. I was desperately worried and very, very much alone and frightened. My mother had returned to New York after the baby's birth and my brother and his wife were not concerned. At last I enticed one of the nurses to tell me the truth about Vicky. She was dangerously ill. She had contracted an infectious disease along with several other babies there in that supposedly hygienic glass walled room. She came very near death and was taken to some other hospital far away to be given mother's milk.

Poor, poor little Vicky, so alone and remote during those important first days in this world. It was hard to know when or even if she would return home. I left the hospital extremely depressed. I had not been able to give my baby what she needed and I felt hopelessly inadequate. Only after several weeks Vicky was brought back to Andover by a lovable nurse called Woodsy. She was still extremely frail and so changed in appearance that I didn't recognize her. What with the earlier ineptitude of the hospital I actually wondered if they had sent me back my own baby. I was still anxious about her health.

A huge bill arrived from Longwood Hospital for Pat with some ambiguous explanation for the cause of the original infection, saying they knew he would be gentleman enough to pay. I'm glad to say he didn't. More and more I wished I had never left New York.

Pat's new persona was becoming his norm, though certain qualities remained that I had known and cared for. Others became sharper, and still others changed sufficiently so that they became different in kind. New characteristics appeared for the first time, such as growing competitiveness, and what I was not expecting, a greedy attitude toward money. The charisma was always there, being used more and more adroitly. The love of gin was still a sine qua non, and the need to be surrounded by admiring people, which had always existed, grew in Andover by leaps and bounds along with his skills as lecturer and teacher. He was a socially oriented person, a superb host. It was hard for me to conceive of giving a party without him. But it was becoming impossible for me to talk to him about things which were life issues to me.

Several months after Vicky's birth, and resulting from it, I painted a small picture called "Face Down". A woman is lying with her head buried in her arms, face hidden, obviously in distress. I brought the painting back from the studio I had temporally rented, put it on the mantelpiece and went for a walk. Pat came home and took it as my farewell message to him. I was sorry to give him a shock, but glad to give him a clue as to how I was feeling, though he made no comment nor took any action. I was desperate. I felt that if he wouldn't respond to this painting enough to talk to me about my obvious distress there was no hope for a profound relationship with him in the future. Sad to say this proved to be true. He was not interested in my problems except in so far as they convenienced or inconvenienced him. The suddenness of the change I had seen in him on my first night in Andover was no accident. It was a thunderous blow, particularly coming directly after our friendly cooperative years in New York. What had been there was no longer, nor would it ever be there again. Now I had to fend for myself, and find another human being to talk to whether I had to pay for it or not. I went to see an analyst, a Freudian analyst, not knowing the difference between Freud and Jung. Little did I suspect then that these sessions would drag on for ten unproductive years. I might have done far better if I had stayed home and taken care of my two children rather than commute to Boston five times a week. "If your doctor was so wonderful," said Vicky years later, "why didn't she do something about us?" Vicky was right. In my Freudian analysis I don't remember Dr. B. saying anything constructive about my children or helpful about Pat. The only thing I remember her saying about Pat's incipient homosexuality was, "Do you want it in writing?"

In our second year at Andover we were moved into a school residence, half a small house on Main Street partway up the hill. Coy House was not distinguished but cozy, with a tiny dormitory in back for four boys with whom we shared the entrance and hallway. That year an unexpected event brought about my teaching at Abbot Academy, the girl's school down the hill. Then independent, it was later amalgamated into the boy's school. Mary Hatch, the art teacher at Abbot, came to me and said, "I have joined the Red Cross Army unit and am leaving today. You are the only person here equipped to take my place. It will be your war effort. You start tomorrow morning. Good-bye."

I had never taught any subject and was intimidated by the thought of teenage girls who were more foreign to me then than their masculine counterparts. But I had no choice. Mary had in effect done me a good turn. After the initial panic, I came to love teaching and my students, especially the ones that showed little talent. The most fun was to figure out ways to get them freed up. Most of the girls were at that difficult stage of being overly self-conscious, afraid of being different. I found as the students' efforts improved, I was able to put the energy I normally put into my own work vicariously into theirs. But in doing this my own creativity was depleted so that, even on days I didn't teach, I wasn't able to work well at home. I never could alter this which meant that I never became a really professional teacher, but I loved the experience for the six years it lasted.

Vicky became a rewarding child, a ravishing little girl with golden curls and a gift for words. At every stage she was beautifully formed. She has one nearly blind eye, as I do, and was treated in the same way. When she was four and five she wore a black patch over her right eye, her good one, hoping to strengthen the weak one. To watch this adorable little person with a black patch tied around her head was a little sad but enormously appealing. The patch never seemed to either hold her up nor improve her vision. She was skillful in everything she did, climaxing by building what was referred to as "Vicky's machine", a Rube Goldberg contraption she created that was the envy of the little boys.

I very much wanted another child. Pat flatly refused. With one boy and one girl I realized that our family would almost inevitably be split down the middle: father/daughter, mother/son. Pat was immovable. I was left to paint out my unfulfilled desire, which I did in "Wishing Well". The woman's body yearns for the foetus which is floating in the water. Gracefully she stands, leaning towards the wishing well, against a dark red background, suggestive of clotted blood, her arms extend lovingly towards the foetus. Originally her long, dark hair hung down over her face as she bends. At this point I had trouble with my composition and made many attempts at a pictorial resolution. Eventually I found the right one. I eliminated her head entirely and the painting was solved, expressing even more fully my longing for the child, which after all, has nothing to do with the head or the intellect.

This painting was so deeply personal that I was shy about showing it. Jo Blackmer, a faculty wife, came for a cocktail when the painting was standing in the corner not quite completed. Pat was saying how he never wanted another child. "But Maud does," said Jo. "Look at that."

I had not realized what I had painted, the yearning was so deep within I had not dared think it out in words. When finished, I put the painting in the cellar and exhibited it for the first time in 1986, about forty years later. Painting helped me live with my feelings, but a painting is not a substitute for a child, and for a long time I regretted not having another child. I still do. I care a lot about this painting and don't want to sell it, rare for me. Usually I am happy to have my work go out into the world to make its own statement.

When we left the city in 1940, I thought, like any typical, insular New Yorker, that I was going to the end of the world, namely a small town in New England. Feeling I would be deprived of seeing good current art work, I decided to start buying paintings and sculpture to take with us. Our collection enhanced our life. In the back of my thoughts was a conversation I had had with Ernest Hemingway long ago in

Paris. He told me the first time he saw Miro's painting of "The Farm", he fell madly in love with it. Though he was a young newspaper writer with very little money, he decided his life would not be complete without that painting. He bought the Miro, paying small sums over a long period of time. He strongly recommended that I act likewise if the real love was there. I did and I'm grateful to him. Our collection greatly enhanced our life as well as that of many students. I spent the profits from my own shows on acquiring new work which came back to Park House for everyone's enjoyment. I purchased a very large Hans Hofmann for $900, paid on the installment plan, a wonderful pocket-sized Henry Moore, several works of Matta, Loren McIver, Morris Graves, Naum Gabo, Pavlek Tchelichef, Arthur Dove, and others. The small collection was rich, varied, and looked magnificent in the beautiful high-ceilinged rooms. I made a lamentable mistake with a big Rothko. I knew Mark Rothko, who was hard up at one point, and offered me a tempting piece at a reasonable price. I had the painting sent to Andover and put it up on the wall. I was evaluating the work carefully when a student walked in and said, "Gee, Mrs. Morgan, that looks just like a popsicle." Reacting too quickly and ill-advisedly, I sent the work back. Of course, I still regret doing so, though I couldn't accommodate anything so large now.

After a few years as a teacher and a great deal of success, Pat began to be more and more enamored of himself as a guru. I once heard his favorite student tell him that he was a modern Jesus Christ. Pat accepted the compliment graciously. I was horrified. Of course the temptation of being seduced by student adulation is there for any teacher. This was exaggerated in Pat's case, both because of his deep need for admiration and because of his sexual ambiguity. I reminded him of Kirk Askew's warning when we left New York, "You will not know when the time comes to quit teaching, but Maud will and you must listen to her." The time had come but my words fell on deaf ears. Pat had already lost his compass and no longer cared to associate with people his own age. Only students or graduates were welcome. He needed to be in a teacher-student situation where he could make the

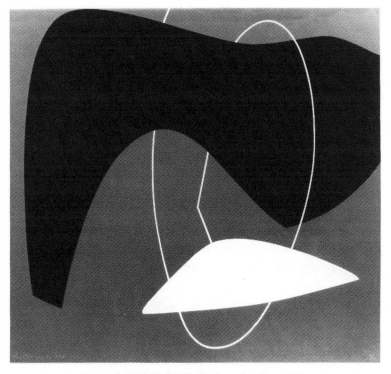

Suspended SS V (1970), Serigraph, 23 ½ x 25 in.

rules or change them at will. His relationships with his students were his first priority.

He was often invited to lecture at prestigious institutions where we would go for week-ends. On these occasions I was very supportive and things always went well. But at other times he resented the fact that I was having more success with my painting than he was and he tried and sometimes succeeded in blocking my work. This area, the only one that kept me afloat in my marriage, was also the one that exacerbated his anger. He always gave me a hard time before my exhibitions. Though I came to know the pattern, I forgot from one show to another the viciousness of his method. For several days ahead of time he would get to me by criticism, argument, a fight on another subject or other means at which he was expert. Then, as I disintegrated, he would say to people, "Pay no attention to Maud, you must excuse her, she always gets nervous before a show." On the day of the opening he would say, "You're really in such bad shape, why don't you stay home and not tire yourself out. I'll tell people you didn't feel well." He never succeeded in keeping me from going to one of my openings, but once in 1955, when he had been chastising me beforehand about my mother who had just died, he came up to me at the end of the show (it had been successful with many sales) and started in on my mother again. I was proud to have gotten through the show well in spite of his harassment beforehand, but this was too much. I broke down in the gallery and had to retire alone in tears before I could join the group for dinner.

My show at the Yale University Art Gallery in April 1951, arranged by one of Pat's pupils, Mark Rudkin, was an aggressive instance of Pat's vindictiveness. Mark was intelligent, observant, sensitive, and more sophisticated than many of the other boys; he was both older and younger. He and I became friends early on and have remained so to this day. After graduating from Andover he engaged in various activities, one of which, as a result of taking a degree in drama and dance at Columbia, was traveling around Europe with Martha Graham and her troupe. Later he came back to Yale for more study in art. He chose my work for his major focus, writing a paper and producing an exhibition. The show consisted of only fifteen paintings, ten of mine and one each of Jackson Pollock, Walter Munch, Richard Pousette-Dart, Calvert Coggeshall, and Marc Rothko. The show was unusual, provocative, and selected with great perception. To be hung in such company was an exciting privilege for me. I cut the ribbon as I walked into the opening through the high arched hallway of the museum. Sandy Calder had driven over from his house in Roxbury for the event, which was to be followed by a dinner given by Mark's mother in Fairfield. After the exhibition closed Sandy asked me to drive with him to the dinner. Pat immediately and strongly negated this idea. I was his wife; I must drive with him. I said flatly that I wanted to go with Sandy. Sandy said he had driven over to see me as well as the show. Pat argued and a wrangle ensued, embarrassing me in front of the guests at my exhibition. For the sake of peace I angrily gave in and drove with Pat. Certainly what I did not realize at the time was that Pat's deep involvement in a homosexual affair was forcing him in an inverse way to make more evident the fact that he was my husband.

The next day, Ted Greene, a popular professor of philosophy and art at Yale, was to deliver a lecture on my work. I couldn't wait to hear what he would say. Pat was determined that he would prevent my attending that lecture. To this day I cannot say how he succeeded. First, by methods at which he was a master, he got me into tears. Nothing new there, but previously I had usually been able to function in spite of him if it was important enough to me. What happened at Yale? I can only presume I was so angry that I have blocked the memory out permanently. Somehow he got me into the car and started to drive back to Andover. As luck would have it, a terrible snow storm fell on top of the already-deep snow on the ground. Well into the highway we were marooned, all cars stopped where they were. We were forced to sit there for three hours not being able to get out of that little car, two furious, bitter people hating each other, each wild with rage – a living nightmare.

One evening at Park House in 1951, Naum Gabo, the Russian constructivist artist, whose ballet "La Chatte" we had seen in Paris, gave me a memorable, hour-long, insightful criticism of a painting I was working on called "Emergence". It had been inspired by the simple comment of Agnes, the wonderful friend my mother passed on to me who had a way of being able to say a simple thing so that it seemed like a totally new idea. She said, "There must be evil in the world in order to have good." For some reason this comment made a tremendous impression and I was impelled to paint it. I stretched a large horizontal canvas. In the extreme upper right hand corner I put two, four-inch squares, touching each other, one black, one white to express the basic theme. They stayed there for a year. The main forms in the painting were few and simple and remained almost unchanged from those I had put down on the first day. A very large oval filled most of the space, with an irregular, large square outlined in black at its center, in the middle of which is a disintegrating yellow square with one solid white and black oblong about 4" by 6" imposed on it. A single, slightly tipped division on the far right breaks up the deep background unobtrusively. Just off center some yellow spikes shoot up from the bottom into the big oval. Gabo liked the painting a lot and thought I must have worked on it for a long time to arrive at these simple forms. I told him that they had been there from the beginning. None of the forms had changed. "Well," he said, "You will make only one change in the future." He indicated the black and white squares in the upper right-hand corner. "You will eliminate those." "Oh, I couldn't. Those are the basis for the whole piece." "Yes," he said, "I know, but you will."

I was having a hard time getting the subtle power I knew was in the painting to emerge, hence the title. I kept struggling with this problem long after Gabo's departure. In all I worked on the painting for almost two years until it finally jelled. Just as Gabo had predicted, at the very last minute I took out the black and white squares at the top. I think it became one of my best paintings. To have a man that I respected so highly totally understand what I was trying to do and help me understand it was a rare and exciting privilege. He thought my work was constructivist, a great compliment from one of the originators of that Russian movement.

Gabo went to a Boston exhibition I was having at the time, writing me a complimentary letter and inviting me to visit him at his studio in Connecticut. The invitation did not include Pat. I was incredulous that an artist as important as Gabo might be interested in my opinions on art, even though clearly he would not have invited me otherwise. I wanted to go but was shy about expressing my ideas. That evening at Park House is the only time I can remember Pat allowing someone to talk seriously or favorably about my work in his presence. He was usually able to switch the conversation to another subject. But Gabo's authoritative presence silenced Pat and I suspect Gabo sensed Pat's negativity and so didn't include him in his conversation or in his invitation. Of course I was flattered, but being ridiculously unsure of myself made it easy for Pat to persuade me to decline the invitation.

Pat, now forty-six, centered his attention on a small elite group of boys, then later on Tommy, an attraction which began when Tommy was in school and continued until he was through college. Pat's aggressive behavior towards me increased as he moved towards overt homosexuality, which depended on family life as a protective cover. The main problem was that Pat wanted this love relationship as well as the family; he wanted it within the family. This led to chaos, compounded by the fact that his lover, Tommy, who was nineteen, also fell in love with me and tried to persuade me to leave Pat and run away with him. The reverberations of jealousy in that house could have made the walls of Jericho fall down.

One of the most distressing aspects of this complicated situation was the lack of privacy. Pat allowed students in all the communal spaces of the house. The only place I could be sure to be away from them was in the bedroom, but that I shared with Pat, from whom I needed distance. One day while walking I observed a very deep ditch at an intersection of Abbot Street, somewhat away from the area of school activity. It had tall grasses growing in it which, along with its unusual depth, made it a perfect hiding place, out of sight of even occasional pedestrians. That ditch gave me the privacy I so desperately needed. In times of great stress I would go there and with relief sink into what seemed like welcoming arms, and lie there and cry.

I wanted the children out of the whole mess but didn't know how to move without exposing Pat and therefore them. As a stop-gap we sent Lex to a five-day boarding school at age twelve, leaving Vicky, age seven, at home alone.

Only now do I realize with horror that for the next seven years Vicky was the only small child in that chaotic entourage of older boys. When her brother left she became her father's acolyte and she had his devoted love. But as she got older his cocktail hour coincided with her homework period and Pat encouraged Vicky to stay around with him and his students rather than do her homework. She was bright, he said, and could easily make it up. My pleas were disregarded, so naturally Vicky did poorly at school, making her feel she was stupid. In Park House family life was at the bottom of the list. To the outside world we appeared to be better parents and partners than in fact we were. In 1955 Vicky was sent away to boarding school at age fourteen.

Under any circumstances it's a rude shock for a woman to discover that her husband is involved with another man, a shattering denial of her feminine being, of her very core. For me it was particularly devastating because my femininity, so late in showing itself, was still insecure and had not grown with Pat. He said the only person who had mattered to him since knowing Whitney was Tommy. As Pat had not been Whitney's lover, or so he claimed and I believed, becoming Tommy's lover, whom he equated with Whitney, may have completed an emotional cycle for him.

I suggested to Pat that he spend a summer with Tommy away from the family to confront his problem and find out where his allegiance lay. He wouldn't hear of it. To think of continuing our life as it had been seemed almost impossible. We were at a dead end.

Just this week, thirty-five years later, as I was walking around Fresh Pond in Cambridge, a different way of looking at this whole situation suddenly came to me: Pat's way. I conjectured how he may have felt and came up with a very different scenario. Pat may well have felt that he did not have a problem to confront other than controlling me. Things may have been exactly as he wanted or even intended them to be. After all, he had his lover under the respectable shelter of the family, at no inconvenience or expense to himself. The only necessity was that I maintain the status quo. All the threads controlling the precarious balance of his life were in my hands. Had I so wished I could have deprived him of his lover, his job, his family, and his reputation. He had to see to it, therefore, that I remained within the traces by whatever means necessary. Such a scenario would shed light on his mounting violence. Certainly none of this entered my head then. I was still far too much under his control, and never dreamt I was the one in power. I knew that Tommy wanted me to marry him and leave Pat, much as Pat had wanted me to marry him and leave Whitney in 1927.

Now in Andover Pat found himself in an untenable position. Having made me an integral, if unwilling, part of his love affair with Tommy, he had placed me once again in a pivotal position, much as I had been in earlier in his relationship with Whitney. This drove him wild, while I remained unaware of what the stakes were.

When I became conscious of his fundamental desire to stop my painting or preferably to reduce it to the level of a hobby, I became deeply angry. I would watch him be his charming self, recognize and hate the effectiveness of it. I would hate him because he forced me into a position of impotence where I felt inferior and apologetic for being myself and pursuing my art, even to the extent of causing me to denigrate my own work and sometimes destroy paintings. Then I became like an animal at bay, vicious, jealous and mean. I saw my self turning into a kind of violent person that I didn't recognize. Sometimes, to release the pressure, I would get into my car, close the windows, drive at an outrageous speed, screaming at the top of my lungs until I was exhausted and even more depressed because I felt I had betrayed my real self and allowed Pat to control me, which enhanced my anger against him and my discouragement with myself. Try as I would, I was not able to hold my own ground and was far too occupied being angry and full of self pity to be effective. For years after I left Pat his disparagements still rang in my ears, and when I feel low, still do. I find in my diary of that time, "Right now I hate him for what he deprived me of and I hate him for making Lex and Vic pay such a heavy price. I hate myself more because I let him do it."

As that remarkable woman Florida Scott Maxwell writes, "Hate may be nature's way of forcing honesty on us," and perhaps that's what happened to me. I had not learned to value myself, and it's hard to stand up for what you don't value. It took me much of the rest of my life and the help of a Jungian analyst to find a sense of self-worth. As Herbert Read wrote, "Happiness can only come to a man who lives along his own grain, who 'drees his own weird.'"

Pat never hit me when he was sober, but he hit hard when he was intoxicated, which he often was. Why is it that women accept this?

When I was hit, I'm glad to say, I instinctively hit back. This was not wise physically, but it kept alive my determination not to be destroyed, especially when, as he was breaking my ear drum, he said, "I'll break your spirit if it kills me." He would have better served both himself and me if he had heeded the words of Lao Tse:

> The spirit of the valley never dies
> This is called the mysterious female
> The gateway of the mysterious female
> Is called the root of heaven and earth
> Yet use will never drain it . . .

My hitting back was a primordial reaction, not a constructive step towards personal autonomy. I was not yet strong enough for that. Even though the physical hurt was great, the psychological hurt was greater, weakening my hope of survival. Sometimes along with the anger there was a strange inverted tenderness in him. Once when he had given me a bad black eye, he came up, stroked it lovingly and said, "It's like a little mouse."

He hit me because of the frustration I had caused him by not fitting into the slot where he needed to keep me, augmented by a grave fear that I might be slipping out of his control. His was more than the anger of one person against another. It was an anger of gender, perhaps a generational anger, his blows expressing the deep hatred and condescension he held for the women in his life. Apology or regret were not in question. To quote Carolyn Heilbrun, "A woman is in total isolation if she has to support male violence alone. It is extremely difficult not only for her to act but for her to even recognize what is happening to her."

I was afraid of Pat, less of the physical pain, which he could and did inflict on me, than by the ruthlessness, viciousness, and heartlessness that I sensed and saw sometimes in his behavior towards me, saw several times in his behavior toward other people, and saw once toward an animal. These powerful, negative qualities could be delivered with grace or in a naked form. As quoted from a student, "Self-justified he could do plenty of damage as well as plenty of good with people on whom he didn't depend for his own self-perpetuation." I had a panicky fear of being confined in the mousetrap into which I had let him put me.

He was revengeful and did not forgive someone who thwarted him. For seventeen years we played out our lives on this level of fierce competitiveness: I fighting for a life for myself, our family, and my work; he fighting to obstruct me; each of us trying to maintain a surface acceptability, a false facade. Henrik Ibsen was once heard to say, "Men and women don't belong in the same century." The only way I knew to combat the wrongs happening in Park House was to take them out on myself. When we left that house, there were deep dents in the plaster wall at the foot of the stairs where I had banged my head against it in frustration. I blamed everything on Pat. Annoyingly and correctly he called me "Maud the Martyr". He felt strongly that I, as his wife, should have his aims as my primary concern, so any pulling away to lay claim to my own interests was regarded as treachery which must be combatted.

Pat and I were both needy, though I believe we often gave an opposite impression, particularly since so many people came to each of us for support. But we each had an aching chasm left empty from childhood that needed filling. Together we made an equation impossible to resolve.

If either of us could have seen our marriage in its proper light, it would have been clear that the differences we had were so fundamental that there was really nothing to fight about or to stay together for. We simply had two totally alternate ways of seeing, functioning, remembering, and feeling. For much of the twenty-seven years I lived with him I did not recognize how basic this generic cleavage was, because we also shared many mutual tastes and pleasures. But on all the deeper issues we fought. Sometimes I became so angry with him that I was delighted if he had a failure.

In a desperate attempt to achieve a little time for us to be a family without the presence of students, I suggested to Pat that we give over every Saturday night to receiving students, keeping the other nights to be with our children. This proved to be a boomerang. The Saturday nights were wildly successful. I made great jugs of delicious drinks and all the living rooms, dining room, and kitchen were in full use. These occasions came to be known as non-alcoholic cocktail parties. In one room a jazz group might be improvising rhythms, in another people might be playing Cole Porter, Benny Goodman or Kurt Weill, in another I might be having a soul talk or 'parent-trouble' talk with an individual boy. Undeniably these evenings were diverting and interesting, fabulous for the students and fun for us. But they made things worse for the family. More students came on week nights asking to be invited the following Saturday. There was no way to keep them out. Park House was a dormitory and the halls were open to all, which Pat encouraged. He was delighted with our popularity.

Amazingly enough, through all of this turbulence Pat and I could, and mostly would, function well together socially, especially in a crowd, the common condition of our house. We worked as a team, avoiding each others presence, but giving the appearance of an ideal couple. This became painful when a graduate would return with a favorite girl, as they often did, asking for our marital blessing since "we were the happiest married couple he knew."

In the bad periods, rather than sleep in the same room with Pat, though we had twin beds, I would sometimes go out late at night and walk for miles. I was occasionally picked up by the police, but they were understanding when they saw I was all right. Sometimes I took the car and my sleeping bag. I found a very high, rocky area in a woods four miles from our house. I would go there, park my car at the base and walk to the top of the steep hill to put down my sleeping bag. One night the police found my car but couldn't find me. They called Pat around 2:00 AM. He simply told them he had a neurotic wife, they should pay no attention to the event, and went back to sleep. Later I wondered if I had decided on suicide that night how he would have explained such behavior. I thought fairly often about suicide at that time at various levels of immediacy. Just lately, thinking about it more objectively, I realized with some surprise that I have known many people who have committed suicide: twenty-one that I can think of immediately. Suicide is always a catastrophe. The loss is so great and the thought of the pain that must have been endured preceding the actual act even greater. Of my friends who took their own lives, only two were old. Four others were couples who made a mutual decision, the rest were all under thirty-five.

I think of how often I considered this route as the only answer to a no-win situation and how deeply grateful I am now for not having taken it. I would have eliminated what has turned out to be one of the best periods of my life. "The acceptance of despair," Spinoza writes, "is in itself faith and on the boundary line of the courage to be." It was this acceptance that tipped my scale.

How could Pat have known in Paris in April 1927 that, by putting a paint brush in my hand to keep me busy while he was finishing his still life, he was creating a life-long problem for himself? As hard as he tried, he was never able to dislodge that paint brush. This fortuitous coincidence that had brought us together during the first few years of our marriage pulled us increasingly apart from then on. Recently one of the students wrote me, "I suspect he hated your being a painter and at the same time relied upon your work as a source and excuse for many things. 'I just want her to be charming', he would often say to me in irritation." Nevertheless, and although unintentional, on that day in Paris Pat gave me the greatest positive force in my life: my work.

It is hard to imagine now, and harder to admit how far I had abdicated from myself in order to do what my husband wanted me to do. To support views with which I disagreed in order to be the good wife: skillful at social disguise, acting out a lie with the intention of deception. Before marriage I had felt differently. Shy but free, with or without a man. When away from my family, I felt I could go anywhere and try anything. I lost that independence almost completely through matrimony.

Because of the superior qualities of a certain group of Andover students during the late 1940s and early 1950s, there arose a remarkable flowering of artistic euphoria and production centered around Park House. Such a period is unusual at anytime, anywhere but almost unheard of in a boy's boarding school. It was a moment when everything seems to come together. The right people in the right place at the right time interact and nourish each other. I had experienced such a moment earlier, in Paris. Now in a more humble but generically related way, a similar ambiance took place in our house in Andover. A group, Frank Stella and Carl André in the arts, Hollis Frampton and Michael Chapman involved with film, William Sloane Coffin concerned with liberal thinking, music and languages, Jack Lemmon intent on theater and acting, and many others, were stoking their creative fires within the receptivity that Pat and I had established in Park House. That they were all brilliant is testified to by the distinction of their subsequent careers. It was an ideal setting!

For the last part of our tenure, I was so involved with my own frustration and anger that I was of little use to anyone particularly myself. Our time in Andover wound down to a diminuendo. It had been full, alternately stormy and jubilant, chaotic and fun. Now it was time to leave. We had faced some things and learned some things, the hard way. We had made a mark for the good, particularly Pat. There were some crescendos to remember, some good friends, and finally the blessing of time that came to unravel our tangles. Tommy returned to California, Vicky went to boarding school, I, now fifty-four, advised by a psychiatrist, left Park House for a rooming house in Boston, grateful to be out at last. Pat's teaching lost its back-drop and he went on sabbatical never to return to live in Andover again.

After a year in Europe Pat came back to live in New York as a single man. He couldn't keep up his old pace alone and was rather lost. He who looked like a teenager when we married retained a youthful appearance well into his fifties, when he aged suddenly and perceptibly. To counteract this, he grew a heavy beard and looked like a handsome old Papa Hemingway. After awhile he abandoned the beard but age was catching up with him, which he saw as an encroachment on his rights. His face became saddened and deeply-lined. Constant smoking and heavy drinking took their toll; earlier he had lost a lung to cancer. It was dreadful to watch him fighting for breath, which he did with an enormous amount of uncomplaining courage. Eventually he alternated his winter months between a flat in Portsmouth, New Hampshire, and Bunny Brooks' beautiful place in Boxboro, Massachusetts. His main involvement was now his Canadian house near Chouette that he had built and loved.

All dressed up no place to go (1946), Oil on canvas, 36 x 21 in.

11. STRANGERS

"The world is filled and filled with
the Absolute – to see this is to be free"
— *Teilhard de Chardin*

From the beginning I felt myself to be a misfit in my family, but comfortable as a stranger in the world. When we dare admit it we know that we are all more alike than we are different, which I find easy to live with. I stand back to observe others but I must learn by experiencing myself since I am my own principal tool. I haven't always been able to keep this tool under control, especially in mid-life, when I lost track of its secret. But it reappeared and I have been reclaiming it as my own ever since, significantly helped by serendipity.

For many years I suffered from what the Germans call "Lebensmüde" (fatigue of life), seeing no path that seemed feasible to take. Now I am more apt to find what Gertrude Stein called "the daily miracle." The older I get the more pleasant I find ordinary life. During the Andover years of estrangement from my husband, I knew loneliness. Winter, summer, spring, or fall I would wander the roads late at night. Often a truck driver would stop, but after one embrace I would run away, frightened and held back by my upbringing. After leaving Pat, when I was living in a rooming house in Boston, I garaged my car seven blocks away and would walk back to my room in the early hours of the morning. A series of lonely men cruise the city at night. I was amazed at how many. Sometimes four or five cars would stop as I walked those seven blocks. Seemingly nice men of varying ages, yearning for the companionship of a stranger. My face clearly showed my age. I was fifty-four. It seemed not to matter. Beyond sex I think there was a search for human contact. I was desperately unhappy myself at that time and felt a kinship with those solitary, cruising males, for, in fact, I was a solitary, though timid, cruising female. There was a place between the garage and my rooming house where I stopped, no matter what the hour, a hole-in-the-wall coffee joint. I always went in there to bolster myself, not with black coffee but with the welcoming remark from the friendly man behind the counter, "And how will you have yours tonight, dear?" Someone had called me "dear" – now I could walk on back to my room. These small things represent salvation at certain times. They have kept me going. Jeremiah, my astrologist, told me I would have made a good prostitute. Who knows? Too late to find out now, but the possibility had crossed my mind.

> In a dark time the eye begins to see
> Everything comes to one
> Which I is I
> I learn by going where I have to go
> We think by feeling
> What is there to know?
>   *– Theodore Roethke*

While I have always felt comfortable with casual strangers, I have for much of my life disregarded the stranger within. I have been unfair to my own strangerhood, at first by following my parents and later my husband's lead, and not taking the risks of acting in accordance with my own nature.

In writing this book past episodes spring vividly to mind. Otherwise these memories would have remained much like the slides that recorded them, still in their original boxes way at the back of the drawer, waiting to be put into some sort of order, a job low on my list of priorities, one usually never done. Now the events come to mind so forcefully I sometimes confuse continents or decades, but not the context or power of the incident recalled.

One is connected to a stranger I never saw. The scene is in my beautiful studio on St. Botolph Street in Boston. I was living alone in that large building and my studio was broken into frequently. The first thief took all the out-of-print art books. That gave an intriguing hint of his tastes. His technique was simple. There would be a phone call late at night, which, on my answering, was immediately cut off. If I was not there to answer, the time was ripe for a break-in. The number of occurrences became alarming. Our family went to Chouette that year for

Christmas. My robber came the day before we left and took all the wrapped-up Christmas presents I was taking to Canada, and, on my return, he came and took all the presents I had received. This was getting too much. The next time he broke down the door and I had to leave, angry that a stranger could force me out of the workplace where I was so happy. After a little bouncing around, I bought a small house in Cambridge, where I still live. I registered under an unlisted telephone. About six months later, just before dinner one night, the phone rang. A man's voice asked, "Is this Maud?" "Yes," I said. "Thank God I've found you, I've been hunting for you ever since you left St. Botolph Street. It's been terrible." Then he went on to tell me that he'd been following me for the two previous years, describing my clothes in great detail. "I liked it best when you wore the red pocketbook with the grey and white suit." I don't think I said much before I hung up. Luckily Vicky and her husband George arrived for supper. They said I should immediately get the operator to trace the call. Something in me said "No." I did nothing. There were quite a few calls after that. Of course I was conscious he was probably following me again, an uncomfortable feeling. Since the man had somehow traced the phone number, he probably had the address. One night he called late. I didn't say anything beyond, "Hello." "You're not talking," he said, "Are you frightened?" "Yes." "Do you wish I wouldn't call again?" "Yes, I do." He didn't call for six months, then he did again and the same thing happened. After two or possibly three years he called one New Year's Eve. "I only wanted to call to wish you Happy New Year." That was the last call I received from him. I never knew if my stranger-caller was my robber or not but I felt sorry for the man.

My second memory of when I saw and came to know a stranger is quite different.

In 1976 I was in Sicily, that beautiful land which, from earliest times, has been invaded by one people after another, all of whose cultures were absorbed by the Sicilians. In today's world Sicily is very much itself, differing even from Italy, its cheek-by-jowl neighbor, and still a wild land.

In 1924, on my first European trip with my parents, Sicilian mosaics were my impressive introduction to great art. I believe that for a total novice as I was, mosaics may well have been easier to encompass than paintings, because a mosaic is tactile, not totally flat. Each small square, roughly 1/4" by 1/4", has, as well as its own color and image, a slightly uneven surface or may be set not quite evenly with its neighboring squares. This gives an organic vitality to the whole surface, each tiny piece an infinitesimal part in a vast apse or cupola, often culminating in a gigantic image of Christ or the Virgin Mary, perhaps twenty feet tall, dominating the panoply. The concept is staggering.

The drive in from the airport to the hotel in Palermo was a long one. I had chosen a businessman's hotel in the center of town because I wanted to be within walking distance of some of the mosaics. It was a nostalgic trip for me, a return visit to a place I had loved and hadn't seen for fifty-three years.

I was elated. My show in Vienna, my first in Europe, had just closed. It had grown out of an unexpected invitation from an unknown dealer who had seen some of my work in a friend's apartment. I responded positively and sent over a sizeable group of oils and serigraphs. It was a risk for each of us but one that turned out to be advantageous for both. The show was very well received. I made many sales as well as friends. I enjoyed showing in Europe where the public is more attuned to art than our public here at home. There is a noticeable difference in the understanding and interest shown in the work as well as in the desire to make personal connections with the artist.

As the taxi trip from the airport progressed, my pleasant anticipatory mood changed. I began to feel very much alone and frightened. Uncharacteristically, I had prepaid my first night at the hotel, through a travel agent in Venice. When I arrived, the voucher was not honored and the hotel's concierge yelled at me loudly and angrily. He spoke neither English or French. I couldn't understand his Italian, which I suppose was Sicilian. One way or another my visit to Palermo started badly. I had wanted to see the Greek temples at a leisurely tempo, not rushed by a bus tour. This, however, was not possible. I discovered that both trains and long distance buses were on strike. Reluctantly I bought a ticket on a Cooke's tour to see the mosaics in the city that afternoon and another to visit the temples scattered over the rest of the island. Palermo is a very hectic city. Downtown the congestion of car, motorcycle and bicycle traffic competes with mobs of people who are often dangerously forced off the overcrowded sidewalks. By the time I got to Thomas Cooke's office, I was relieved to get into the protected private bus and looked forward to renewing my experience of the mosaics.

Early next morning I started to walk to the chapel for a quieter, second look at the mosaics I had seen the previous day. I found myself on an elevated terrace paved in stone that I did not remember. The area was deserted. I couldn't see the chapel I was looking for and felt I must be in the wrong place. As I realized this, I was quite suddenly and forcefully thrown face down onto the paving while my pocketbook was pulled roughly from my shoulder. Stunned, I lay there watching a young man run down an alley, my pocketbook clutched under his arm. I lay there motionless, aware that with the exception of my passport that young man now had everything that was important to me: my glasses, my money, my tickets, my traveler's checks – the works. Slowly I got up.

Then an amazing thing happened. As I stood there, totally alone, on what now seemed like a vast terrace, empty of humanity, I had a moment of ecstasy, a true epiphany. For the first, and so far the only, time in my life I experienced the thrilling reality of belonging completely to humankind. I saw and knew myself as a creature in proper proportion to the eternal, an infinitesimal speck but part of the whole. I was an isolated old woman in a strange country, knowing no one, having lost everything. But something new had happened, something greater than anything I had ever experienced, which completely changed my sense of reality. I was not alone. I was a strand in the fiber of life, a tiny component in the grand plan of the universe of the spheres. I was ecstatic and elated, feeling lighter than air, uplifted, to a different level.

Then I looked down at my hands, saw a lot of blood, and slowly I started to walk. A kind woman came out of her house. "Mama mia, Mama mia!" she cried, and told me to wait. She came back with a bowl

of water and a cloth to wash away the blood. I continued slowly towards
the hotel, anticipating having to cope with the disagreeable concierge.
As I came into the lobby, I heard a voice speaking American English. A
man came up to me, saying he was the owner of the hotel and that he
came there only once a month. He said I should immediately go to the
police station and the hospital, he would take care of the cab.
Registering my accident at the police station was interesting. There
was a line of waiting people, mostly injured, crying women accompanied by caring husbands. Clearly my experience was not uncommon.
Next we went to the hospital. I never could have found it by myself, as
it was on the fifth floor in a business building. In a very large room
tables were arranged into a big open square. Doctors were on the
inside of the square and patients sat around the outside, waiting their
turn. The taxi driver came in with me and led me to a chair. After a
while a doctor sat down opposite me and listened while the taxi driver
told my story. The doctor examined my hands and said the nail on the
left forefinger was split down the middle all the way to the lower cuticle
and would have to be pulled out, otherwise the nail would not heal and
would fester. He could not give me an anesthetic. The taxi driver
repeated this to me and I agreed to go ahead with the procedure, there
was no alternative. When this process was about to begin, the taxi
driver stood directly behind me, put his hands on my two shoulders,
and pushed down with such enormous pressure that I felt a sharp
spasm. This took attention from the extremely painful process of
having my finger nail pulled out, first one half, then the other. The pressure on my shoulders made it possible to tolerate the finger pain. Then
the finger was bandaged up and we left. When I got back to America,
my doctor said that if the two pieces of the nail had not been pulled
out with dexterity, I would have had a deformed finger. Now I have a
perfect new nail which took a year and a half to grow.

Leaving the hospital I suddenly remembered I had no money, but
as I had bought a Thomas Cooke ticket for the Greek temple tour, they
would probably forward me some cash. It was rush hour, fifteen minutes before closing time. I jumped into our waiting cab. The trip was

hair-raising. At one point we drove through two backyards to get to the adjacent street. As we pulled up to Thomas Cooke's, a man was pulling down the steel shutter. My driver spoke to him urgently; he pushed the shutter up again and I rushed inside. I was given some money for dinner and agreed to be there at 6:00 the next morning to start the tour. Then my taxi driver took me back to the hotel. Somehow I got myself to Thomas Cooke's the next morning and boarded the bus, my hands bandaged and my wrist hurting. Once in my seat I passed out. Many hours and one temple later, I started to come to. The bus whirled along a high road as an attractive blonde young woman walked up and down the aisle giving the history of the temples of Sicily in three languages. When I was fully awake I said to her, "You don't look Sicilian." "Oh, no," she said, "I do this on my vacation. I'm a trained nurse from Switzerland." This was just too good to be true. I told her my story. She gave me a pain killer. That night after dinner she took me to the hospital in Syracuse to find out if my wrist was broken. I had first class hospital care all through the rest of the trip.

By the time we got to the famous old volcano of Mount Aetna, placed in the very center of the island, I was feeling fine. Our group went into a hotel for lunch. I sat beside a German book dealer from another tour. We got on splendidly and even had an acquaintance in common, a German book dealer we both knew in New York. My new friend photographed me standing on the nuggets of old lava which surround Mt. Aetna's snow-capped peak and later sent me the prints. I liked the photos because of the contrast between my obvious happiness and having an arm in a sling and bandaged fingers on both hands. These pictures inspired my self portrait, "Mount Aetna after Palermo Mugging," that I painted for my show "An Autobiography" at the Massachusetts College of Art ten years later.

The tour ended the day before I was to fly home. I was in the lobby with my bags, about to leave, when the nice hotel owner came up to me. I thanked him for his considerateness but especially for having found that extraordinary taxi driver at the time of my accident. "I had never seen him before," the owner said. "And I thought I knew every taxi driver in Palermo. I have been trying to locate him ever since or at least to discover where he comes from. I have not been able to find out anything about him." "Well, I must go to the airport now," I said. "Would you call me a taxi?"

As we went out the front door together, an empty taxi drove up. My taxi driver got out, greeted me, put my bags in the trunk and said, "I'm glad you're going back to Boston now." I got in. I didn't have to ask him where he came from, I knew. He came straight from heaven.

FREE AT LAST

Blue Balance (1991), Oil on canvas, 42 x 30 in.

Kernel (1991), Oil on canvas, 42 x 30¼ in.

12. EN ROUTE

Fifteen years prior to my Palermo mugging I drove across the country in my Volkswagen bug, top down from coast to coast with George Benedict, who later became Vicky's husband, though at the time of the trip he knew her only slightly.

I had always wanted to drive across the country and now with Lex at the Army Language School, it seemed the perfect moment to do it. George wanted to go with me. He was a boarding school friend of Alexis and a close neighbor in Andover, a lonely boy who when he discovered that I did a lot of cooking at night would often walk over from his house around midnight and sit in my kitchen talking to me as I worked. It was in those kitchen talks that the plans for the trip shaped up. I felt that he should have the approval of his parents before taking off for several months with an old woman in an open car who was planning to sleep out anywhere except in a campsite or in a motel. They agreed, but warned him that probably one night in a sleeping bag in a rocky field would change my concept of travel. It didn't. As we departed from his parent's house, George's father yelled out with a laugh, "Don't run out of gas in Death Valley!" Fortune seemed to be with us and for the whole two months of our trip we never had to put up the top. We were both elated by our adventure. George did most of the driving. I often cooked in the car. I had a little stove tucked under the hood at my feet on which I learned to make simplified gourmet meals while travelling at seventy-five miles an hour. We amused ourselves by writing a long narrative poem as we went along, congratulating ourselves liberally on our rhythms and humor through mile after mile. It was of course atrocious poetry but an excellent time filler. We agreed that neither of us would refuse to do anything because of personal disinclination. I knew George hated social events but I felt we should be open to anything that came up. We also agreed to make a big effort not to sleep near a main road but to try to seek out more interesting spots. We found some delightful ones: beautiful rolling fields in Illinois where we had two flat tires simultaneously, a mountain forest in Colorado where we slept by a rushing stream and George cut down a little tree in the middle of the night to make a fire to keep me warm, a wondrous canyon in Utah. Late one hot afternoon after Lex had joined us our road headed directly toward the Colorado River. Anticipating a picnic near the freshness of its water, we stopped at a supermarket for supplies. There were few customers at that hour so we fell into conversation with a father, mother and daughter, a nice all-American family finally making the trip they had looked forward to for years. The three men fell to talking about roads. The father said that within ten miles of where the road reached the Colorado River, one branch turned left the other right. He said he was planning to take the left, and asked which way were we going. Lex and George told him that they had decided to go to the right. As we left the supermarket we all said good-bye and wished each other happy travel. It was dark when we reached the river and chose the slab of rock on which we planned to eat supper and sleep. We went into the water, immediately loving its cool temperature but being careful not to get too far out because of the strong current. Then we had our picnic and went to sleep refreshed. At breakfast the next morning the river looked less tempting. It was a deep chocolate brown. We were glad we had enjoyed it before seeing its color.

Sitting on the rock drinking our morning coffee we listened to the horrifying news that was coming over the radio. Our friends of the supermarket had turned left as planned and a bit down the road passed a man standing beside his car with the hood up. They asked if they could help. The stranger said he couldn't figure out what was wrong and asked the man to have a look. As he did so the stranger stepped back and shot him from behind. Next he shot the woman. He tied the girl up and put her in the car while he threw the bodies of her parents into the Colorado River, then came back to rape the girl and drive away with her. The police had been on his trail and caught up with him shortly after these incidents. It was a chilling and sad warning. We persisted in our mode of travel though with considerably less bravura. I wouldn't do it today.

Only once we reneged on our agreement. After a big night of gambling in Las Vegas we gave in and slept in a ditch by the road. One other night when George and I were alone I was dead tired and tried to persuade him just to stop anywhere, but he held out. By then it was way past midnight as it often was when we found a campsite. Finally a little dirt road showed up. He drove in, we threw down our bags exhausted and fell asleep. I was awakened early by the sounds of big machines. I jumped up alarmed. Our little dirt road had, in the dark, led us to a dump site. We hastened to escape the unloading of the big garbage trucks. Not too long afterwards, in Kansas City, we were guests of a former Andover student who included us in a gala dinner of his friends, followed by attendance at the Jewel Ball, a party known as one of the most elegant coming out parties in the United States which it certainly must be. It is held in the Kansas City Art Museum. About fifteen lovely young girls in long white dresses come down the great stairway on the arms of their tail-coated fathers. They are introduced to the matrons of honor and the dancing starts. There was wonderful music on two of the terraces, one traditional, one rock'n'roll. Champagne was served by red-jacketed black waiters at little round candlelit tables in the Romanesque courtyard. To his amazement George, who had claimed he hated dances, was having a fabulous time dressed in a tuxedo which David, our host, had rented for him. Much to his surprise he proved himself to be a great social success. The following night we were back in our sleeping bags in a hay field, relishing the variety of our trip.

Eventually we arrived at Death Valley. We drove around in its awesome beauty as the sun began to set, feeling as one does there, totally removed from any previously known world, when the car made an unpleasant sound. Quickly we looked. Yes, it had happened! The needle pointed to zero. I couldn't believe it and was unable to restrain my uncontrolled laughter, the ultimate joke. George took off his white shirt and stood on the hood of the car, waving it energetically to no one. It really felt like a grim situation. After what seemed like a long time, in the distance we saw something moving in the opposite direction, looking about the size of a ground hog. He waved the shirt even more wildly and to our joy we saw the distant vehicle change direction and head back toward us. As in all normal trucks in Death Valley, there was a can of extra gas in the trunk. We were given enough to get back to the lodge where we gratefully ate supper, taking the comment of George's father a lot more seriously.

Our fabulous trip eventually ended back at Chouette where Pat and Vicky awaited us. Vicky came to know George better and three years later they were married in the beautiful Saarinen chapel at MIT, followed by a wedding reception in the snow on a barge in Boston harbor.

The Couple XXXII (1976), Serigraph, 24 x 18 in.

would do anything to make his woman happy. I found him totally unpredictable. Our affair flowed like a river following its winding course through small or larger waterfalls as it carried us along in its current. Many day-to-day life experiences took on different meanings.

The locale of our affair was my apartment on Commonwealth Avenue, and later my wonderful studio on St. Botolph Street with its 18-foot ceiling and large, high, rounded windows that let in a gorgeous light. Perfect privacy. I painted the studio white. I can see Darcy now sitting on the top step of the ladder I used, looking out at the heavily falling snow and talking to me as I lay naked on the bed below. Most of my friends did not get on with him. He drank too much but in a way it was better so, giving us more time together. We were enclosed in a capsule having little to do with anything beyond ourselves and our lovemaking. Through him I came to know myself, especially my body. I also came to see more clearly where and how I had fitted into or jutted out of the frame into which I had been born. In 1962, after many robberies, I bought a little house in Cambridge which became very much our house. I built a studio in the front where I painted pictures that expressed our lovemaking. Darcy was delighted by these. His love of my body gave a whole new dimension to my painting.

I believe that my last ten years, which have been so productive in terms of work, so expansive in relationships and activities, and so happy have taken place because of the fortuitous good fortune which brought Darcy into my life.

We were both on the wagon when we met, but that didn't last long, because basically we were both heavy drinkers. From a young age I had been taught to drink at home. My mother said it was rude for me not to have a drink with my brother before dinner. I didn't like cocktails and gin for me was associated with menstrual pains, for which it was a good remedy, but regardless, I had a martini every evening before dinner with my brother George when we were both living at home in New York and I was at Barnard. It soon became a habit, and I could drink a lot without getting a hangover. Heavy as my own drinking was, I was shocked at the drinking at some of the faculty parties Pat and I went to in Andover. I would sometimes leave the party and walk in the night to escape. When I started living alone I didn't try to curb my drinking as it gave me the courage to go to a party unaccompanied, which I found hard after twenty-five years of constantly being with Pat.

Then came Darcy, another heavy drinker, with whom I went along. We drank far too much but I presume neither of us were generic alcoholics because later Darcy gave it up completely without much trouble, and I drink very little now. But for a long time drinking was a threatening volcano that had to be held in check. The winters of 1960, '61 and '62, when our romance was at high pitch were snowy ones. If a storm came Darcy would stay in town and we'd have the night together, and often the next day, making love. We'd only get up to go out for something to eat and come right back to my studio. I was the only person living in that big building then, which made it very private, but also very dangerous.

Finally, after years of working at it, Darcy made me believe that someone could adore me, and I could accept his caring. Once he said, "I think the thing I'm proudest of in my life is to have developed a grand passion for you and you had nothing to do with it." I understood exactly what he meant.

Darcy had a glint in his eye and a lilt to his life. He was a whimsical Southerner of Irish descent, a wonderful father and lover. A tender and sentimental man, he was so sure of his masculinity that he was not embarrassed to cry, which he often did. Being with him was like night and day for me compared to the men I had previously known, most of whom were full of complexes and sexual insecurities. We were very good friends too, but my main feeling when I was with him was that of being a woman. I exalted in the new sensation.

One spring we took a trip south. Darcy wanted to show me his country. He knew a great deal about American history, which was a total blank in my education. Somehow, though I had completed college, I never had a course in American history anywhere along the line. I absorbed with interest everything he told me. We went to Monticello, a thrill for me. Like most people I marvelled at Jefferson's ingenuity and beautiful sense of landscaping. For Darcy the trip was sentimental and nostalgic. He had adored his childhood in West Virginia and especially his grandfather. He left home as a young man and had been emotionally unable to go back, fearful of losing his dream. But now here we were at the turnoff from the main road in a rambling, undistinguished, little town. Miraculously there was still the dirt road he remembered, meandering through the small hills of that beautiful country. He told me of his youthful experiences; stories floated back clearly. Around the next curve would be – or used to be – the grandfather's house. There it was, a handsome, two-storied structured with double balconies, set back from the road in a field with a little stream running behind it. He couldn't believe it. Some member of the family had put on a new roof, so it had been protected from the weather and looked fine from the outside. Inside the place was a ransacked shambles. Darcy wandered around looking at old books on the floor, some of which he remembered. Then he stopped short. Lying at his feet was his grandfather's old change purse, from which he remembered receiving his weekly childhood allowance more than fifty years earlier; what a treasure! Later we went walking up the valley passing between wooded hillocks. He remembered the young trees that had grown bigger by now and the big trees that hadn't changed that much. This wonderful walk gave him back his childhood. He hadn't dared to return before, though the place was constantly in his thoughts. He could only go with me, someone from another world, but someone he loved enough with whom to take the risk.

Many happy years followed that trip during which we met often, customarily at my house where both my children came to know and like him. A compulsion to focus on my work finally caused me to break off with him. I knew it was something I had to do alone. In the beginning when I was expressing the feelings which came from our lovemaking Darcy reveled in my art. But after that, when I turned more towards abstract work, he wasn't so involved. His diminished interest in my painting was a loss. Still he was averse to ending our relationship, saying neither of us would ever have anyone else. I thought differently but he was right. Later after I'd gotten through the particular hump I needed to surmount in my work, I thought and hoped that he and I could have an old-age romance. It would have been pleasant and fun for both of us. Unfortunately he had a series of small strokes which terminated all such thoughts. I visited him after these but finally there came a stroke severe enough for him to say that he didn't want me to see him as he then was.

For several years I was completely out of touch. I knew that his son, Puck, who is a scientist living in California, habitually came East with his family for summer vacation to the lovely old house Darcy had moved into at Woods Hole. One July 4th I called him, knowing in my heart that Darcy had died, which indeed he had just a few months earlier, as had his wife. Puck was extremely gracious, inviting me to come down saying, "There are five grandchildren here waiting to meet you." I went and was warmly welcomed into this big family where the children range in ages from thirty-two to two, all very much of a clan, the older girls enjoying comradeship with their father. The experience was uniquely rich with Darcy's presence strongly felt. I was happy to see some of my work in the house, things I had given him, which had hung there and been loved by the family for many years, especially a painting of the church at La Malbaie. They all knew a great deal about me. I was touched and pleased that Darcy had included them to that extent in our romance. To be with this lively family, who I felt were being honest and open with each other and with me, was heartwarming. The whole day was like rounding out a final, wonderful gift from Darcy, of what he would have felt to be natural for his family to feel about me and me about them. To have things come full circle so beautifully is rare. How nice to be old enough to have it happen. I'll always think of Darcy with great warmth, gratitude, humor, and love.

I have long been interested in off-beat relationships, a joining of two people of disparate interests, religions, colors, nationalities, social status, or ages. Nothing is taken for granted. Both people start from scratch with bedrock material. I wish I had been more successful with this in my own life. I enjoyed the film "Harold and Maud", about that nice nutty old woman and the young boy. I used to drive my car just the way that Maud did. I've become a more reasonable driver now but fortunately, there are other legitimate areas in which to exaggerate. One such opportunity presented itself to me in a sauna.

Two people are attracted to each other: he, European, twenty-five, she, American, seventy-five. The temperature was delicious, as was the lovemaking it engendered. Later, as I was lying naked on the bed, enjoying the interval of peace of that particularly pleasant after moment, he, standing beside the bed, looked down at me carefully and lovingly and said, "You are so young." I was happy. It seemed like a minor miracle that the fifty years between our ages had been eliminated so beautifully for a time.

In Peking in 1930 I remember a handsome, extremely attentive admiral my father's age. There was the same age gap in reverse. His chief anxiety was that I would consider his feeling for me to be ridiculous. I'm glad to say I never did.

The old age romance of my teacher, Hans Hofmann, also interested me. After his wife's death – he must have been eighty or more – Hofmann fell in love with and married a young woman, Renata. The explosion of the paintings that resulted from this union, "The Renata Series," declare the joyous crescendo of renewed masculinity. Erotic ecstasy springs out of these canvases in a glorious freedom reminiscent of the satyrs of Greek vases. The emanation seems more forceful for being that of an old man. I was lucky to see the entire series of these works when exhibited at the Metropolitan Museum and vividly experienced their sexual vitality and excitement.

When lovely Venus lies beside her Lord and Master Mars,
they mutually profit from their scars . . .
            — *music by Kurt Weill, words by Bertolt Brecht*

14. WORK IS HOME

"Art is the axe that breaks the frozen sea within us."
— *Kafka*

Recently I dreamt that I was in my mid-twenties, standing before my parents who sat in two Imperial-looking armchairs. I spoke to them as I never had in real life.

"You make me feel that I don't belong in this family. You never wanted me in it anyway, especially as a girl. Why didn't you put me up for adoption? I'm a decent human being, somebody would have been glad to have me."

I was surprised by the uncharacteristic tone of anger and came to realize that the dream was closely related to writing this book. Maud was an autonomous person, although only in the dream. In actuality I had docilely followed the path laid out for me by my parents, a habit I continued into my marriage.

In the dream I told my parents I had never had a home, that I had never been at home in their house. Since then I've had four homes, all places of work. Of the many studios I've had, two were pivotal: the one in Park House, from 1947 to 1957, and the one I recently lost at 69 Harvey Street in North Cambridge, from 1967 to 1986. Each was a true home, embracing, intimate, and my own. The Cambridge studio, even more than the one in Andover, was a place I centered out from and went back into as though physically reentering my body, eventually finding there long repressed feelings: hopelessness, resolve, excitement, elation, amazement and delight and, not infrequently, dancing for joy. These feelings no longer submerged were transferred to canvas from the safety of a secure base. There was a solid feeling to that space. My studio was on the third floor of a large old Catholic school building, Notre Dame de la Pitié, built in 1900. High-ceilinged, with six windows and ample hallways built to accommodate crowds of children. The entire building lived up to its name and protected me.

Another home space was Yaddo, the artists' colony in Saratoga Springs where I spent parts of seven summers from 1954 to 1976. My first visit had been quite unexpected. An invitation came out of the blue to spend two months there. I had never heard of Yaddo, nor any other artist's colony, nor did I know how one functioned. In the previous twenty-odd years of marriage, I had taken only one vacation strictly on my own, a week in Provincetown at Hans Hofmann's school. To think of extending such an experience to two months stretched my imagination too far beyond its limits, so I accepted for half the time. When the moment came I was terrified by the thought of all the brilliant people who would be there. Would I be able to pull my own weight? I decided to arrive late at night, hoping to slip in unnoticed. As I drew near Saratoga Springs, I stopped at a bar, bolstered myself with a strong cocktail, and proceeded. I reached my destination around midnight and was met by Clifford, a pleasant young man, who had waited up for me. He showed me my room in West House and asked me if I'd like to see my studio that night. Yes, I would. We walked down a meandering road through gorgeous tall pine trees to a group of three studios in a long, low, stone-based building. Clifford flashed the light on showing a high-ceilinged room with a row of top windows on one side opposing a row of low windows on the other. There were large tables, stools of various heights, and a sink in the corner. I couldn't speak. He handed me the key, said breakfast was from eight to nine, and bid me good night. Holding the key tightly in my hand, I sat down in order to feel the reality, as well as the overpowering unreality, of the situation. This space would be my very own for a month!

The adjustment to this unique place and interesting people proved far simpler than expected and far more pleasurable. The problem lay elsewhere. For many years I had been leading a highly stressful, demanding life. Could I now handle the luxury of having all day, and all night if I wished, to do my own work, uninterrupted, with no responsibilities? It was a dream come true, but could I handle the dream? On the first day I outlined the key to the studio in ink on a small piece of paper. I wanted to hang onto the significance of that key. For days, even weeks, nothing I painted got beyond the level of the work of a beginning student; I had difficulty even dragging that much out of myself.

What was occurring was not happening on paper but within me. I was beginning to accept myself as an independent person and to take myself seriously as an artist. That month was a gift beyond price.

My six subsequent trips to Yaddo through 1976 were each different, all rich in experience. Besides learning how to paint super large canvasses, I made life-long friends and had my first extra-marital affair, with a lover twenty-five years my junior. One later summer when I was involved with Darcy, he came to spend a week-end. He reached Yaddo and somehow located my studio in that huge place. I came in to find him talking to a writer I was friendly with, who immediately recognized Darcy's position in my life. Although Darcy was only six years younger than I, having him there as my visiting lover gave me a sense of our being part of the younger generation of lovers around us, of belonging where I had never belonged before. Yaddo was inevitably the background for deep kinships and loves. They used to say that the first bell in the morning is for people to get back to their own rooms, the second is for breakfast. I never understood how I had been lucky enough to be invited until many years later, when I learned one of the trustees had seen a show of mine in New York, liked it and acted on that impulse to invite me to be a guest.

I recall the excitement (and fear) of painting my first so called "oversized" canvas, "Gold Coast I". The stark reality of being faced by a vast empty canvas is so intimidating that you find yourself stopped short, wondering "Why am I doing this? Where should I start? Top? Bottom? Middle? Perhaps it would be best to leave the nice new canvas as it is, clean and white. One stroke of the brush and its purity is gone forever. Eventually the battle with oneself lets up enough to take some timid action. I penciled in grid lines which would at least divide the space and help me find my bearings. After completing a few of these gigantic pictures I found that I no longer needed a grid but could start an oversized painting with no more nor less trepidation than a smaller one.

Yaddo generates its own creative energy. The very power of so many artists, writers, and musicians in one place, each working hard at their art was cumulative. There is an unspoken feeling that each person is doing something important. One sensed it indoors and out.

Unquestionably this mingling of divergent talents was one of the main assets of Yaddo. In the evenings we might listen to the composition of one of the musicians or the poems of a writer, or see an exhibition of a fellow painter. The experience of being there brought the arts together in a setting where one's eyes, ears, and heart were particularly receptive. Behind and beneath it all was the spirit of Polly Hansen, an excellent poet, who, in her daytime hours, filled the role of protectress of our powerful, sensitive, and often demanding egos. She was a jewel and made Yaddo home for me, my third home.

Even before Yaddo music was an important influence on my art. In 1949 John Cage's phonograph record "Sonatas and Interludes for Prepared Piano" accidently fell into my hands. In one way or another he has been in my life ever since. I played this record over and over again, to listen and savor certain notes held in isolated vibration and sustained individually for protracted periods, giving time to hear the sound of the note and the sound of the silence that follows and letting both sink into one's being. This quality was an exciting new input into my painting. The thrust of this early impression of the power of the single sound or the single spot of color related to my love of Oriental art and has never left me. I had to wait forty-three years to meet the man behind the thrust. John lived his life and composed many of his works according to the *I Ching, The Chinese Book of Changes* whose origins go back to mythical antiquity, whose words are the roots of Confucianism and have influenced Oriental thinking for the last three thousand years. He gloried in the unexpected: whatever came his way was what should have come his way, whatever didn't, shouldn't have. I loved John and deeply admired the measured benevolence with which he accepted life.

In 1990 John Cage gave the Charles Eliot Norton lectures at Harvard in Memorial Hall. I attended several. He chose words at random from books or newspapers as directed by a computerized program derived from the *I Ching*. Rational sense is irrelevant. I was attentive throughout the first lecture which lasted about two hours, thinking that I would learn something. I came away mesmerized by his voice but feeling I had learned nothing, and also extremely fatigued from the concentration. However, every time I met John in person, which happened on and off during this period, I felt turned on, exhilarated, and captivated by him and his cheerful approach to life. I met him at Rugg Road Paper Mill where he was experimenting in making edible paper. The proportions for the ingredients, all elements of his macrobiotic diet, had been chosen by the *I Ching* and pressed into paper. They were beautiful, earthy colors, variegated dark greens and browns, but frail; several fell apart, a fault which was later corrected. We didn't try eating them. Still the idea is good; perhaps some ingenious person can make it a reality. Why shouldn't there be edible junk mail? It would minimize trash and perhaps taste as good as some of today's cereals. A cook book I liked, in describing a certain cereal, recommended, "Open the package, empty the contents, and eat the container."

Another night I went to John's lecture, not to learn this time but to listen, to listen detachedly to his sonorous, poetic voice. This changed my focus from words as intelligence to words as sound with only an occasional recognizable meaning intruding before lapsing back into a liturgy of pure tone. I sat spellbound for an hour and a half, came back briefly to factuality, then lapsed again into the meditative world John was creating. The lecture ended after two hours, leaving me full of emotional richness, rested and in excellent spirits.

The prolonged applause let me know that many other people had sat there attentively for two hours also listening to "what they didn't understand", to use John's phrase, and probably experiencing much of what I had, an exciting, quiet, optimistic involvement. John's simplicity and proverbial happiness were a drink of pure water from a mountain spring, a rarity in today's world. At seventy-six he was in his full prime, combining youth and age, wisdom and wit along with his unusual abilities for music, writing, speaking, and making art. I became part of all that, smiling to myself, happy to be friendly with him and grateful to have the privilege to live in this marvellous Cambridge where such events are a five minute walk from home.

In talking to Phillip Guston about painting, John Cage said, "When you start working everybody is in your studio – the past, your friends, enemies, the art world and above all, your own ideas – all are there. But as you continue painting, they start leaving, one by one and you are left completely alone. Then if you're lucky, even you leave."

Later I visited John in the New York apartment he shared with Merce Cunningham, a black cat, two hundred plants, and at least two hundred rocks. I felt a peaceful participation in the communal joy of wonderment having supper there with John and Merce. I was totally at home with them, happy beyond selfhood. I felt I belonged. "Oh, Lord, reveal to us thy Peace that surpasses all our understanding."

∾

When I first started painting in 1927 my work was representational, although extremely personal. I set myself a level of proficiency that I wanted to reach. An early small picture, "Green Landscape", represents a cow in the distance, grazing in a field of grass and trees. When I had finished, I was surprised to see that the evergreens were easily distinguishable one from another; a spruce from a larch, a larch from a cedar, a cedar from a pine, etc. I saw that I had reached the representational standard I had aimed for and needed to move on to abstraction, toward capturing interior states of being and feeling with as much veracity as I had the natural scene in "Green Landscape". I chose a subject no less ambitious than the creation of man, titled "In the Beginning". I placed twenty-five small human figures in a cosmic type landscape. Slowly and hesitatingly these were eliminated and replaced by areas of color, letting the forms follow their own devices. Finally all the figures had disappeared except one small, central one. The spatial quality of the painting had become enlarged, which encouraged me to remove the last figure, changing it into a vertical line on which the entire picture now depended emotionally and structurally. Without representational elements the meaning of the painting also changed. Instead of symbolizing the beginning of man, the work came to represent creation itself as the critical event. Made in 1941, this picture was my initiation into abstraction. I struggled the whole summer to come through that passage. Although I have made many

Ides of March (1990), Oil on canvas, 42 x 29 ⅞ in.

representational paintings since "In the Beginning," my work has been largely abstract.

Now for the most part I do not attempt to portray recognizable landscapes or material objects but rather to create shapes and colors that represent my interior images of emotions, movements (physical and psychic), ambitions, fantasies, or celestial yearnings. As Dorothy Adlow wrote in the *Christian Science Monitor* in 1950, "Mrs. Morgan...does not seem concerned with imagery which is familiar or with symbols of common currency. She originates forms and creates moods in patterns of her own invention. She tries to convey ideas of universal character. She also tries to distill a subtle pattern of emotional states. The pictures must be pondered and explored." I have always painted from the inside out even when working on a straight landscape, I become a hollow reed, a vehicle through which something passes.

While some viewers find it difficult to enter the emotional world of the abstract artist, others find that these paintings evoke powerful responses. One of them, "Descension," was painted in 1949 when I was in a depressed mood, expressing strong, downward feelings albeit in a flamboyant way. If I was going to go down, I was going to go down with pizzazz. At the top of the canvas are two white forms that look like disintegrating airplane wings from which bits and pieces fall, catching fire as they descend to the base of the painting and on out the bottom. The strong cerulean blue background at the top moves down, mingling with the orange flames below: all highly dramatic. When I'd finished the painting I brought it downstairs from my Park House studio to look at in a living room setting, something I always like to do. As usual boys were present. One whom I didn't know came up and, without preamble, asked if he could borrow the painting. Although surprised, I realized that his question was urgent. "Yes," I said, "but bring it back before Commencement." When he did he explained his request. He had suffered from acute agoraphobia all his life. On seeing the painting in the living room, he experienced the all-too-familiar sensations of terror. He took the painting back to his dormitory and placed it at the foot of his bed. For three weeks it was the first thing he saw on waking and the last thing before going to sleep. Slowly the terror began to diminish until, by Commencement time, he had cured himself of the problem that had plagued his childhood. I was happy to hear of this healing experience through art and admired that boy's approach to life.

Each concept of an art work demands its own manner of presentation which must be devised by the artist through known or invented means. With me, the original concept usually comes directly from personal emotions or experience and its power springs from the strength of the ability to put myself inside those emotions, in a sense becoming an aspect of them personally and universally. Often in this process what seems random or a mistake may, in fact, be a necessity, although not recognized as such until the work is finished. It's the power of the originating idea which dictates the ultimate conclusion.

As Nancy Raine wrote of my work at the time of the 1986 exhibition, "Maud Morgan, an Autobiography 1928-1986" at Massachusetts College of Art, "Medium, image and technique are secondary to emotional representation. ... However it is portrayed or symbolized, the real subject is always her own feelings or state of mind... this non-intellectual approach, which was fundamental to the development of abstract expressionism... has been the key to the growth of her work in intimate synchronization with her life." Painting in some ways is like athletics, you have to push yourself, but at the same time, if you push yourself, you can't make it. You must stay loose.

At my Cambridge studio during 1973 and '74, I embarked on a series of large, romantic paintings of the seasons that now hang in Boston City Hall. I was excited when I painted "Spring Love" (6 1/2' x 10'). As I was working, my daughter Vicky came in and was delighted with it. "All those happy little sperms," she commented. "But it's not finished. It needs to be longer." I followed her advice, doubling its length and then adding another ten-foot panel. Now thirty feet long, "Spring Love" was my largest canvas to date. The painting demanded its own format.

There was no preconceived idea for this series beyond my wish to have a wide, irregular, angular, hard-edged, yellow stripe move through the lower section of the entire sequence, in contrast to, but coordinated with, the highly fluid, loose painting of the main body of each canvas. This apparent contradiction gave structure to a romantic conception. In "Summer Solstice" I interrupted this stripe halfway; I didn't want to hinder the feeling of midsummer foliage with its falling petals seen against a timeless sky. I didn't want the rigidity of the stripe, but it reappears again briefly in the winds of "Autumn Equinox", and then fully across the entire base of "Winter Narrative," becoming progressively wider and stronger as it moves towards spring. By the time I painted "Winter Narrative", I was completely at home with the scale. Like "Spring Love", it was composed of three sections framed together, each 6' x 10'. I completed the last two sections of "Winter Narrative" first and was left with the first section to do last. At that point to undertake ten more feet of canvas did not loom as a difficulty. I knew what I wanted to say and how I wanted to work through the impression of a snow storm towards spots of yellow sunshine where a large, yellow, flying bird-form announces spring. Finally three, very bold, irregular and jagged verticals of blue, pink and white cut the canvas from top to bottom, declaring that winter is over. Then the basic yellow stripe leads into spring, starting the rotation of a new cycle of life and hope. At that point the yellow stripe changes to blue and, above it, a vigorous pink, irregular, serpent-like form, the thrust of spring, moves through twenty-five feet of canvas, growing stronger as it progresses towards "Summer". The seasons are by far the most romantic of all my works.

∿

Though Cambridge was my center, I also had a wonderful home base in New York. From 1948 to 1970, Agnes was the main influence in my life. Originally my mother's friend, then mine and, at exactly the midpoint of age between us, she was my mother's greatest gift to me. A magnificent matriarch and at the same time an extremely private person, Agnes was sensitive, shy and strong. Rather a large woman, graceful and flowing in her movements, her clothes always seemed to have accessories, a scarf, a little fur cape or some detachable element that often slipped to the ground or got mislaid, giving the appearance of casualness. She was the least casual person I have known in my life. Nothing escaped her discerning and discriminating eye. Her generosity and love were so great that a word needs to be invented to describe them adequately. Her whole life was feeling, her awareness a full circle. During much of the time I knew her, I was having difficulty with Pat. I once wrote her, "I'm lost, I can't get to the core." Her answer, "But you are the core and it's hard to get to where you already are." Less than a year after Mootzie's death in 1955, Agnes took me on a long trip. She had always wanted to see the Taj Mahal. We spent extended periods of time in India, Lebanon, Greece and Italy. Her sister and her daughter had both married Italians so when we visited them, relatives of all ages were always around. To live intimately in an Italian family, to experience it from the inside, was a rare treat for me. Throughout our twenty-five years of friendship, Agnes was also my patron, one of the most discerning I have ever had, choosing quickly and with discrimination, helping me to be objective in judging my own work.

The long trip with her, away from Pat, gave me an unexpected and much needed interval. The sights we were seeing daily in the different countries we visited were so engrossing that our time and thoughts were focused on immediate experiences. I did not think of Pat nor of the troubled life I had left behind in Andover. Passing through Paris on the way home from Italy, I saw my brother Quin, who lived there. He said, "You look ten years younger and twenty years happier; try to stay that way." Only when I finally got back to Andover did I realize how much I had changed, feeling myself to be more my own person and less subservient to my husband. The time away had strengthened me.

Indeed this period of travel sowed the seeds for my gaining enough confidence to separate from Pat the following year after our sabbatical.

It was in Andover, however, in 1956, on my return from the trip with Agnes that my self-portraits appeared which unequivocally exposed my unhappiness. The first two of them were pivotal works for me, "Woman in Grey" and "Mood".

"Woman in Grey" (48" x 36") was a three-quarters length view of a woman sitting very upright, dressed in a simple, severe, short sleeved, grey work dress. In her lap she holds a gigantic uterus, the infant form visible within it, the umbilical cord showing. The enlarged uterus is about the length of the distance between her elbow and her hand. This form came out without my realizing what I was painting. The woman's curly white hair tops a delicate, pale, sad, elongated face.

Her head is frail and wistful, her body strong and capable. As I look at the photograph of this painting I see how powerful and successful it was and am filled with shame and sorrow at having destroyed it, an act I can best explain in retrospect by the fact that I was probably frightened when I saw what I had produced, and by the despair I felt on my return to Pat after the carefree trip with Agnes. I wasn't able to see then, or more probably, wasn't able to accept what this painting was telling me about my continuing sorrow of having been prevented from having the third child I had longed for, a sadness I had originally expressed in "Wishing Well" in 1946. But at least I had had the courage to paint the internal foetus as an external symbol to show my grief.

The second grey painting was "Mood" (31" x 26"), where the foetus is eliminated but the sadness is retained. A friend said of this painting, "It is a great picture. It is young and old, very old even, but it changes from one to the other and back." The head occupies most of the canvas, the neck and shoulders merging into shadow at the bottom of the painting. The intense and despondent face has a reserved feminine beauty. Audrey Bensley fell in love with the second grey painting and for many years "Mood" hung over the family mantelpiece and was very much a center of their lives. One evening when the parents went out for dinner they left the house in charge of the children, who were entertaining a group of friends. Of course one doesn't know how the kids spent the evening, but I suspect there was some experimentation with drugs going on. In any event, when Audrey came down to breakfast the next morning, she found her favorite painting desecrated by holes, many holes. Poor Audrey. When I happened to drop in later in the day, she was still distraught. We discovered that the fire poker had been the weapon. It was an exact fit. I could understand that as the young people sat around the fire, a little high, the presence of the powerful, sad and penetrating image of the woman above the mantelpiece had been just too much. They had punched holes in the background, in the hair and in the neck. I felt strangely pleased that the face itself had been sufficiently arresting to ward off direct attacks, as though its spiritual quality had gained the upper hand. I took the painting off the wall at once, put it into my car and drove to the restorer who did a superlative job. Now the wounds don't show and "Mood" hides her secret story. Audrey and her husband Diz have been wonderful patrons of mine for a very long time. It adds an enriching element to our friendship.

A torrent of self-portraits of many sizes and emotions continued to pour out all through the following summer at Yaddo and into the next winter, part of which I spent in a Boston rooming house, having by then left Park House. In my one rented room in Boston, moving my easel every few hours from one window to the other to get more light, I painted six self-portraits in four months. These paintings were anathema to my husband, but to many people they are the quintessential aspect of my work. They certainly create strong feelings. On viewing a portrait of himself, Saint John the Evangelist wrote, "The portrait is like me yet not like me, but like my fleshly image, for if the painter desireth to draw the very me in a portrait, he will need more than colors and things that are seen with the eyes." My aim was to paint the "very me."

Pat disliked all my self-portraits because they made my unhappiness evident, but also because he thought my drawing was atrocious. Our last conversation before his death in 1980 was on this subject. Again he begged me never to do another self-portrait, or, if I had to, never to show one. He complained vigorously about their unacceptable draughtsmanship. He said Audrey told him that she liked them, and he had been very, very glad for me that somebody did. As he belabored his point, I suddenly saw with startling clarity the whole plan of his well-worn game. Since it was almost impossible for him to get inside my painting; I was too idiosyncratic there and too secure he focused on my drawing which he knew to be my weakest area. That night, in our final conversation, the scales fell from my eyes and his criticism rolled off my back like that of the proverbial greased duck. I was amazed as I detachedly observed the intricacies of his strategy, to which I was no longer susceptible.

Once in 1957 I exhibited some of the self portraits at Betty Parson's Gallery in New York. Betty strongly disliked them too, which may have been a factor in the twenty-year gap from 1957 to 1977 during which she did not exhibit my work, a fact that was hard to take since after my first show with her, she had written, "I hope that I can go on being a satisfactory dealer as you are one of my most talented and intelligent painters."

In 1978 I said to Nancy Raine, who produced the film about my work, "Someday I would love to have a show of 100 self-portraits and maybe I will have it in 1986." Amazingly enough this wish was partially fulfilled in my Massachusetts College of Art show held that very year. I didn't have one hundred but I did show twenty-eight, which is a lot of self-portraits.

After the first inundation of these portraits in 1957, there was a long break into other kinds of work until I surprised myself by painting a large pencil and gouache head in 1963, "Woman in Tibetan Necklace" (36" x 44"), which intended to portray the vigor of age. It is a powerful work showing age, but not despair. After that there were no more portraits until 1978 when they appeared again in conjunction with the filming of my documentary, first shown in 1980.

I think these self-portraits were too personal and too revealing for Betty's taste, but I showed them successfully at the Margaret Brown gallery in Boston and in Cambridge, where I became involved in a small cooperative gallery under the direction of Patsy Hoffman, above Josefina Yanguas' coffee house, the Pamplona. Our aim was to offer good, inexpensive paintings for sale in Cambridge. The situation suited my needs to perfection. I was somewhat estranged from my work after all the confusion of separating from Pat and establishing myself in a studio on St. Botolph Street in Boston, only to have to move after a year due to break-ins and robberies. Now I was eager for a fresh start.

Through the Hoffman-Yanguas Gallery I began selling paintings like hotcakes. Paintings on paper sold for fifty dollars each unframed. The turnover was so quick that Patsy started recording the time between my bringing a painting into the gallery and its going out under the buyer's arm. The shortest was fifteen minutes. This support was exactly what I needed. Through these small pictures I was

Woman in Tibetan Necklace (1963), Gouache, pencil and
charcoal on board, 44 x 36 in.

building back confidence that had been badly burned during the
period of my life with Pat. I was off and running, starting to rebuild
myself as a single woman, it felt wonderful. I began to paint my yearnings and aspirations in cosmic terms. I did a lot of work, exhibiting

wherever I could, in movie theaters or openings of model houses built by architect friends. In both these settings many paintings were stolen, but I knew it was essential to keep working and showing.

A beautiful and supportive person came into my life at that time, Isabel Whiting. She was a cultivated, sensitive, charming older woman who seemed to understand exactly what I was trying to do in my work. Her appreciation was way beyond any I could have hoped for. I was shy about accepting it but kept every word she wrote to me.

"I find myself standing before your created forms in light in masterful mobility and color as belonging to a cosmic confrontation. You seem to have visioned our point in this universe in a cosmic experience, giving us a viable sense of our whirling world, of the depth of sun, sea and earth and the mysterious moon in its shimmer and withdrawal and ourselves involved."

Since my aim was and has always been that stated by Pythagoras, "To make a construction of the seen order capable of providing for the needs of the unseen," these comments by Isabel Whiting were total affirmation.

There was also a man whose opinion meant a lot to me, a learned, artistically-sensitive man, Mr. Bornstein, who had a high quality art bookstore. He wrote, "Every one of your paintings is a quintessence of an idea marvelously conceived and beautifully executed and fulfilled. I look forward every year to seeing your work and every year you bring forward remarkable if not startling results." Again I kept his letters, although I didn't reread them until 1977 at the time of my fifty year retrospective at the Addison Gallery in Andover. Like Isabel Whiting's, these letters sustained me at some very interior depth since I wasn't able to accept them at a surface level, my self-esteem still being far too low.

Of course there were other opinions too. A Boston review said, "Highly individualistic. If she has any message it is for the few, unless elusive combinations of forms and colors are enough for all."

Around 1969 I started making brightly colored, hard-edged serigraphs of simple abstract shapes, which I continued through 1974. They were fun to do and were enthusiastically received. Except for two small etchings, I had never worked with multiple prints before. I made the serigraphs by cutting up Color-Aid papers into the shapes I thought I wanted, pinning them to the wall, taking them down, altering the shapes and pinning them back up until I was satisfied with the design. Then I'd have it printed and throw the mock-up away. One day a client came to my studio and wanted to buy one. I told her I was about to have that edition printed. "Not the print," she said. "I want the mock-up."

This is what gave me the idea of collages, which became another refreshing break-through for me. I had loved the clean beauty and precision of the hard-edged shapes of the serigraphs and kept thinking of Hans Hofmann as I made them. I could hear his triumphant voice when he would make one of his dramatic dynamic lines, saying, "It's a matter of a millimeter." I made an enormous number of these silk screens before abandoning them for collages where, instead of the precise hard-edges cut with scissors, I now used Japanese mulberry paper which I wet and pulled apart, giving shaggy edges, often placing one layer over another, almost the opposite of the serigraphs. I felt a free and sensuous response to this material, very female. I experienced an 'at homeness' I had known earlier in Paris when I first put brush to canvas.

The collages started in 1974 and I am still making them. Now I'm up to number three hundred and thirty-six in sizes varying from six inches to eight feet. People liked this new work and Betty Parsons did too. She gave me a show in her small gallery in 1977, the first in twenty years. Also in that same year I was given a large, comprehensive show at the Addison Gallery of American Art at Andover, superbly hung by Chris Cook, its able director. My work occupied almost the whole museum, enabling me to include all the types I'd done so far, ranging from the huge "Seasons" to the little 6" x 9" etchings with many different sized oils and prints in between. In the catalogue Lucy Lippard wrote, "Too much is made of the fact that she is in her seventies and 'still' working with such vitality." (Now that I am in my nineties, this period seems like ancient history.) "Women tend to be livelier than men in old age and we almost always get our chance later."

About the collages, Lucy Lippard wrote, "They convey the same elegance and 'joie de vivre' as their author. These collages could only have been done by a woman. The collage papers are roughly woven, ragged-edged with a life of their own that demands formal order but at the same time transcends it. Their whimsicality incorporates dignity and wit. They seem to me her best work so far." In all, one hundred and twenty-four pieces were hung at Andover, and sixty-three sold. It was a great occasion, starting with a glorious lunch given by Neva and Walter Kaiser in their Cambridge garden, followed by a private bus trip to the gallery.

The following year I had another large show at the Boston Museum of Science. Different from the Addison show, this one was all collages with only one exception, a small self-portrait in oil, "Passe Montagne I" (20 ½" x 16"), which I thought of as a sort of calling card. Having a show without a single painting felt incomplete. I needed this little head as an affidavit to myself as a painter. The portrait was serious and severe. I was wearing my black knit ski cap which hugs the head, exposing the eyes and mouth in two openings, but covering the nose. One lock of white hair shows over the forehead.

Packing up after the show, I found that the calling card painting was not there. Someone had just picked it off the wall and put it in their rucksack. I loved this painting and felt sad at its loss. Since it had been sold and paid for, I returned the money to the buyer who sent the check back with the comment, "Paint another." Far easier said than done. I tried many times, wearing the same ski cap and using canvasses of related size. Of course I didn't want an exact replica, there was no chance of that. I can never copy my own work, but I did want something similar and I was having great difficulty in getting it. Finally the following year I produced a painting that I thought was good. Where the first one had been serious and severe, this one doubled those qualities. There was no lock of hair to soften the forehead, no reprieve in the eyes, no softness in the lips. The painting was totally uncompromising. I was startled and frightened by it. I knew the painting was good but couldn't look at it. A kind friend came into the studio, saw the reality of my fear and said, "Hang it in the farthest corner of the room and forget it." I did just that and after several weeks was able to begin looking at the work. I gradually came to be able to accept the painting's strength but I felt it would be too much for the original buyer. Only my wonderful friend Josefina, who had lived through the Spanish Civil War, had the courage to buy it. She has lived with the portrait now for many years. Each time I see the work in her house I like it better and admire her increasingly for the strength of her valiant personality.

~

Along the way I have painted two paintings relating to my mother, "Matriarchal" (52" x 50") in 1976 and 1977 and "Bravura" (65" x 48") in 1976. I like them both. Each is powerful but in very different ways. I started "Matriarchal" at a beautiful artist's colony on Ossabaw Island off the coast of Savannah, Georgia. The painting shows a shape like a great, medium blue, mountain whose slightly pointed top and hefty bulk stand out against a lighter blue sky. Just one small white cloud-like form touches the mountain from behind. Within the mountain is a huge, medium cerulean egg bisected by a white line whose end hangs down like a string. The egg is traveling toward a vast, free, orange-red space. I am that egg on my way out to the unknown. All the shapes are big and powerful, each has its own strong color and is in full command of the place it occupies. This work has a quiet brilliance, a rightness, and joy. The picture is not one of escape but of a genetic process in which each shape, and there are not many, fulfills its function in order to carry out the intention of the painter.

"Bravura", on the other hand, although a large painting, has for its composition just one line that changes shape, contour and color as it moves across the picture from left to right, at first upward and then taking a deep downward dip in mid-canvas as it travels on a dynamic, orange-red path through a pale lavender ground, widening out as it gets to the upper right-hand corner. While painting this I thought of my mother's extraordinary energy and her freedom of unrestrained action in the context of a vast space. The man who bought and loves this work objects only to the title, which he claims is a total misnomer. He sees the painting as highly sexual, the essence of the ultimate, unattainable female. Another man who also loves the painting gives it a similar interpretation. Clearly one doesn't always know what one is painting.

During my lifetime I have made three large triptychs. One is an oil painting made in 1949 and the two others are in hand-made paper from 1986. The 1949 work started with just one 40" x 20" panel. From the top a suspended, rounded form, hangs like an opened Chinese lantern, exuding light. A friend, recently out of the military service, asked to borrow the painting as he was having a hard time re-adjusting to regular life and said the painting helped him towards quietude. When he returned the panel after a year, I discovered that the painting also soothed me, but seemed incomplete, too small. I decided it should become the right panel of a triptych. When open, I wanted the triptych to have the effect of a religious apotheosis devoid of religious symbols or recognizable personalities. I wanted it to express pure elation, which is why it mounts from a bluish area mid-canvas to a crescendo of yellows and pinks with powerful black markings rising up towards the top. These colors spread through all three interior panels with some darker reds at the base. I also wanted the element of surprise. When closed, the outer panels are very quiet. Muted greys and soft browns in geometric forms melt into each other with a centered, darker area that gives the feeling of a lock guarding the hidden glory of the interior until the outside panels are opened and the spirits soar. Open, it measures 40" x 80". The finished painting was exhibited at the Margaret Brown Gallery in Boston. I had recently met a young man who looked like an Assyrian king with whom I'd had an instant rapport, Arthur Kohlenburg. I felt I had known and loved him in another life in Egypt or Assyria. Authur felt deep affinity for the triptych and wanted to buy it. I told him I thought he was too young to encumber his life with such a large piece of art, but I would lend it to him. I never saw it installed in what I'm sure must have been a very small apartment. He told me that every night the triptych was in his possession he ceremoniously closed the panels and every morning ceremoniously opened them. I felt wonderfully gratified that he had understood the religious power in the piece exactly as I had hoped.

The other two triptychs from 1986, one 36" x 56 ½" and the other a gigantic 8' x 12', I made at the Rugg Road Paper Mill in Boston. Both are primarily involved with abstract spatial considerations and gain their power from implied motion, intervals, shapes, and negative space; all qualities which need to be seen and experienced rather than written about. While working on the large pieces I thought of the Standing Stones of Callenish in the Outer Hebrides that I visited in 1974. There, across open fields, one saw these glorious monoliths, standing free, twenty-five feet above ground, counterbalanced by their reciprocals twenty-five feet below ground. Their immensity is over-powering as is their magic, about which we know so little but whose effect we can still feel centuries after their creation.

I have always been interested in what becomes of my paintings when they leave me. I feel personally about them but not possessive. I like to have them go out into the world and enjoy meeting them sometimes years later, like bumping into an old friend and catching up on how well they have worn in their new homes.

My first patron came early in my career, even before I had exhibited. Mrs. Nathan Porter bought work every year from 1933 on. In 1938 she donated a piece to the Museum of Modern Art and another to the museum in Montclair, New Jersey. At a later period a very different kind of patron was a very young man, Steven, who for many years paid me a hundred dollars a month. When one painting was paid for he'd buy another on the same basis. Ed Diehl and his wife Mary in Cambridge have also been wonderful patrons. An unusual scheme was devised by Eunice and Julian Whitlessey. Their small New York apartment had only one good wall for hanging a painting. Julian designed a handsome metal frame just the right size for the wall. They then asked successive artists, for a minimal fee, to make a painting the size of the frame. The Whitlesseys would live with the work for three years, then return it to the artist to do with as he or she wanted when another artist's work would fill the empty frame. This gave them variety on their one picture wall and the artist a stimulating project. When they gave me the commission the 40"x 60" size was considerably larger than my usual canvases so I enjoyed the challenge.

This painting, later bought by my friend Agnes, was called "Early Morning Maze". A soft yellow haze is combined with other muted colors in geometric shapes. The painting is a pleasant one to wake up to, an idea which pleased me, so I followed it with a painting of the same size to go to sleep to, "Jam Lucis", a title taken from a Gregorian evensong. This is in soft greys and blues and also has geometric shapes. I would love to see these two hanging together. "Jam Lucis" still belongs to me. So far no one has wanted to buy it, but one day someone probably will. This frequently happens even after a twenty or fifty year interval.

More recently still I have become my own patron, for the first time falling in love with "The Heavens as Meadow" (88"x 70"), painted in 1974, a period when I made many such gigantic works. This picture was recently returned to me from the Art in Embassies Program after hanging for seventeen years in various embassies as one of the large group of works loaned by artists to our government for the enjoyment of our ambassadors and their foreign guests. No money is involved in these transactions, but human graciousness often is.

From Mrs. Sallie Lewis I read, "There is no way to thank you personally for the real satisfaction of living with a piece of art that one loves, and publicly for representing the best of American art to the literal thousands of our Israeli guests. Two thousand booklets have been distributed to our acquaintances, each one containing a photographed facsimile of your work and a brief autobiography of you. I hope that in some small way this compensates you for your generosity in loaning it to the State Department and to us." From Ambassador George Vest, "I cannot resist writing to thank you for something which perhaps you are not aware of; one of your paintings, a glorious large yellow canvas called "Pale Rubric" has the place of honor in the Embassy drawing room where it lights up the room and our lives and the Brussels overcast weather makes it shine all the brighter." This is an effective kind of diplomacy.

In January 1983 I met and started paying weekly visits to a Jungian analyst, Robert Bosnak, an experience I had wanted for forty-six years. Soon I realized that I had found the person with whom I was eager to investigate my dreams and discover whatever might flow from them, which proved extremely rewarding. Through my visits to Robbie I was enabled to release enough energy to produce a huge volume of new work, as well as gain a better sense of my own identity. I saw him for seven months then went up to Chouette for a short vacation that turned into a long stay because of a fractured ankle. This period of quiet was valuable as a hiatus, a time to let things seep through without too much thought. It was a beautiful, unpressured time of being with Lex and being with myself in a particularly spectacular autumn at Chouette. Since I was on crutches I couldn't do much outdoors. I was fortunate in finding a box of postcards from earlier travels and sent a hundred of them to friends around the world which amazed Lex. What I could do outdoors was to look. Those autumn hillsides became deeply implanted in my memory, to emerge later in paintings.

On returning to Cambridge I resumed my weekly visits to Robbie. During that first month I had a dream of a carrot, a large, isolated, red-orange, vertical, freestanding carrot with no background. On waking I wrote, "I see a carrot grow, orange and red. At the bottom of the carrot tiny new roots have grown. It is impossible, but it is that way anyway. And the new tiny roots at the bottom of the large carrot go deeper." I painted a picture of it, 48" x 24", a large painting for a single carrot. As it sometime does in nature, a beginning of a little carrot emerges from the side of the old one. In my painting this has definitely become a provocative pregnancy. I was rather startled by this painting, especially after such a long, non-productive period; but I got accustomed to it, encouraged by my friend Carol Rankin who saw the canvas in the back of my car when I went to visit her. She was very ill at that time. The carrot painting seemed to give her enormous pleasure, a sense of life came back into her face, which was wonderful to see and one of two reasons that make me care about this painting. The other is that it was the precursor of one of the most intensely creative periods of my life, an explosive outpouring of work. As the dream said, "the new tiny roots at the bottom of the large carrot go deeper." I had painted pictures from dreams before but never a whole sequence. I decided to be as open to the new roots as possible, new subjects, new inspirations, new ways of painting, taking each as it presented itself. For the first time I painted several large paintings from photographs, two of Chouette in October foliage and one of Ossabaw's beaches. I painted some works in acrylic, which I hadn't done in eight years, and several naturalistic landscapes, which I hadn't done in forty years. These strangely diverse paintings kept coming out like water from a faucet. The flow ended only when the date of the exhibition, called "Maud Morgan, an Autobiography 1928-1986", was at hand in February 1986. The installation was in the very large space of the North Hall of the Massachusetts College of Art in Boston. As well as many paintings and drawings from all periods, there was also work I had made that year at the Rugg Road Paper Mill in a technique new to me, called "Work in Paper". Essentially this involved making the paper from cotton pulp that is floated in water on a vacuum table into which other colored pulps can be introduced before draining the water out, leaving the pulp as a flat surface on which one can work either before or after the pulp dries. The changes made when the work is wet will become a part of the structure of the paper; those made afterwards will be part of a superimposed image. I became very involved in both small and very large pieces done in this medium. My big, black 12' by 24' triptych bowled me over when I first saw these three huge pieces framed and hung together. They had been lying flat to dry for the three previous weeks, and I had put them out of my mind while coping with all the other works for the show. My great and long time friend Kyra Montagu bought them. Unfortunately they were too large for her house so she kindly donated them to the Addison Gallery of American Art at Phillips Academy in Andover where they will remain as a triptych, as I had always hoped.

Macedonian Coat (1985), Oil on canvas, 61½ x 35 in.

Victoria Munroe came up from her New York gallery to hang that show for me. This continued the magic surrounding the whole affair. To watch her sort out, make sense of and bring that show into existence was a new experience. To observe the pieces I had made over a lifetime being formed by another person into a cogent, powerful unit with its own life was exciting. Two of the landscapes from this show were particularly important to me, "October in Quebec I" and "October in Quebec II, Birth by Water." Both were paintings of Chouette seen when I was there with the fractured ankle when autumn was in its full regalia, more beautiful than I had ever seen it and I had not seen it, at that season for fifty years. Both paintings were sold.

One had a subsequent life of its own several years later. Through Ran Blake, a musician who came from New York to work with Gunther Schuller at the Boston Conservatory of Music in order to create the Third Stream Music Department of contemporary music, I was invited to partake in a concert at the conservatory in which the musicians composed works inspired by individual paintings. I entered "October in Quebec II, Birth by Water" (36" x 84"). The central motif of this painting is an image of a mountain in brilliant yellow and orange foliage, framed by dark spruce and larch trees at both ends and by dark water at the bottom. When I saw the slide enlarged on a 20' by 30' screen, I was immediately involved, drawn into the work in a different way than I had been while painting it. I found myself busy trying to locate the little places I vividly remembered working on. I couldn't. I was thrown off by the scale, which seemed to change the interrelationship of the parts. Clearly I needed to look at my work with different eyes, especially at the water in the lower middle canvas. In the center, beneath a magic golden tree, I had painted an implied whirlpool, dimly visible, expressing the thought of the subtitle, "Birth by Water". Now in this vast scale I could no longer see the small form of the whirlpool, but instead the concept of birth by water was powerfully expressed in the entire expanse of the dark lake which had become profound and mysterious. I was being shown what I didn't know I had actually painted, but knew I had felt deeply all through the time of working.

Now I saw the painting in its universality. I became increasingly fascinated, curious and delighted.

The musicians came on stage. Joe Maneri was on tenor saxophone and clarinet and Mitch Haupers played guitar. I was surprised that Joe was an older man. I had expected only student performers. Obviously he was a faculty member, grey-haired, fattish with a powerful aura of vital energy. Immediately his clarinet hit on a high, piercing tone, challenging to the listener and challenging to the painting. He was addressing the work with tremendous vigor. Clearly there was a confrontation with the mountain. The more he played the more it appeared like a vibrating, mythic golden dome containing as yet undiscovered secrets. Mitch was backing all this up with his guitar and some electronic sounds that were like voices calling from within the painting. Joe was putting everything into his triumphant approach; his right knee bent, his torso forward as though he were going to charge into the sacred unknown place. From time to time he switched to the tenor sax, making a conversation out of the interplay, reinforcing the urge to advance. The distance between him and the mountain was diminishing. He was about to enter the mountain, to go beyond it. For the first time I was seeing my painting from within. I had become the spirit inside the mountain, the spirit born of water. I had learned its secrets. Joe was about to find them. Later I went back to meet these men who had led me within my own mystery. Joe was even shorter in reality than he had appeared on stage. He was delighted to meet me. "We got to the back of the mountain," he said triumphantly, "to the other side of it." "You certainly did," I said as we hugged, "and within it, too." What a miracle. Strangers had taken me inside myself while I, a stranger, had led them to their own outer reaches. I was so moved by this event that I sent a copy of the description you have just read to Joe. He was overwhelmed that I had caught in words the emotional verity he had felt and rendered while playing. I too was awed by the strength of my original response to the autumnal glory of the yellow birches on the Chouette hillside that inspired the power of the painting and became the inspiration for the musical interpretation which is turned into words.

To spend fifty minutes each week touching ground with Robbie has been wonderfully supportive to me both personally and professionally. I welcomed his encouragement through the preparations for my Mass Art show and the next one the following year at Victoria Munroe's Gallery in New York. This totally different exhibit was all recent work made at Rugg Road, unified instead of diversified, almost all done in three months. No retrospection here. It was all new and now. I felt great and was tickled to have produced two good shows so close together in time and so far apart in concept. I felt I never needed to have a show again, a satisfying sensation. Of course the reality was different. A show with Gyorgy Kepes came the next year, and my drawing show at Barbara Singer's house in Cambridge, "Surprises from a Lost Portfolio", the year after that in October 1988. How pleasant to realize that I was having as many shows and being as productive in my eighties as I had been in my best years.

I have been seeing Robbie for nine years now, and I think of him as a friend rather than a doctor, a friend to whom I can put any question and get any answer. He often surprises me and I think sometimes I surprise him. At first it did strike me at a bit odd when I decided to go to a shrink again at age eighty, particularly with the track record I had in that domain – (ten years of non-productive Freudianism) – but fundamentally it made sense. To see a Jungian doctor had been a life-long wish still hanging fire. Now here was a chance to try out one of the many unfulfilled desires floating around in my head. For some of them, indeed for most, fulfillment was too late. No third child was possible, no passionate love affair probable, but here was something I wanted to do to which I could say "yes." For a while, Robbie became my fifth home.

One day recently, while walking around Fresh Pond, I found that I had to go into the bushes to pee. Afterwards I continued my walk, having just the right amount of time to complete it before going to my appointment with Robbie. When I got back to my car, my keys were gone. At once I realized they had fallen out of my pocket when I'd gone into the bushes and were irretrievable. I was downcast and a little frantic at missing my appointment without being able to communicate with my doctor. At that moment my friend Katie jogged by and offered to go home, get her car, come back and take me to my appointment. She very kindly did all this, but by the time she got back to me, there were only twenty minutes left of my hour. "That's worth it," she said. "Let's go."

My doctor had been worried about my non-appearance and said so at the door. I walked into his office and sat down in my usual place but it was not my accustomed chair. Instead I was in a different chair in a different place. I was sitting in a white canvas officer's chair in French Indochina. The weather was deliciously warm. There were other people on the terrace, but they were not close to us. Slender waiters in white jackets were moving gracefully among the tables. "What shall we drink?" I asked. "What are you going to have?" "Well, I think, I'll take a piña colada," I said. "Then, I will too." He looked well in his safari jacket, tanned and a little more mature than the last time I'd seen him. He must be about 37 or 38 by now. Three years ago when we were both on the same assignment for different papers at Phnom Penh, we had had a delightful love affair – just the right intimacy, just the right length. I was tickled to bump into him unexpectedly like this and wanted to know what had been going on in his life since we'd last met, just as he did in mine. Now we were on different assignments, heading in different directions. Each had just stopped in at this familiar Saigon bar for a quick drink en route to the airport. Our meeting was a pure happenstance.

"Now we must stop," said my doctor. "I don't know where I am," I said. "It's been overwhelmingly real. And you dressed for the part." "I've never worn my safari jacket to the office before," he said as I left.

The front steps to the office to which I had come once a week for the last nine years, now seemed strangely remote, less real than the Saigon bar where I had just parted from my lover, looking so pleasantly familiar in his safari jacket. I was reluctant too, to leave the semi-tropical climate of French Indochina. But slowly reality gained control over this, the most vivid space disorientation I have ever experienced. Along with the strangeness I felt a detached stimulation as I walked along the Cambridge street. I was not quite the same person who had lost her keys in the bushes earlier that day. My horizon had broadened. Like a break-through that sometimes occurs in a painting, when discouraged by what appears to have been a mistake, one comes to recognize that out of it has developed an opening to a different resolution. It is said that an important qualification for a painter is the ability to accept not knowing where one is going or where an inspiration will come from. In 1989 I surprised myself by finding the inspiration and material for my next show in a portfolio in my own cellar. I knew it was there but I had not opened it for twenty years.

The portfolio contained figure drawings from various periods. Some were from the early years in Canada before Lex was born, 1934 to 1936, others from the Hofmann school years, 1936 to 1940, some from the early period in Cambridge, 1960 to 1965 and others from various times in between. With hesitation I showed these to my friend and framer David Murphy. My insecurity about my capability as a draughtsman had been reinforced by the sculptor Alexander Archipenko, who after a season as my teacher said, "You should choose another field. You haven't made one beautiful line all year." Pat agreed and found my drawing, particularly the self-portraits, quite unacceptable. So I was totally unprepared and disbelieved David's enthusiastic reaction to this work that I had almost totally disregarded, although to be sure I had kept it. There was one drawing that I had torn up at some earlier time when, I presume, I was planning to destroy them all. But something changed my mind, for I kept the drawings, even the two halves of the one I had torn up. I asked David to frame these two pieces for me (only one small section got lost along the way) as a strange and sad reminder of how far afield I had allowed myself to go, persuaded by Pat of my inadequacy, while thanking God that my painting had not suffered the same fate. For painting was my blood stream. Had it had been dammed up I would not have survived.

David showed the drawings to my dealer Barbara Singer, who has occupied herself on my behalf. She carries out her role with great pleasure and élan. It has been rewarding to work with Barbara as she and I have a real accord. From our very different positions in life, we meet easily with sudden and deep understanding. In quite a different way I feel equal friendship and love for her husband Leonard and her daughter Jessica, for whom I acted as an ersatz grandmother when I accompanied them to Jerusalem for Jessica's bat mitzvah. I have become a part of their extended family, a great enrichment to my life. Barbara agreed with David on the quality of the drawings and together they gave me a beautiful show in her Cambridge house in October 1988, appropriately entitled "Surprises from a Lost Portfolio". Because I completely trusted both Barbara's and David's judgment, I stood back as an observer watching this exhibition coming into existence, trying to look at the work as a stranger might, seeing it for the first time. The more I was able to do this, the more I first appreciated, then really liked, and finally became excited about the drawings. Some people found this the best work I have yet exhibited. What a strange journey to travel in these few days while they hung the show. Starting from nowhere. I just looked on bewildered.

There is a parallel between this 1988 drawing show and my first show at Julian Levy's in New York in 1938, fifty years earlier. The parallel of surprise. In each case I was taken aback and startled by the degree of appreciation the work attracted. In some ways, the surprise of the 1988 show was the greater of the two. After all, I'd been showing for fifty years by then, so a surprise was not to be expected, but the 1988 show consisted of work which I had been made to feel was of no value. My gratitude to Barbara and David is great. Quite possibly if I hadn't had that final conversation with Pat, I might not have been able to exhibit these drawings, or even to show them to David. "It's the unexpected, the unknowable, the divine irrationality of life that saves us", writes Florida Scott Maxwell in *The Measure of My Days*.

A disturbing thing happened at that show. For forty-seven years I've owned a charming little book containing clipped out reviews of my work from the late 1930s with some photographs of the paintings, a photograph of me, and one of me with my husband. It's a nicely designed and crafted little book that I treasure, made by G. Alan Chidsey of Plandone, Long Island. He is a man who loves art and has built an excellent collection in an interesting way. He would make such a book about an artist he admired, and send the book to the artist, requesting that if the artist was pleased thathe or she acknowledge it by returning some small piece of their work. Since Mr. Chidsey clearly knows how to fabricate a superior book, artists can't help but be pleased and flattered. Often I take my book to my openings especially if they are not in large spaces. I took it to the opening of the drawing show at Barbara's. When I went to pick it up after the opening, the book had disappeared. It's easy to see why someone would like to slip it into a pocketbook; it's a unique little document. When I realized that the book was gone I burst into tears, unusual for me in recent years. Later when I got to my car, I couldn't stop sobbing. I was completely thrown off my track, disrupted as I haven't been for thirty years. The following day the same thing repeated itself. What amazed me was how totally knocked out I was. Listless, the interest in writing gone, feeling that this book didn't matter. There's enough done, I thought, someone else can finish it after my death if it's worth it. They won't know first hand the difficulties Pat and I had, they can just smooth it over, maybe better so. I didn't want to eat, couldn't sleep and didn't want to see anyone. I saw the missing book as the sustaining corner-stone of all my subsequent work, the tangible proof that my art had been good enough from the start to tide me through the barren places. The book had been a rudder, the one art object that was important for me to leave to my children: all the good reviews, a picture of me, and one of their father and me together when things were going well with us. The book said everything I wanted them to hear about my art life, and it was irretrievably gone. Even as I was experiencing these emotions, I was unable to believe their intensity, wondering what was happening to me. I realized I was crying for more than the loss of the little book, even though I felt it represented my entire life in art. I was crying for the loss of Whitney, I was crying for the wasted years in Freudianism, I was crying for the years of self-created martyrdom in my marriage. I was crying for all my losses, crying for my life. Finally, and for the first time, I recognized I was at the Wailing Wall.

I went to a Jim Dine show at the Museum of Fine Arts, trying to change the subject from myself. When I got back into the car, the sobbing started again. There was a terrible mid-rift emptiness. The interesting part of my life seemed to be over and I didn't care. What had happened to all that euphoria of the last ten years? Gone in minutes, through the loss of a tiny, slim book. For me, who cares little about possessions, this loss was worse than the loss of the twenty paintings that have been stolen from me over the years, or of all the beautiful rings and other jewelry which has been taken. This was far worse. The tenuous fragility of my equilibrium frightened me. What keeps us on track anyway beyond the habit of daily familiarities and the deeper urge, drive and hope of accomplishing one's goal? Usually that is enough, but in the case of the little book's disappearance, that had not been enough. I had lost my bearings. Those two days were a painful and exhausting passage of witnessing the disintegration of personal balance caused by the physical loss of a symbolic object.

In Oklahoma during the 1935 Dust Bowl period it was said that the dust storms struck so quickly that people sometimes got lost in their own backyards. I felt I was lost in mine. I had not known that I considered the little book to be an affidavit of my life in art until it was taken away. Then somehow it became a statement of my lineage. Without it I had no credentials. I was no one, which caused a kind of terror I recognized as a fundamental aspect of life from which I had previously been sheltered. Mostly I have lived a life similar to what Lao Tze describes in writing to an artist, "You are like the river which only knows as yet its shimmering banks and has no knowledge of the power that draws it forward inevitably to the ocean." That was the way of life that had always been enough; this loss made me know it was not enough. Slowly I began to accept what had happened and to realize that, through it, I had become more impersonal, stronger, pared down closer to the bone, more able to live without the written word to prove my veracity. Many weeks later the little book was discovered with a pile of other books. It had accidently been taken to the Singer's attic, where it had quietly been sitting on a shelf waiting for me to get through my turmoil. Having it back was gratifying and quieting. I also knew that it had come back to a different and somewhat more resolved person. I think I had learned that an affidavit of one's veracity is not a necessity. Attempting to be a complete human being is challenge enough. At a spiritual conference a while back I was sitting on the edge of my bed, when I saw a blackboard rise before my eyes as in a marijuana image. On it was written in heavy white chalk, "I forgive Pat."

15. ENTRE-DEUX

"Do not hurry, do not rest"
— *Goethe*

Tonight I am not feeling the exhilaration of age which Hans Hofmann must have felt at the end of his life, but the reverse. I am feeling old, tired, and sad, going around the house groaning out loud as old people do who live alone. I have been watching the episode of "The World at War" in which Berlin is taken by the Russians, Hitler marries Eva Braun and shortly after shoots himself. She takes cyanide. The story is told by women friends of Hitler's, seemingly caring women. I had just come from a Saturday matinée of Lily Tomlin's one woman show called "The Search for Signs of Intelligent Life in the Universe". These two experiences seem related, inversely related, perhaps simply by the contrast of the final defeat of Hitler's evil juxtaposed to the vigorous stamina of Lily's fight for good. Her's is a remarkable tour de force: night after night she has the grit and chutzpa to be on stage alone for two hours, holding the audience in suspense through laughter, breathing life into Jane Wagner's brilliant text, pin-pointing our fads and fakes, and ridiculing the lunatic nightmare we have created through our computerized efficiency. Yet throughout she manages to keep herself personally intact, remaining kind, sensitive and extremely generous. In spite of Tomlin's buoyancy, I am feeling ancient and static. Am I trying to explain away things that keep me from knowing how I feel about them down in my gut? I know I feel exhausted and am blaming it on old age, ashamed of letting myself do so. It's a cop-out. Feeling old can easily become a habit, a habit that people fall into at fifty or sixty or forty. I think one must fight hard to hang onto and nurture every shred of vitality as one proceeds, giving in only when essential and adapting to the limitations of age gradually. Recognized at the proper time they are welcome to oneself and comforting to others.

Of course one must accept diminishing returns, particularly in the areas of seeing and hearing. This can be irritating, particularly as one discovers that most people telling a joke drop their voices at the end of the sentence to add dramatic effect to the punch line, particularly in a dirty joke, so one is left stony-faced as the rest of the audience is convulsed in laughter. But one can learn to live with this and perhaps learn to tell a joke oneself to fill the next gap.

By and large through my long life I have been blessed by good health, which like many young people, I abused in usual and some unusual ways. At twenty-three I lived in Paris for a winter and inexplicably decided to give up bread, good French bread, to lose weight. At one time it seemed so important to be thin that I scarcely ate anything except liver extract and fell down from weakness. At that point the doctor who was advising me said I could eat an apple. I woke up, realized what I was doing and changed doctors, fortunately not having injured my health irreparably. Finally at age sixty I saw these follies for what they were, and now I am blessed by working with a trainer three times a week. Under Aviva's skillful direction my back has become more limber than at any previous time in adulthood. I actually see improvements in my body, something I had not been told to expect with advancing age. It seems to me like a minor miracle and stems the tide a bit.

I woke up Sunday morning and decided to go to service at Trinity Church, the large, beautiful edifice built by Henry Hobson Richardson in 1877 on Copley Square in Boston. Just before Richardson's death in 1885 the Architect's Association voted Trinity Church to be the best building in the United States, and Richardson himself was considered to be one of the great American architects. This handsome, ample building dominates the large open area of Copley Square at the heart of the city. It has a sculptural three-dimensionality ahead of its time and is bold in form and detail. Richardson worked closely with the craftsmen, altering his design as job conditions warranted. This church has a massive solidity that came to define Richardson's architecture, but it also has a welcoming, friendly feeling of belonging.

Richardson developed his own style in architecture, drawing much from French and Spanish Romanesque, adapted to American uses in a very personal way. Trinity Church is exceptionally large but it looks

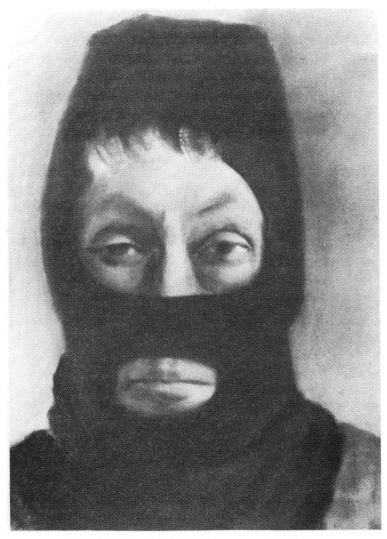

Passe Montagne I (1978), Oil on canvas, 20 x 15 in.

small, though not diminished in strength, by its neighbor to the rear, the towering, 60-floor, spectacular glass obelisk of the John Hancock Tower, built by I. M. Pei in 1973. His fascinating use of a reflecting glass curtain wall produces an endless series of changing effects. In certain lights and from specific points Richardson's entire church is reflected in Pei's skyscraper. It's an extraordinary sight, a surprisingly harmonious one. These two outstanding buildings, designed by two great architects, augment each other across a hundred and twenty-five years of time and a century and a quarter of architectural change.

Such lapses in the history of architecture serve as instructive clues in understanding broad sweeps of time. I think the same thing is true on the smaller scale of personal lives. Recently I came to appreciate this when an incident came my way that significantly helped illuminate my own life. It came in the shape of a hitherto misplaced diary, an abortive one in which the first two entries were 1935 and 1936 and the next and last entry was in 1962. It showed me where I had come from and indicated where I should go. To my amazement I read from May 1935:

"I come from a tribal family, a masculine tribe. I, the only female, am the most masculine of them all. My energy is a man's energy, my desires a man's desires. Underlying this is a completely feminine nervous apparatus weakened by neglect. I feel that I have power and greatness in me, greatness for myself or my child. I don't know but it is there. It should have a different tone and strength now after all the weeping over the lost years and my lost love. I must paint this. I must do some work about women, they have so little to turn to in the arts, work made by other women. I write this that it may one day help me to stick clear and straight to the path through which I think I can touch people, humans, and have reality. I had a life in Whitney, a life and a first death, the most valuable chapter of my youth, then nothing but waves of hopelessness about the future and a great fear of what will become of me if I don't paint. What is this driving urge? Is it for paint? For power? For sex? For peace? Peace I have been given these last two years, the first peace I have known. I wonder, is it the last? I shrink from this baby."

The reference here was to the foetus that miscarried. Clearly I was not emotionally ready for a child. Happily, however, I became pregnant again and, after six months in bed and considerable spiritual growth, Alexis came into the world very much wanted and loved. Nature had done me and him a good turn of timing. His birth was on July 6, 1936.

August 1936: "It's extraordinary what they do to you, there he is now lying upstairs, the most patent evidence that I am a female, Pat a male. He is seven weeks old and has made everything in our lives different.

"Yet there is still a cloud between me and reality. Partly it must be the resurgence of the shame of being a woman so firmly implanted in me in childhood which began to dwindle only when I knew Whitney. But Alexis has come out of my body. Why is the unreality still there?"

The next entry skips to 1962, twenty-seven years later. My second child, Victoria, had been born in 1941 and we had spent seventeen years as a family at Phillips Academy. I was then living alone in Cambridge, separated but not divorced from Pat. The earlier courageous statements about my belief in my own power had dimmed during those twenty-seven years, only beginning to show signs of coming to life again when I started living alone in 1957.

August 1962: "And so I knew all that in 1935, twenty-seven years ago, knew so much more than I knew I knew, was so much more than I knew I was. Since then I have painted and painted well. I have faced the masculine in myself by finding out that I was an erotic and evocative woman, which took me half a lifetime to learn. How marvelous it is for me now to be loved by such a masculine man, to be loved totally as a woman, not as a woman substituting for a man."

These sweeping reflections took me traveling back through several decades before I returned to Trinity Church and found myself sitting in exactly the same spot as I had been before embarking on them. The speed with which one can relive big chunks of time with a good deal of detailed accuracy has always seemed incredible to me. Still we are told that everything is always present and available in our memory if one knows how to trigger its recall. The knowing how is difficult to learn.

Trinity Church was packed, balconies and all; there was scarcely an empty seat, just like Lily Tomlin's show. Everybody's seeking meaning and purpose in their lives. I hadn't been to a Protestant church in a long, long time. There was a lot of kneeling, which hurt. I am still feeling the effects of several falls last autumn. Much of my time in church was spent putting my glasses on and off, hoping to be able to read the words of the hymns, but since I couldn't I realized I must have brought the wrong pair. Then I attempted to adjust my hearing aid, with only minimum success. I was sitting between two devout men who tried to help me find the right book and the right hymn in that book. Only later did I notice that the hymn numbers were written in big white letters directly over my head. I enjoyed hearing the man on my right saying the Lord's Prayer in a strong male voice, pronouncing it clearly. I felt lonely listening to him. I only relaxed when I heard the large, excellent choir begin to sing. During communion Bach's "Sheep May Safely Graze" was played.

Immediately I was taken back to my Andover studio of forty-five years earlier and to Wilfred Freeman, my friend and muse. It was he who introduced me to that music of Bach's. I loved both the music and the idea and painted two pictures of the pastures of Heaven. The smaller one I painted especially for Wilfred. The larger one was bought by Agnes. I thought of him throwing pebbles up against my studio window to get my attention before coming up to visit and I thought of his deep love, commitment, and connection to the Episcopal Church. There was also another painting inspired by Wilfred, my large "Jam Lucis" (40" x 60") whose title comes from the Gregorian Evensong by that name.

Now at the ending of the day
Creator of the world I pray
That with thy wonted favor thou
Wouldst be our help and keeper now.

I realized that while part of me misses attending church, I don't feel less religious for not doing so and at this point I am not drawn to make a commitment to an organized faith. So I decided to leave those ideas hanging as an "unanswered question", a phrase that brought to mind Charles Ives' beautiful musical composition known by that title, a composition that invites speculation and philosophical ramblings.

The sermon followed. I could hear the sound of the clergyman's voice but I couldn't distinguish the individual words which gave me a pleasant hiatus in which to think about my current religious feelings, my past religious experiences, and to recall some of the religious people I have known.

I thought about Buckminster Fuller, whom I knew and cared for, that tiny, all-powerful, world-famous man, the ultimate world citizen, equally at home in Japan, Scandinavia, or Andover, his wife Anne's home town. Bucky adored his wife, whom he would call every day from whatever part of the world he happened to be in. Bucky said that without her he could not live. He was a deeply religious man, although a non-conformist. Every day he would re-think or re-phrase the Lord's Prayer. He told me he thought the wording "Forgive us our trespasses as we forgive those who trespass against us" was an unworthy bargain to ask of the Lord. Forgiveness has nothing to do with quid pro quo. His belief in God was the motive force of his life; his intermediary was Anne. At the end, when she was extremely ill, Bucky, visiting her in the hospital, saw that she was dying. He lay down and died too. His last statements, written on Chinese New Year's, February 14, 1983, from Penang, Malaysia reads: "Human integrity is the uncompromising courage of self-determining whether or not to take initiatives, support or cooperate with others in accord with all the truth and nothing but the truth as it is conceived by the divine mind always available in each individual. Whether humanity is to continue and comprehensively prosper on Spaceship Earth depends entirely on the integrity of the human individuals and not on the political and economic systems. The cosmic question has been asked, 'Are humans a worthwhile to universe invention?'"

Thinking of Bucky's tiny stature led me to remember another tiny, all-powerful, world-famous man, Mahatma Ghandi, and my early absorbed interest in him. I had been swept off my feet by his religious fervor, dedication, and power, inducing hordes of the Indian population to believe in non-violence as a religious way of life, non-violence even in the face of armed troops. I thought of the glorious dedication that was his life and of its tragic, though expected ending. What a great privilege it had been to meet and talk with him when my mother and I attended the National Congress in Lahore in 1929 and he invited us to follow him to his private tent when the speeches ended. He walked ahead very fast accompanied by Mrs. Slade, his chief secretary, the beautiful, middle-aged daughter of a British admiral who was devoting her life to serving him. My mother and I followed directly behind as closely as we could. A square was made around Ghandi, Mrs Slade, my mother and me, consisting of bamboo poles held by volunteers trying, with only moderate success, to isolate us from the crowd. It was a struggle to stay near enough to Mrs. Slade so that the mob would not come between us. They were hoping to kiss Ghandi's feet or at least touch the hem of his garment. Their force was like that of the ocean rushing into an empty cave. One felt that had they been able to make a wedge between Mrs. Slade and ourselves, we would be forever lost in that vast, seething sea of humanity. As Ghandi passed they chanted with suppressed reverence and awe. "Ma-hat-ma-ghan-di-bee-ja;ma-hat-ma-ghan-di-bee-ja – Long live Mahatma Ghandi." I recognized it as the most intensely religious moment in my life.

Mrs. Slade devoted her life to Ghandi. To see that dedication of service, which she fulfilled in a total way, was moving. But there are other roles for women now, and always have been. We must understand their appropriate application to our period of history. Women today must undertake work beyond the traditional heritage imposed on them through millennia, and we must give our wisest and most creative thinking to our societies. We have the capabilities, skills, and compassion to bring about drastic and much needed change in our world, but many women still have a deep fear of taking the steps we have been trained through centuries not to take, opening ourselves up to the epithet 'unfeminine'. However, the new world which we are entering so rapidly promises to be one where womens' values are given consideration.

I have been tremendously interested and excited by Mary Robinson in the short time I have known about the attractive, lively, brilliant, forty-seven year-old woman who is serving a seven year term, begun in 1990, as president of Ireland. At the start of her campaigning for office, the bookmakers gave odds of one thousand-to-one. She ran on an independent ticket on a platform for change and was put into office by the grassroots villagers and the women of Ireland. She said that her election was "a catalyst for women's self-development and empowerment." She is a radical crusader for women's rights and human rights. "I want to develop Ireland," she said, "the way one would want to develop oneself." Mary Robinson is anxious to break down the fear between Ireland and England and between the North and the South of her own country. She acts directly in a womanly way, inviting mixed groups of Protestants and Catholics to visit her home. Some from the North have never been to Dublin before. Her father, Dr. Bourke, says that the mixed marriage of his daughter is "a big advantage, a very uplifting situation for this country."

"Being president," she said, "means that I must reach out to the people of Northern Ireland." Being a Catholic married to a Protestant can only help. She is the first of Ireland's presidents ever to visit Britain officially and the first to see that Ireland can be a bridge between a rapidly evolving European Economic Community and the United States. She has fought for homosexual rights, winning the case at the European Court of Human Rights. Up to that point homosexuality had been a crime in Ireland. This remarkable woman is a brilliant lawyer. At twenty-five she was the youngest person ever to be appointed as law professor to Trinity College, Dublin. She is a beacon of light on the horizon, a liberated but sober voice, reminding all women that we "must ensure that the whole movement of feminism is not narrow and exclusive, for if we as feminists don't value the career of child-rearing and homemaking, how is society going to value them?" So she is working for change within. She herself comes from a family of "equal opportunity," a family free of conventional sex roles where she and her four brothers shared family chores, cooking included. Both of her parents were doctors and practiced together before they had children, when the mother gave up her profession. But Mary and her husband Nicholas have three children and both are going full-steam-ahead. He is very supportive of her and is himself deeply involved as chairman of the Architectural Archives, dedicated to preserving old Anglo-Irish mansions and even the storefronts of entire villages.

It is extremely fortunate for American women to have such a role model to observe and learn from, just as President Robinson claims she has learned from us while earning a degree at Harvard in 1969. Even those of us who are too old for active participation can help the process by expanding our point of view and by encouraging younger people or grandchildren to enlarge their outlook to encompass our global world. The prominence of a woman like Mary Robinson is helping to turn that vast concept into a tangible reality.

Though not usually so considered, I think that the later period in a woman's life is one of the very best. Today it is not uncommon to hear of a woman over sixty taking up a new career or having a resurgence of youthful energy. "Isn't it amazing," a man friend said to me recently. "Since my father died my mother, who is seventy-six, is kicking up her heels like a spring chicken, taking trips, doing new things, even dancing. She's like a different person." Aside from the fact that chickens don't kick up their heels even in spring, it is less amazing than he believes. Rather than his mother being a phenomenon, I suspect that she might represent one of a growing thirty percent or so of single older American women, widowed or not, who are ready to change their lives, to become actively involved in something new. They have fulfilled their apprenticeship and are free to focus on their own needs. There is time now, and often along with it comes a desire for a new sense of exploration in fields which necessarily had to remain dormant through child-bearing and child-rearing years. Being a wife and a mother is a demanding, important, constantly changing job which, because of its complexities is good training as preparation for other fields.

It is my belief that at this time in a woman's life a great deal of new energy can be at her disposal, post-menopausal energy. The vital support system for the foetus is no longer needed or operative. What happens to that life force? Does it just wither away, or is there an alternative? We know that nothing in nature is wasted. Is there biological energy which is no longer tied up by the body's needs now freed to be used by the woman in other ways? It seems there can be, as I saw there was in my own life. It's an energy which is new in many ways; sexually, certainly, minus the fear of pregnancy. It was then that I had my first extra-marital affair with a man twenty five years my junior. It was then that I developed a different point of view which let me think about myself for myself rather than about myself for the family. I gained a whole new sense of freedom. I began building up the emotional energy which allowed me to make an entirely new life in a new place, living alone and doing new work that was closer to my real feelings. I started painting more self-portraits, revealing ones, wanting to show who I was. I began to find a new phase of life that I had not been told about, that I had not expected and that perhaps not many women were focusing on. I knew only that it seemed real and reassuring to me. I just observed my own experience and don't claim to state a clinical reality – only, for me, a functioning one. In a general sense I realized that this post-menopausal period was an increasingly important time in our lives since we are all living for extended periods now, and especially as women are outliving men. This relatively new phenomenon partially explains why women are increasingly wielding more power and undertaking wider responsibilities beyond the family. We are getting time to live our own lives; infusing feminine values into our culture which have been absent for centuries.

Though young girls mature more quickly than do young boys, men peak sexually earlier than women, roughly twenty compared to forty, and women's psychic cycle develops later than men's and differently. Postmenopausal mid-life is a time when a woman is coming into her prime. Able to use her abilities unencumbered, she brings in a much-needed, different language. It's a time of great involvement for her and an effective one for society as a whole. There is a lot of good living left for her to do and an enormous amount for her to give. Essentially too, it is a time which is conducive to men and women's being able to work together more equitably, to establish a different kind of work ethic where the feminine plays a vital role to the end that as a well-rounded culture we would be utilizing our full potential.

To quote Isak Dinesen, "Women when they are old enough to have done with the business of being women and can let loose their strength must be the most powerful creatures in the world."

In our current American culture the male ego is often so fragile that it must be upheld by the female in the manner to which he has become accustomed. We have gone astray and allowed wrong elements into sacred places. We women want to be ourselves, to act and love directly. We want to believe that men want that of us as well as of themselves. We are not giving enough credence to the glory of our differences. They are more than the spice of life, they are also the meat and potatoes. There is no question but that women will become more and more involved in the managing of the world, not as an infringement on man's terrain, limiting his vital contribution, but as an added power, given from her own different province, supplementing his views with her female insight and compassion. I believe that most women do not want the ultimate power but would prefer working along with men, meeting as one of two opposite entities each giving what is theirs to give for the profound purpose of healing the planet together and ourselves in the process.

> "For the Lord himself being asked by someone when his Kingdom shall come, said, 'When the two should be one and the outside (that which is without) as the inside (that which is within) are the male with the female, neither male nor female'"
> — *from the Apocryphal Gospel of the Egyptian.*

I don't know how many of the Trinity Church congregation would agree with this text. I suspect a great many.

16. DIVORCE

"If we love enough, we almost understand"
— *Pauline Hanson*

My husband had been so successful in one-upmanship gambits during our marriage and long separation that he doubtless thought he was home safe. When he finally received the letter from the divorce lawyer, the shock must have been truly horrendous. All my friends and several members of my family advised me strongly against taking such a step. "What's the point now?" they said. "You've waited until you are seventy-five and you haven't even lived with him for the last twenty years. What do you think will be changed by a divorce now, beyond creating a lot of pain?" They also pointed out that he had suffered from lung cancer and had emphysema. The shock of a proposed divorce might kill him. Rationally, of course, there was no answer to these comments. But I was now in a different place.

In 1977, when a friend pointed out to me that I was not taking responsibility for my own competence and power or, in other words, that I was the negligent one, an idea was put into my head which caused me to review my life from a different standpoint and remove the inhibition towards action. Once I understood this shift of responsibility, the door that had been sealed tight since Whitney's death stood ajar again and I saw the possibility of pushing it wider open. The observation may have been something that was evident to many people, but to me it was a revelation. I had never thought of myself as the powerful one in our relationship, the one setting the tone of the marriage. But once I had allowed the idea to sink in, its validity became apparent and I had no hesitation about proceeding with the divorce. Although I felt that a new opportunity had suddenly opened before me, in reality nothing had changed in our marital situation in the last twenty-one years. What had changed was my point of view. Pat had not lived up to our separation agreement that we accept each other's individual liberty. He had also increased his psychological pressure on me to an untenable extent. From the house that he had built for himself, a few miles from my house in Canada, he kept tabs on me and closely involved with my family and our friends, putting me in an awkward position with my own relatives. He entwined his life with mine more and more insidiously and acrimoniously so that I would only go to Chouette for a few weeks a summer and never without house guests as foils. I came to dread those summer visits, much as I loved Chouette and enjoyed working on it once I was there. In essence he deprived me of summers in my own house.

I knew that I had tried, almost beyond my endurance, to make the marriage a pleasant one. I had failed and Pat's deep anger was increasingly targeted in my direction. At age seventy-five I was finally able to see the opening that might clear the decks and bring in fresh air for everyone. I was making into a reality something I had been talking and thinking about on and off for forty-five years. Now it was high time to carry it out. I would certainly have done Pat and myself a service had I been able to send the divorce letter thirty years earlier, but I had not. As Lex said in answer to his father's query, "Finally she's cleaning up her act and I think it's good." Even though we had not lived together for twenty-one years, it took two years to get the divorce. Quite naturally Pat was stunned. How had I dared? That must have been the unanswerable and most difficult question.

Since it was clear that both Pat and I were going to leave everything to our children, the division of property would only be for a brief time. Nevertheless there was terrible bitterness, anger, and emotion. Divorce is a horror that transcends reason and turns decent humans into misers. "You took away your love, I'll take away the candelabra, all the silver and everything I can lay my hands on." The scale swings between the strong but weightless feelings of the heart and the deadweight of worldly goods. Its a sad transaction no matter how played out, but late and imperfect as ours was, it still proved therapeutic for all of us.

I had finally been honest to myself and to others and was pleased that I had succeeded in carrying out the divorce. I also knew that I had a great distance to go before becoming an integrated, whole person. For so many years I had trained myself to live by a double standard that to come to know my real self would be hard work.

Only as time went on did I realize I had spent most of my adult life trying to solve an unsolvable equation, due in large part to my exaggerated sense of misplaced responsibility, guilt and an obtuseness and stubbornness about recognizing and accepting reality. I had also spent too long reliving many hurtful episodes. Although Black Elk is right when he says, "I did not have to remember all these things, they remembered themselves all these years," I am happy to say that now the agonizing incidents no longer hurt as they once did, for they have been amalgamated into the past.

There is one anecdote from this time which is perhaps symbolic. In our kitchen at Chouette there is a long, low windowsill above the kitchen table. Placed on it for the last fifty years has been a very beautiful, large, wooden, Louis XVI, elaborately carved clock, standing about two-and-a-half-feet tall. Pat's mother had it made in Paris at the beginning of the century, copied from one in the Louvre. Its incongruity in the kitchen always pleased both of us. People used to say, "If you want to give the Morgans a present, give them something that can be used for what it's not meant for."

The clock had become the central symbol of our family life. At the time of the divorce, Pat came into the kitchen one day, intending to take the clock. Helène, by then our cook of forty-five years, looked at him horrified and said, "You can't take away my clock." "Oh, yes I can," said Pat, picking it up and walking out the door. "Well," she said, "it will never work for you."

It was an idiosyncratic clock. It needed a penny under its right foot and had to be wound on an intuitive schedule known only to Helène; then it kept perfect time. Pat installed the clock in his new house, but no matter how many pennies he put under either or both feet, or what intricate schedule he devised to wind it, the clock never ticked again.

When I moved to Cambridge and was living alone, my two children gave me a seventieth birthday party in my studio at Notre Dame de la Pitié. Fifteen years later people still talk about it. I had three studios on the third floor. One I rented to my good friend Carol Rankin, the photographer. The second was my own, and the third I needed as an extra for its thirty-foot painting wall. I was working on my big 'Seasons' then, two of whose panels measured thirty feet each. Lex and Vic and others transformed Carol's studio into a perfect imitation of a Paris café in winter, striped awning over little round marble topped tables. All it lacked were the small heaters used against the Paris chill. Sally Scoville provided superb food; beverages flowed. The studio with the thirty foot painting wall was taken over by the wildly vibrating music of the North Star Jets Phase Two steel band. Several hundred people were there dressed in jeans or tuxedos. The unusual mix of people and ages, the intensity and quality of the music and dancing enhanced the elated feeling of joyous surprise which lasted through the whole evening. Somehow it was an out-of-this world occasion. Recently a friend spoke about the party. She said a man had come up to her and said, "If you were walking down a straight garden path and at the end one path led to the right and one path to the left, which one would you take?" She answered, "You must be Maud's husband."

Pat's nature in relation to people was a complex mix. In relation to plants, it was simplicity itself – always at home, very sure and in harmony. I have walked through the woods with him when he heard a bird make a certain cry, realized there was trouble, go towards the sound, find the nest from which a baby bird had fallen to earth, pick it up and put it back in its nest. This was the world in which he was magical, backing up real botanical knowledge with his deep love for growing things. He took enormous pleasure in seducing plants to grow further north than their normal habitat, and had a gut knowledge about what you could dig up in the woods and place in some precise spot where it would continue to grow without realizing that it had been moved from its original home.

In August 1989, after Pat's death, I visited Lex in Pat's former house, which now belongs to our children. It goes by the name "Cache-Cache", French for "Hide and Go Seek", a concept dear to Pat's heart which he tried to induce in every way throughout his life. He did so with particular success in his romantic garden. There, some of the secret little paths lined with flourishing mounds of maiden hair ferns lead no where but back into native forest. Others turn and twist over rivulets running through narrow rock passages traversed by stone bridges, or stepping stones midstream, or contrived waterfalls which betray no human hand, opening upon beautiful quiet pools with Japanese iris growing between large flat boulders. Great slabs of bedrock which he laboriously freed of green growth are its structural bones.

Inevitably one thinks of the evanescence of a garden, its temporary quality being in some ways its greatest allure. Leave it untouched for even half a season and it demands attention; clipping, pruning, weeding, but leave it unattended for a year or two and it's a tangled jungle. Does this matter? Doesn't the joy of a garden come from the work put into it and from the momentary beauty which repays that work? I was thinking of the comparison to the work put into a painting. There, if one has succeeded, its quality can remain long after the work has been completed, but that, too, is subject to the threat of death, by hanging on someone's walls where it is never looked at, or sold to a museum, which stores it a subterranean vault, or simply dying naturally because the life-spark of creative energy put into it at its inception had not been strong enough to keep it alive through generations of changing taste. But with both the garden and the painting, what is important is the thrust of constructive work invested by the artist or the gardener without thought of the future, that energy which is one's own salvation, as well as the life force of the created object. It was wonderful that Pat built himself a place and a garden that he loved in Canada. His deepest and most sustaining attachment throughout his life was, I think, to plants.

Pat's garden, when he was alive to labor on it daily and care for the many unusual plants that are scattered throughout, each one holding a special part of his love, was an exquisite thing. Though now its surface is a tangle, the structure is still there, as is the spot he prepared for his ashes, which lie under a cedar tree with a small head stone on which is carved a saying of Colette's, *"Ici git Patrick Morgan et les débris d'un rêve" (Here lies Patrick Morgan and the shards of a dream)*.

But Pat's true and lasting achievement was Chouette, Chouette which he dreamed of and planned for from the start, and on which he worked for most of his life. Now sixty years later Chouette still holds the contained beauty and indefinable seduction that has always captivated and nurtured the people who knew it. I take pleasure in seeing these qualities expand to include a younger generation in the same enriching way, and delight in the fact that it will now belong to my great-nephew Colin and his children.

Separating from Pat after our European sabbatical had given me the immediate freedom that I had needed for many years, the liberty of living alone, of being responsible for myself, of overcoming the shyness, of walking into a party as a single woman and the freedom to have exhilarating and rewarding sexual experiences. But the divorce gave me something deeper, a liberty of my soul. Hedging was no longer possible. This was the real challenge.

After Pat's death in 1982, Lex moved into his father's house for the summer months. He and Vicky are now co-owners. It's hard for her to get there and her husband John is almost never free to go, however Vic and I usually pay Lex a short visit every year. We both love it, and when she is there she joins Lex in working on the house and place as he always does. They are each skilled in carpentry as well as many other trades and the house is flourishing under their hands. They have not been able to keep up Pat's garden, but Lex had a different idea when he saw a few wild lupines growing nearby. Every year he has collected the seed after the tall, beautiful flowers begin to wilt, and now in July the house floats on a vast bedspread of solid blue. At various spots in the more distant fields he has planted more lupine in large patches, which stand out like strong cobalt brush strokes against the light green of the meadow or the dark green of an occasional spruce tree. Frequently people stop, asking if they may photograph their children in this fairyland. Being with both my children is one of my greatest pleasures and each year we all seem to get closer. I have the satisfaction of feeling that age helps towards my better understanding of them, as well as of myself, and makes me a more attentive listener. We are all growing together.

17. AFRICA

"You and the other are one"
— *Joseph Campbell*

"Sequence is a fiction in human life", writes Jerome Bruner in *Knowing, Essays for the Left Hand*. "What follows may precede what went before. It is difficult to know who you are until you feel what you do." Only in Heaven itself could a project have been planned more suited to my needs than my six-month trip alone to Africa at age seventy-seven, one month after my divorce was finalized.

On departure I was serious and fully aware of the difficulties and risks ahead. At a farewell party a friend asked, "Do you realize that you may die on this trip?" "Yes, I do," I said. But at the same time I felt young, strong, virginal, and free. I was deeply involved in beginning a new phase of my life. To this day I am unable to understand how, in spite of my having lived a rewarding life on my own for twenty-three years after separating from my husband, he had still been able to exert such a negative psychological influence on me. The existence of the divorce paper eliminated that fear at once and forever. In Africa I would observe who I was by what I did. Often what I did astonished me, judged not by its rightness or wrongness, but by its unexpectedness or effectiveness. Flying from Boston and landing in Africa is in itself an exciting shock. I came down in Dar es Salaam, Tanzania, and visited friends stationed there. This time was delightful and gave me a period of security and comfort in which to let Africa sink in a bit before taking off alone into such a different world.

For me Africa was a fantasy fulfilled. I had wanted to go there for over forty years. Before I went people said, "If you really let Africa get to you, you are never the same again." I let it get to me.

It is difficult to write about Africa because it is magical.

Africa overpowered me. Although the wild animals are fascinating to watch and interesting to study and the land as beautiful as any anywhere, the African people themselves most captivated me. The stately way the women stand, as in many cultures where the women habitually carry loads on their heads, and how these women tie an ordinary piece of cloth around their bodies and an unexpectedly different piece of cloth around their heads is an eye-opening lesson in sensuous design, learned by them from their tropical birds. The jewelry they make with the round bottoms of tin cans or with the left over parts of inner tubes or worn-out shoe soles is the essence of invention.

Wherever you go you feel the mystery of Africa. Why should I, a single, old, white woman feel so completely at home there where every other face is black? Why did they accept my presence without question and disregard it?

I cannot answer the "whys" of Africa. There are too many. Its secret is deeper than skin, deeper than custom, deeper than history. When I was there, I was at home and very conscious of being a part of the human race.

Africa inspires generic love.

Like most first time visitors I took safaris to game parks in several countries. The first and the best was a small trip organized by the American Ambassador Richard Viet to the Selous Reservation in Southern Tanzania, a long drive down from Dar. The Selous is comparatively unfrequented compared to the better known Kenyan reservations. Our party of four stayed in a delightful, simple camp run by a German who had spent his life in Africa. We were the only guests. It was a perfect camp, individual tents and an open air shower with water from a gasoline drum. We could hear the hippos grunting in the river below as we sponged our bodies or as we lay in our tents before going to sleep. Once when we were walking in an area where the jungle gave way to beautiful, open fields reminiscent of an English countryside, we were suddenly stopped short by a large herd of impala, beautiful deer-like creatures bounding gracefully across our path and on through the trees. One young one lingered behind the pack. He leapt over low branches and jumped over high ones, bouncing around and around, circling the open space, doing a dance for his own delight and seemingly showing off for ours. One thought of Nijinsky. Another evening at sundown, moving silently and smoothly along the river where the hippos lived, our boat floated beneath a ledge of land about ten feet above our heads. As I raised my eyes to the ledge I saw a lion sitting there quietly. His majestic silence made me catch my breath. From his Sphinx-like pedestal, slowly turning his dignified head away then back to look again, he deigned to observe us mortals. Later when his musing was over he loped off through the underbrush.

Once I met a giraffe when we were visiting a neighboring camp. The rest of the group went indoors but I wanted to be by myself for a while. I was alone, as he was, when I first encountered him with about fifty feet between us. Our eyes met. I stayed totally quiet, not shifting my gaze, nor he his. Then very, very slowly I moved towards him. I had read that if annoyed a giraffe can raise one leg and strike a person dead. We never lost eye contact and I knew he would not harm me as long as I could hold that contact. I had a tremendous urge to get close to him, to get near enough to touch him. I could almost anticipate the feel of his slightly harsh hair against my fingers. Slowly, very slowly, I kept approaching. He never shifted his gaze nor I mine. I was elated by an extraordinary joy which overtook my body. I prayed that the people who had gone into the camp would not come out, but alas they did. At the sound of them his long legs started to move him away in a slow lope and his endlessly long neck, with its imperious little head, swung into accompanying rhythmic motion. The magic moment was over, but I can still feel the awe of that encounter.

～

My most exciting adventure in Kenya was a week-long trip to Lake Turkana and the Jade Sea. We travelled in two old German army trucks with wooden planks placed lengthwise for seats. Each bus held about twenty people. Starting north from Nairobi we stopped every night at a different place, each with its own climate. We put up our pup tents before making the fire to cook supper. When we left Nairobi the temperature was seventy-five degrees but by nightfall we had climbed so high that even though I kept on all my clothes inside my sleeping bag, plus putting my towel on top for added weight, I shivered all night. The next day we came back down into the very hot Horr Valley. We camped with the Sambura tribe, an offshoot of the Masai who had parted from the main group due to some alleged cattle thefts. They were a peaceful tribe except if cattle were stolen, when, as our driver told us, they became extremely fierce. Beautiful young Sambura warriors, probably about eighteen years old, led us up a steep mountain path to a waterfall. Observing us as we swam, they stood around in arresting postures, their black skin shining against the diagonals painted in red earth on their backs, cheeks, and foreheads. Their hair, sticky with red mud, fell to their shoulders in long locks and was held out over their eyes on a leather visor fastened by a thong strapped across their bangs. They were a staggering personification of the vigor of masculine youth. As we swam three of them sat on a high rock above us, singing. I gave them an old brown shirt of Lex's that I was wearing. They loved it, argued over it and we all laughed a lot. They didn't want to be photographed but I did take a beautiful shot of two of them from the rear, their strong backs cross-hatched in red, and then found I had forgotten to take the shutter off the lens.

The young warriors suggested taking us up to Mount Na, a rain forest full of marvellous animals where their god lives and where watches stop. It would be a four hour climb. Unfortunately our group had to move on so we couldn't go.

We went to many extraordinary places on that trip, which was known to be rough and hard. The management was hesitant to accept me because of my age, but I managed as well as any and better than most, suffering only from one scorpion bite. As I emerged from my tent one morning, the young man in the next tent said, "Maud, I just saw a scorpion come out of your tent. I think it was a grey one. It's the black ones that are fatal." I had felt nothing up to that moment, but five minutes later there was a sharp pain in my rear which lasted for several months. Fortunately for me, my young friend saw correctly, the scorpion must have been grey.

On the trip I met Bob Lang, a Canadian film maker who had previously made a documentary for CBS in Ghana on the funeral of the last king of the Ashanti. We teamed up to go to Ethiopia. He was a wonderful traveling companion with whom I still keep in touch.

My first impression on reaching Ethiopia was of the beauty and graciousness of its people. Walking along the streets of Addis Ababa, one passed one person after another of strikingly beautiful, dignified bearing: old men, young women, children, all of them. It seemed strangely incongruous and almost surrealistic to find a dominating statue of Lenin at the end of the same street.

Unfortunately my permit to go to Lalibela was granted only after Bob had to leave me. Lalibela must be one of the most amazing small towns in the world. Its roots go back to the first century AD when the ruler of the Aksum people, King Ezana, was converted to Christianity in 314. Under him a notable civilization developed. Tradition has it that the Ark of the Covenant was brought there by the son of King Solomon and the Queen of Sheba.

This ancient mountainous town was the seat in the twelfth and thirteenth centuries of a burst of rock-church building under King Lalibela. Some of these were razed by fanatic Moslems in the sixteenth century but eleven of them are still standing and in use in the town itself. These churches are cut directly into the rock. They are below the surface of the ground, carved inside and out from the rock to look as though they had been constructed from the ground up. As one approaches Bet Giorgis, the first thing one sees is its flat rooftop at ground level with a large, raised cross carved upon it, following the shape of the church. The open space that surrounds it has all been cut away. One looks down at the church itself, a free-standing monolith with interior aisles, bays and windows, all below ground. Nothing is built up; everything is cut down directly out of the solid rock. The concept staggers the imagination. Some of the other churches are not free-standing but only show a curved facade, a portal through which one enters to find a completed church inside, invisible from the outside. These rich ecclesiastical treasures and the priests who serve in them express all that is most fascinating about the Ethiopian Middle Ages. The churches continued to be built through the fifteenth century and there are still one hundred and thirty rock churches in use in the Tigre area.

There are no seats in these churches. The priests have tall, crutch-like, canes with curved metal tops to use for support in one's armpit, under one's chin or simply to rest one's hand on. We were given two, which made me feel very much accepted.

My time in Lalibela was all too short in spite of being given two unexpected days due to airplane re-scheduling. It was the end of my time in East Africa. By now I was anxious to get to West Africa where, for some reason, I felt my real challenge and adventure would be.

~

I landed in Douala, Cameroon, where I stayed for ten days, living at the Procure Generale des Missions Catholique, a delightful center for French Catholic priests who took in six or seven guests. I had heard about it from a young American on the Turkana trip. One could sign up and pay ahead for excellent, simple, ample French meals, served on long tables. This gave me a chance to eavesdrop on the tales the Brothers would recount to each other about situations out in the countryside as they came and went to their various mission stations. Sometimes I was included in the conversation of these gossiping monks. This place was an oasis, a welcome refuge providing a clean bed and shower room and, wondrously, a swimming pool, a welcome asset in weather above 100°. This time was a wonderful and safe hiatus for me.

My plan was to travel into northern Cameroon and from there by bus into northern Nigeria. Bob Lang had been very apprehensive about my going to southern Nigeria. Lagos, the capital, was considered very dangerous. He said that, as a somewhat absent-minded, old, obviously American tourist, I would almost certainly be robbed or even killed there. It sounded terrifying. The daily paper published the number of people killed on the streets by having a tire put over their shoulders, gasoline poured on them and ignited. The numbers ran in the thirties each day. But by coming into the country from the north and avoiding Lagos, Bob thought I would probably be all right.

When I left Douala going north I traveled through the beautiful mountain country of northern Cameroon towards Mokalo by bus. We drove through places that are unbelievable except as fairy tales. In long,

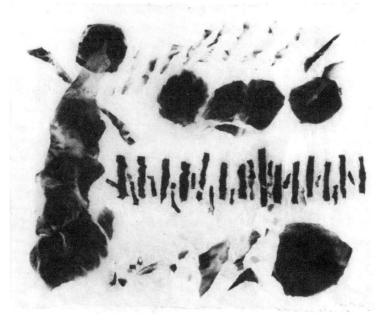

Blue Collage #43 (1975), 22 x 26 ½ in.

beautiful, soft, hazy valleys great shafts of flat-topped rock pyramids arise suddenly from the plain like fountains. On the lesser heights dirt houses cling to the slopes in camouflaged clusters of hanging villages hard to recognize as habitable. These are the Kapsidi Mountains inhabited by the Kirdi people. Mokalo seemed like a good central place from which to make excursions. On one such excursion I took a truck trip to Rimsiki. It gave me a fascinating and unexpected experience.

I was sitting on a sack of onions resting my back against the cab, always the most sought-after position. A handsome young man in a shell pink robe and a white Mohammedan hat came to sit beside me. As I turned to observe him more closely I caught my breath. His face was scarified with striations in concentric grooves from his temples over his cheek bones and down to the jaw bone, exactly as in the early Nok sculptures. I was struck by how much his beauty seemed to be enhanced by the scarification. Seeing these markings on a living person for the first and only time, I suddenly understood the early sculptures as I never had before. A concept of African beauty that had eluded me became clear.

I had almost no money left when I finally boarded the bus for Maiduguri, Nigeria. The Campement, or inn, in Mokalo had been more expensive than anticipated. I hoped to change an American Express check at the border even though it was Sunday. We reached the border in the late afternoon. There was only a small fruit stand with one vendor to whom I expressed my dismay and asked for advice. "Go to such and such a hotel," he said. "Say I sent you and that you will cash a check at the bank on Monday morning and pay him back." This sounded promising. Arriving at Maiduguri, I took a taxi but became apprehensive about my funds. The hotel seemed unduly far away and the fare was mounting. On arrival I had only exactly enough to pay the fare, no tip. The driver was annoyed, unloaded my bags and left. The owner came out and flatly refused to take me in without money – French money. My only cash was a five dollar American bill which I offered him but he wouldn't touch. He was disagreeable and curt. Was there anywhere I could cash a check? He suggested the Customs House, indicating its direction. I asked if I could use the bathroom in his hotel before going. The answer was a flat no. I was beginning to be concerned about having come to Nigeria. I started to walk towards the Customs House. It was about 100° F. The high road was jammed with bustling people. My anxiety about my lack of funds was now compounded by my anxiety about finding a toilet. Opposite the Customs House there was a hotel. The door was open. I went in hopefully. No one was around so I rushed down a corridor, and luckily found a bathroom which, contrary to custom, was not locked. This removed one of my problems.

On coming out I ran into the angry owner who asked me what I was doing there. "Looking for you," I said. "I'd like to take a room here." "We have no free rooms, and in no case, none for people like you." I left secretly grateful. Now to try my luck at the Customs. The building stood in a very large shady courtyard surrounded by a high iron fence. Two men were chatting in the shade of a spreading tree. I joined them, telling them my problem and saying I wanted to borrow some money. "And what do you want us to do?" they said. "We have no money." At least they were nicer than my two previous contacts in Maiduguri. I didn't want to stop talking to them as I had no idea where to go or what to do next. Finally I just said what I was thinking, "I am very tired and I haven't had any breakfast or lunch." To my delight one of the men handed me a few coins and said, "Here, cross the street and buy a Coke." That Coke tasted like champagne. I felt made over.

When I returned to my acquaintances under the tree, they had been joined by a large fat man dressed in a long, elaborately embroidered garment and hat who was sitting astride a huge felled tree trunk. He examined me as I approached. For some reason, which surprised me as much as it must have him, I came up quite close to him, put my leg across the wide tree trunk and sat facing him, also astride. We started to talk. Quite suddenly he asked me if I could ride a bicycle. "Yes," I said. "You won't fall off the back?" he asked. "No. Do you mean a motorcycle?" Yes, he did. He summoned a boy who went to fetch a motorcycle and rode up to us. The fat man in the embroidered clothes told me to get on the back. We started off into the dense Sunday traffic. Every chauffeur in Maiduguri seemed to establish his ownership by blowing his horn and then speeding up. We whirled in and out of these noisy vehicles. I hung on as firmly as I could to the boy driver. Finally we stopped at a rundown place in front of which a filthy man lolled in a deck chair. The boy spoke to the man, went into the house and, after a short while, emerged, jumped on the motorcycle, and we were off again. He took me back to the fat man who spoke to the boy and then told me to follow him. He led me to quite an elegant car, told me to get in, and asked me if I'd like anything. "I'd love a cup of tea," I said. I knew that was asking a lot as tea is scarce. He was kindness itself as he drove me from one little restaurant to another asking to see if they had tea. We must have gone to five or six before being successful. There we got out and sat down at a sidewalk table to which was brought the cup of tea I had asked for and a roll. My enjoyment must have been evident. We were beginning to like each other.

Then he took me back to the filthy house with the filthy proprietor whom he said was his great friend. He went in. When he emerged he said, with a strange look on his face, that there was a room that I should look at. I went in. The room had no window, and the light didn't work, though they said it would later. There was an excessively grubby bed covered by an unpleasantly dirty sheet, and a large hole in the wall near the floor about four feet square which looked black and ominous and led Heaven-knows-where. When I came out, after a hesitation, the fat man asked me if it would do. He was noticeably relieved when I said it was just fine. He paid for the room and, happy day, gave me enough extra for a beer. I wrote down his name, said I would return the money the next morning at the Customs House, thanked him and said good bye. I had not dared to risk my luck and refuse the room, fearing I might be left with no place whatsoever off the street. So I calculated the time before it would get dark in order to space the best moment to buy my bottle of beer. With care I could spread its consumption to a half an hour before I would have to go into the horrible room. I didn't feel safe in that city and didn't dare stay on the street after dark.

When I came back in, the light was on in the room, but not for long. One only had electricity when the town allowed it. I had a little flashlight but didn't want to risk using up the battery unless necessary. Luckily I had a large handkerchief in my pocket on which I could rest my head, I hoped my clothes would protect me somewhat from the fleas. I wanted to save the battery in case there were rats. I'm frightened of rats but if there were rats I'd rather see them than not know where they were. The lock on the door was reassuring. I was disciplining myself to remain calm, not to question where the black hole in the wall led nor what might come out of it, nor to become too disturbed by the increasing noise in the hall. People were running up and down, men and women screaming at each other. I tried to envisage these yelling people as I gained comfort from the fact that no one, in this obviously low-class brothel, had tried to get into my room. Since I knew the night would be long, I invented games to trick myself, only letting myself look at my watch every fifteen minutes, flashing on my flashlight briefly only every half hour. The shouts and chasing went on in the hall until the very small hours of the morning. Six o'clock was the time I had decided upon as the earliest safe time to go out into the street. To wait from 9:00 PM to 6:00 AM was a long discipline, but the time finally did come to an end. I left the building and walked slowly to the other part of town where I found an impressive bank building on whose steps I gratefully sat until ten. After getting some money, I found a sidewalk café and enjoyed a coffee and a roll, and reflected on my horrendous night. One might not think of such a night as a salvation but under the circumstances I think it probably was. My big, fat friend in the embroidered costume had saved me from something that could have been far worse, for after all, here I was having coffee and a roll, frazzled and exhausted but alive and intact. As soon as I had refunded my debt at the Customs House and collected my bags at the hotel, I went to the bus station and bought a ticket to Kano. I wanted to get out of town. I had totally forgotten the remark of the charming Canadian ambassador, Hugh Vernon Jackson, whom I had met in Addis. He had said, "Above all don't go to Kano. They've just killed fifty people there."

When I got off the bus all was calm, and I went to a mission house that had been recommended to me by a man I met on the bus. There I was welcomed by born-again Christians and given a room and access to a clean bathroom. I washed everything that had been with me in the brothel and had a pleasant supper and a wonderful sleep. I stayed there for five days. Although I am not a born-again Christian they accepted me graciously into their simple, pleasant surroundings.

I can again feel the immediacy of that challenge and the very real fear I experienced when I write the story of my night in Maiduguri. It is hard to imagine living through that experience again, because now I would not allow myself to be in such a position. Self-protection would have prevented it. I see that I must have needed the challenge, not only of that night, but of the entire trip. To stack myself up against the unknown entity of Africa for six months alone indicates as much. Of course I had done my homework before leaving Cambridge. I had an itinerary written in my little black book with names of places and people to look up. (I vowed from the start that I wouldn't stay in any American-style hotel.) But as fate decreed, on my second day in Kenya the little black book with all its wisdom and security had been stolen, along with my glasses. Fortunately I had a second pair of glasses, but I was not a sufficiently knowledgeable traveler to have made a copy of my address book. The loss had been stunning. I had to choose. Was this a bad omen that I should pay attention to and go home? Was it a signpost indicating I should change the kind of trip I would take and proceed? I went to African Heritage, a lovely shop in Nairobi, and had a particularly delicious lunch, bought myself a handsome African neck-lace and decided to go ahead with the trip. I wrote down as many names as I could remember and the general plan of travel and decided not to think of the little black book again. This gave me a different kind of trip than I had set out on but probably the kind of possibly dangerous trip I really wanted. I was single again and doubtless needed to prove myself to myself. Whatever shaped the final form, my African trip was one of the best moves I ever made in my life and I was blessed to have made it at the last possible moment when I still had the physical strength to survive.

When I reached Ghana I was told that I should see the lovely sea-port town of Cape Coast. It was the last bus stop and had the pleasant feeling of being so. It was a charming, quiet, coastal town where in every little street one felt the sea, even though one might not see it. I looked around for a place to get some information and went into what appeared to be the only store in town. A well-upholstered, handsome, self-possessed woman was sitting behind the desk, sipping a trans-parent liquid from the glass she held. We engaged in conversation. She told me that the house next door was a hotel but there were no free rooms, nor any other hotels. She was positive, intelligent, and easy to talk to, definitely an attractive woman with a pleasant smile. When I inquired I discovered that she was drinking gin, which surprised me at first but then seemed to be an appropriate thing to be doing. She owned the store and she had to be there even though its shelves were empty. This woman was Ottelia Ackon-Mensah, who originally organized and had been for many years the head of the Woman's Police Force of Cape Coast as well as the owner of its only store. On her empty shelves just two objects were displayed: a quart of gin and a very small can of mixed fruit from England. I bought the fruit and ate it, and three days later in departing I bought the bottle of gin for fifty dollars as a present in gratitude for the extreme hospitality this woman had shown me, taking me into her house, giving me her own bed for two nights, feeding me along with her numerous children, and taking me with her to church on Sunday morning to an unforgettable service. The brilliant sun from the courtyard shone part way up the church aisle as the impressive procession of big men (all well over six feet) slowly progressed towards the alter, chanting. They were dressed in calf-length black and white kentecloth garments, each of a different, dramatic design. Their chant repeated some key words over and over, coming finally to a crescendo, after which they took communion and sat down in the front pews. Certain things were said by the elder in the pulpit to which the audience responded in unison. One felt that these people lived their Christianity. No one stared at me or made me feel uncomfortable, as might have happened in a reverse situation among whites. Doubtless people asked Ottelia who I was and why I was there, but in no way did they make me feel ill at ease or cause me to ask myself if I was intruding. The hospitality was almost always like that in Africa. As I write this now, twelve years later, I have a lump in my throat and a wonderment in my heart at having been given the privilege of being accepted on such occasions. I was very interested in and talked a great deal with Ottelia and her oldest son, who wanted to come to study in America. Ottelia was black as the ace of spades, but her color was not enough to counteract the fact that her father had been a German. Despite her obvious abilities and many years of service, the town had recently decided that they must have an all-African police head and Ottelia was voted out of office. But her German blood showed in her capabilities and achievements. Next to her store she had a large house and garden, and it was clear from seeing her talking to other townspeople after church that she was an important member of the community. I was interested that in spite of her capabilities, non-African blood was considered such a drawback.

~

From the town of Ferkessedougou in the Ivory Coast I took a train to Ouadagoubou, Upper Volta. I remember walking about half a mile down a beautiful, wide, deserted road lined with huge trees. It was evening, yet I was totally without fear in this lovely and unfamiliar place, of whose whereabouts I was uncertain and whose name I was having difficulty in pronouncing. I just enjoyed the softness of the air and the peacefulness of the scene and felt a strange serenity at being there. The train took me to the bus stop. When I got there the crowd had already gathered so I hastily boarded. A very fat man came to sit beside me. He spread his large legs and placed a sizeable radio on one thigh which struck against my arm. I would have liked to change seats but it was already too late, all seats were taken. I was shocked to find that the seat I had chosen was at the place where the two boards which made up the backrest were held together by a protruding bolt. The bolt was at the exact spot where my back bone would rest if I leaned back. This was worse than the radio pushing against my arm. I would have to keep my back erect, away from the bolt, for the entire trip. Since I expected that to be approximately three hours, I thought I'd probably be OK. Opposite me were three other whites: Swedes, big men, well accoutered with an extra-large water bottle. I had only a small one with me; my larger one was in my bag strapped to the top of the bus. They were talking together eagerly, not anxious to speak to me. Despite this it seemed like a good idea to try to make contact, so in a lull in their conversation, I asked, "Am I right in thinking that this will be a three hour trip?" "Probably twenty-four," was the curt answer as the speaker turned away. I thought longingly of my water bottle on the roof and wondered if they would offer me some of theirs later. They certainly didn't seem friendly.

There was a long wait before the bus started, over an hour. One didn't dare leave one's seat. Outside a man was walking up and down alongside the bus selling beautifully woven straw hats. I bought one through the open window. I still wear it with pleasure thinking of Ouagadougou. There was trouble with the ignition. After endless discussions many men got together and pushed. We were off. An hour later we had a minor breakdown. Magically the driver and some of the passengers were able to fix it with a little wire and a lot of conversation. Everyone got back on and we were off again. The Swedes talked constantly and loudly. They were water experts going to confer with another water expert at Fada N'Gourma. Nine hours later we broke down for real. Everybody out.

I admire the African women on such occasions. They get out of the bus quietly, untie the baby from their backs, spread out the carrying cloth on the ground as a resting place for mother and child, sit down on it, and wait. There is a lot of waiting in Africa, but along with it a lot of patience, learned the hard way from childhood on. I don't remember in all my time there, traveling in fourteen different countries, hearing a baby cry. What I was most conscious of was the contentment of the babies everywhere. They reflect the security gained from constant, close physical contact with the mother during the vital early months in life. Strapped to the mother's back whether she is pounding makabo, acting as a store clerk, or striding along the highway with a bundle of six foot branches on her head, the baby is always within the mother's reach for a reassuring check-up pat. When that particular baby is superseded by the next, it is passed on, still as a back pack, to one of its older sisters. At least in 1980 the start in life for those African babies seemed more supportive than that received by many of their Western counterparts.

By now the Swedes were angry, complaining at the inconvenience, referring to the high price of the bus ticket and asserting that they would report it to the authorities. After a few months in Africa one is apt to think, "What authorities?" A half an hour later a miracle occurred – an open truck, in good condition and of fairly recent vintage came along the road, the only such vehicle I had seen in Upper Volta. Perhaps it belonged to the water expert whom the Swedes were en route to visit. At any rate they stopped the vehicle and after a short talk got in, all three of them squeezing into the front and only seat with the driver, putting their luggage in the back. They were about to set off when one of them called back to me saying I could get in the back if I wanted but they would not wait to have my bag unstrapped from the top of the bus. Without hesitation I got in, abandoning my bag. I felt it was my only choice.

When we reached Fada N'Gourma, the Swedish experts dropped me off and directed me to a Campement, a sort of rest house, not too far off. I walked over and came into an open room with a bar in one corner – very reassuring. "Was there a bedroom?" I asked the owner. "Yes, one." He showed it to me. It had no light or available water. I thought he was asking a big price. I refused and said I'd rather sit up in the bar all night. That, he said, was impossible as the bar would be closed. I often astonished myself when I heard myself making such decisions. Clearly there was no other place to sleep, and yet I automatically refused to take the room, as I felt something was being put over on me. This subjective reaction may have been totally erroneous. I often have trouble switching from one currency to another and may have calculated wrongly. Perhaps the room was reasonably priced and my arithmetic wacky. My children always tell me I have a lot of trouble with zeros. In order to change the subject, I asked the owner if he could give me a cup of tea. He didn't have any but called a little boy to show me where the market was. We walked over in the pleasant, cool darkness. Tea was scarce in many parts of Africa and I had no expectation of finding any. To my utter amazement and delight I saw three separate Lipton tea bags lying on a table piled with mechanical junk. I was ecstatic. I bought them and a cup of hot water was produced. It tasted deliciously good. The little boy left me and I walked slowly back through the soft night to the Campement. I stood for a while pondering what to do next while the owner started putting out the lights. My back was to the door when I heard an American voice saying, "Are you the woman who was on the bus that broke down? I am Ed Lochstampfer, the Episcopal missionary here. Would you like to come home with me for the night?" The Swedes must have alerted him, proving themselves kinder than they had seemed at first.

I was delighted. Never have I had such a welcome invitation.

The luxury of having a cool shower and a clean bed is still memorable. Around 2:00 AM Mrs. Lochstampfer woke me to say that the bus had been repaired and had reached Fada N'Gourma. I could continue with it if I chose. If not I would not get a refund, but they would get my bag down from the bus roof. The driver, she said, was dead drunk. I started to jump out of bed to go for my bag while there was still time, when she told me her husband would attend to that for me. Happily I went back to sleep, grateful to the missionaries, who had more than fulfilled their role. They had saved me, body and soul. Ed Lochstampfer left at 5:00 AM the next morning to go on some mission. I was never able to thank him for his kindness. In the morning Mrs. Lochstampfer gave me a delicious breakfast with muffins she had baked. As we were eating, a handsome young man knocked at the door. It was Béat Schneider, a doctor from Northern Ghana, one of only two doctors functioning in that country. He was from Holland, the other doctor from Germany. He joined us for breakfast. Mrs. Lochstampfer questioned him about his work and destination. He said he was en route to Niamey in Niger. I couldn't believe my luck, since that was my destination, too. He invited me to come along.

Driving with him was extremely interesting as he told me about his life and work. He had studied medicine in Holland with the intention of becoming a doctor in Africa. He was on a four-day vacation, his first in two years, and hoped to meet a friend in Niamey. We stopped for lunch by the roadside, where he chose delicious things to eat. When alone I had been hesitant about eating at roadstands (above all I didn't want to get sick while in Africa), but with him I knew all would be well. Several grateful patients came up to him as we were eating. When we arrived in Niamey he dropped me at the museum and went to secure a hotel room. He hoped to find his friend but failed, so we spent the evening and the next two days together. We were extremely congenial. He was an attractive, intelligent, pleasant man, 30-years-old. Like his name, Béat (meaning "blessed") he had a shining purity and zeal, a beautiful stranger.

As we parted, I suddenly realized that I had no money. He said he'd give me some. He raised the mattress on the bed and picked up the equivalent of seventy-five American dollars which he handed to me. I thanked him warmly and wrote down his address in order to return it. This took me a year to accomplish, as due to some technicality, he was obliged to bank in Upper Volta rather than Ghana, where he lived. The check was returned several times. After I got home I began to worry, fearing that I would not be able to repay him, but I had the pleasure of receiving several letters from him.

After giving me the money, he started to take me to my flight for Timbuktu, but his car gave out in the middle of the traffic. I tried to push it but had to give up as time was short. I jumped into a passing taxi and just made my plane. It was sad to leave Béat, we had had such a rewarding time together.

Oberstammheim, October 28th, 1981

Dear Maud!

Your letters are too intense, full of warmth, that I could not permit myself not to reply. There is the sun of september in your words, gentle and kind.

You have crossed this Africa in very courageous six months, you visited Legon and you didn't know how to use a bucket of water to wash down, you were impressed by this astonishing continent and its people. And at an american breakfast table in Fada N'Gourma we met and the other day in the early morning we said good-by and you pushed my car... (I had to buy a new battery, a complete wheel and in the end the gas-tank was leaking – no wonder I then got a terrible headache which only passed in the evening.

Peter Delahaye, my UNICEF friend, who I missed, has now come for a short holyday from Angola where he is working, over to Switzerland. So we climbed together a very high mountain in two days, 3071 m, with a superb view.)

In two days I will fly back to Bawku/Northern Ghana for another two year stay. My suitcases are packed, I've had beautiful three months holyday here in Switzerland and Holland, where I visited Van Gogh museum. But I'm longing to go back. I have friends there and patients.

I do not know if the money you sent me has reached yet, when I'm there, I will inform you.

All my best greetings, and che Dio ci benedica.
Béat Schneider

Bawku/Ghana, 29th May '8x
Dear Maud Morgan,
Saturday before Pentecost, we wait for new inspir-Holy Spirit-ation. I read some poems in the coolness of the very early morning, went to feed the chicken, drank a cup of coffee, was thinking backwards and forewards.

They called me at three in the night to the hospital for a prolonged and protracted labour and when I came back the watchman had just killed one of the big bushrats rushing around the house. Quickly he lit a fire, slaughtered and roasted the animal, very handy, very enthusiastic.

Africa is good.

Africa is tough.

Well, hunger, revolutionary times, we eat two times daily the same rice with nearly the same soup. (I like red wine and the Toscany). But I'm equally thrilled by real commitment, par un engagement vrai.

Dear Maud, I would probably enjoy seeing some of your collages. Faute de mieux, I imagine the spirit in them which I met one, two, three days. I got your money! Thank you.
Yours, Béat Schneider

Finally I was en route to the legendary Timbuktu. The plane held about twenty passengers. There were to be two stops, Gao and Timbuktu. We reached Gao and were told to get out since the plane would not go further. Gao's airport consisted of an empty corrugated tin shed. There was no one about. I enjoyed watching the Africans who debarked. They put their bundles on their heads and walked off in different directions, quickly becoming invisible, amalgamated into the desert. Four people were left standing there in the emptiness of the tin shed as the plane flew off. I later learned that someone important had been on board who wanted to go elsewhere, and had simply commandeered the plane. The four people left standing were one very black, affluent-looking man with a beautiful, younger café-au-lait woman, one pale blond, young, white male, and me. We realized that something had been put over on us, or to be precise, on the young man and me, for we found out that the black man had intended to debark at Gao. He had grown up there and was returning for the first time as an adult. He had made money and wanted to show off to his lady friend. He quickly told us that there were no taxis in Gao and that we must wait, hoping that a truck would pass by to give us a lift to the hotel in town, Hotel Latlantide. A truck finally came. The hotel had an attractive ambiance of better days, a slightly shabby Somerset Maugham quality. There was a large, well-used lobby, clearly the center of intrigues, alliances and rendez-vous. I priced a room. The blond young man, Brian Lindbergh from Australia, was doing the same thing. We both found them expensive. Of course one was conscious, as was the hotel keeper, that there wasn't another hotel for several hundred miles.

I was surprised to hear myself turn to Brian and ask if he would like to share a room. He accepted and we were shown into a large room with a single bed against each wall, a large window at the back and a screen behind which was a washstand. We'd probably make out satisfactorily. Relieved and somewhat tired I sat down on my bed. As I did so the tops of the two upholding metal ends started to come in towards me as their bases moved away. I jumped up, startled to find that the ends of the bed were held up by cement blocks which slipped the moment pressure was put on the mattress. I would certainly never be able to sleep with the apprehension that one active turn over in the night might mean being clobbered on the head by a cast iron bed end.

I laughed at the infeasibility of the whole thing. Brian and I had to invent a different solution. We succeeded delightfully. Every night Brian carried our mattresses up to the flat roof, where we slept through the delicious southern nights with brilliant stars overhead. It was perfect and nobody seemed to mind. For toiletries we were each given a pail of water a day. This had to do for washing oneself and one's clothes and flushing the toilet. For drinking there was beer. At first to have beer seemed wonderful since it had been unavailable in other places, but one's taste for beer diminishes rapidly when it is the only liquid available all day from brushing one's teeth onwards. Brian was an experienced traveler and one of the things he had with him were tea bags. Every night we looked forward to a cup of tea in lieu of a cocktail. We kept trying to persuade, cajole, or trick the waiter into giving us each two cups of hot water for our tea bags. We succeeded rarely. Water was scarce.

It became apparent that our time at the Hotel Latlantide would not be short. There were no airplanes scheduled, going anywhere. Cars were useless as there was no petrol in town. I checked out hitch-hiking on a lorry which sometimes came through en route to Mopti, Mali. This would involve three or four days sitting on top of the merchandise in the hot sun (the temperature was over a hundred) and carrying one's own food and water. I proclaimed, "No interest." I would stay in Gao and take my chances. Also I was becoming fascinated by our life. I had never before been in a place from which there was no exit. We constructed a routine life around simple things, like breezes. Usually at 6:00 PM there was a slight breeze coming from the back gate through to the front of the hotel. Everyone moved their porch chairs to take advantage of it. We'd line our chairs in a row in the path of the breeze, like musical chairs, first come, first served, in the hopes of being able to read without the sweat dripping onto the pages of the book. The evening cooled a bit and we'd walk to the ends of the various streets in the town until each just melted into desert sand. I had never lived in a real desert town before and I loved it. What an excellent time to write letters and postcards. When I took my stack of mail to the post office, the post mistress looked at the pile and said, "C'est fini." The stamps were sold out.

Once we were taken in a car by our airplane acquaintances, the black man and café-au-lait woman, to see the important sights. Gao was the ancient capital of the Songai Empire and has two important monuments which still stand just outside the town; the large and impressive mosque of Kakan Moussa and the tomb of Askia Moussa. Both are built of packed earth. The tomb completely captivated me. The rectangular building is made of long trees not more than six inches in diameter which form the structure. Onto these wet mud is packed and hardens. What is so beguiling is that the trees are left at their full length and protrude beyond the building, some long, some short, giving the effect of a sparsely bristled porcupine. Not only do trees jut out at different lengths but each also follows its natural bend. There is a feeling of vitality and life throughout the whole structure, a delightful lightness, especially for a tomb.

Finally it was announced that a plane would come. At last it seemed I would get to Timbuktu and indeed in no time we were there. But at the airport there was a line of twenty-two would-be passengers waiting to leave. Only two vacant seats were available; the other twenty would have to wait for a week or a month before flying out. I figured I'd done my share of waiting and I was eager to see as much of Mali as possible before going to Senegal and then home. The end of my wonderful trip was approaching. I skipped a visit to Timbuktu but at least I had had my feet in its airport.

Brian and I stayed together for another ten days in Mali and went to the Dogon country. From there he flew back home to western Australia where he is a teacher. He travels extensively on vacations and communicates with me from all parts of the world. These strands give me enormous pleasure, changing a trip from being an isolated experience to being an integrating one, linking the various threads of my life's cat's cradle.

18 : LIGHT COMING THROUGH

"In the night of the womb, the spirit quickens into flesh"
— *Black Elk*

In 1978, at a Cambridge dinner party which I did not attend, a woman whom I had known for a long time but not intimately said, "A film should be made about Maud." That was her initial and final involvement in the project. Various people took the idea on from there, picking it up and letting it drop. Its future seemed improbable. However I spoke to Rickie Leacock, then director of the Film Department at MIT, whom I knew as a dancing partner, about the possibility. He had an unexpected opening in his schedule and was willing to take on the project. As producer he brought Nancy Raine into the picture, a woman newly come to Cambridge from The National Endowment for the Arts in Washington, where she had been working for many years with films, although she had never made one. Little by little we raised the money, by donation and by an auction of my work. It took two years, beneficial years, for the film to ripen into its present form. It's like an impressionist collage. Except for one comment by Rickie, mine is the only voice. The paintings are shown in silence. One sequence particularly delighted Rickie. He photographed me looking into a mirror, seeing me, painting a portrait of myself. All told you see at one time: the real me, the reflection of the real me looking at the painting of me, painting a portrait of myself.

Nancy based the whole structure of the film on a French Canadian fable of a fisherman, who one night when he went to the fishery to collect his catch, found a gorgeous mermaid with long flowing blonde hair swimming among the fish. Immediately he fell in love with her, and neglecting the catch, took her in his arms and carried her up to his bachelor cottage. There he opened his wedding chest and took from it the unused linen sheet spun and woven for him by his mother, put it on the bed and rested the mermaid upon it. All night long he sat by the bed gazing at her in adoration. In the morning when he went to take her in his arms again she was dead. He hadn't understood that she could not live out of the water. Nancy showed unusual imagination and courage in using this story as an unstated parallel to me and my life in art. It proved to be surprisingly successful. The film premiered at the Boston Museum of Fine Arts on October 19, 1980, with a gala Bloody Mary opening and a Sunday Brunch, and was shown later at the Museum of Modern Art in New York and Place Pompidou in Paris. Its title, "Light Coming Through", was chosen by Neva Goodwin, who was helpful throughout.

I went with the film crew down to Southold, Long Island where Betty Parsons lived in her beautiful studio designed by Tony Smith. As she had been my dealer for such a long time, we wanted her to be included in the film. Betty's feelings about my film were complicated. Earlier Ruth Stephen, a poet and editor of the short-lived but distinguished art magazine "The Tiger's Eye", had begun a film about Betty but tragically had ended her own life before the film was finished. Various books had been proposed about Betty, but none of these efforts came to fruition during her lifetime. There were many excellent articles but no books or films at that time. Fortunately Lee Hall, one time director of the Rhode Island School of Design, has now produced a beautiful book. After our trip to Southold, whenever the subject of my film would come up in conversation, Betty would say, "What film?" I'm glad to say that when she saw the final version, she was delighted, saying, "There wasn't a banal moment in the whole thing." Because of the fact that the film did not pin me down as any particular kind of woman, it helped me develop an objective view of my own life.

My earlier relationship with Betty grew more complicated because of my own emotional imbalance. I had become overly critical of my work due to Pat's antagonism to it. When I saw my 1952 show hanging in the two rooms of Betty's Fifty-Seventh Street gallery, it looked like the work of two different painters, all rage in violently-colored angularity in one room, all tender in soft, modulated, rounded shapes in the other. I witnessed that I was "split down the middle." I told Betty that I could not have another show until I had brought these two disparate parts of

Dipody (1952), Rubber base paint and oil on burlap, 48 x 37 in.

myself together. She agreed and said she would show me again at that time. She kept me waiting for twenty years. I know now that there was at least one exceptional piece in that 1952 show called "Dipody" and there may have been others. But I was too insecure to be a good judge, and Betty offered no opinion.

I now recognize "Dipody" (48" x 37", 1952) as one of my best pictures. It came directly from a dream which I then sketched during a faculty meeting. The final execution was rapid; it almost painted itself. Uncompromisingly split down the middle, the two different ground colors established the difference between two kinds of time: the tick and the tock of daily living versus the long distance time of infinity. Infinity is expressed on the right side of the painting by a dark green door-like shape with three small rectangles of bright Persian blue within it, like windows to the beyond. On the left side a large heavy pendulum-like black and white form appears to move back and forth in its narrow, featureless, earth-colored space. The strong vertical color separation between the two sides heightens the question that the work asks of the viewer, and adds rather than detracts from its impact.

Had I remained with the Betty Parsons Gallery, enjoying the vital input which that association added to my work, I might have been able to continue to incorporate my "split down the middle" direction as a positive asset, the way I did in "Dipody" and in many of the self-portraits which followed where it became a plus rather than a minus, but I withdrew because of my own insecurity. Betty recalled "Dipody" for her group show celebrating the tenth year of the gallery. I felt proud as I saw it hanging with Rothko, Pollack and others, feeling it carried its own weight. Edward Albee, who bought the painting, told me later that "Dipody" is one of the best liked works in his outstanding collection. That withdrawal caused a significant break in my career, separating me from the Parsons Gallery where I had been one of the early members of the group. By the time Betty took me back into her gallery, that group, by then referred to as "the Irascibles", had become giants of world-wide fame, who for the most part had moved on to diverse, larger, and more financially desirable galleries. Their work swept the world due to its very American expansiveness and freedom. Each piece of work was its own inherent subject rather than a work about a subject.

Betty and I remained good friends but the relationship was not easy. I would stay with her in New York in her beautiful apartment overlooking Central Park and the Natural History Museum, but my work was never mentioned. When I began making collages out of Japanese mulberry paper, Betty became interested again and gave me a show in her little gallery in 1977. I showed with her again in the main gallery in 1980 and again in 1982, after my divorce and my trip to Africa. "It's a very beautiful show," she said of the last one. "You have finally pulled it all together. Congratulations." I was extremely pleased and again felt the value of my divorce. 1980 was, I think, the most fulfilled year of my life so far, encompassing the finalizing of my divorce, my long trip to Africa, the debut of my film, and my reentry into the Betty Parsons Gallery.

I admired Betty greatly. She was a tough, great lady. I believe that mine was the last show at her gallery in her lifetime. At her death John Russell, the New York Times art critic, wrote, "It's as if a favorite compass had lost its needle and would never be put together again." Betty was a rare person, a child of nature, yet someone of great sophistication, a poet and a passionate flame. She was the mistress of apt phrases. "There is no truth beyond magic." and "The world stinks but life is marvelous." I hope her poems and phrases will be collected and printed. Her mind was like a butterfly moving incredibly fast, lighting down briefly on a specific point, then off again to another. "What the caterpillar calls the end of the world, the center calls the butterfly."

After Southold we decided that we should film in the Province of Quebec to capture parts of my childhood background. Rickie Leacock, Nancy Raine, Greg Baden, an MIT student of Rickie's, and I went up to La Malbaie. Rickie got a good sequence of me climbing on the roof of the chapel being stung by a swarm of bees. Greg shot a beautiful waterfall scene with me under it, along with many other pleasant sequences. For the fishing shots we all went to Lac Gravel, where surprisingly, Rickie, man of the world, went trout fishing for the first time on his sixtieth birthday. After fishing we came back to the cabin, eager for a shot of whisky before the supper of trout we had just caught. Unpacking our gear, I found that the whisky, which I had wrapped in a bath towel, had broken on the trip to the lake – a disaster! There was just a little left in the bottle so Rickie and I set ourselves assiduously to the task of attempting to squeeze enough whisky out of the bath towel for each of us to have a drink, while Nancy laughed at our efforts. I was glad that he could photograph Lac Gravel since it's been part of my life, yearly, since early childhood.

My grandfather built the first cabin there, probably around 1907. It was one of the many good fishing lakes on the Seigniory property. Much later the cabin burned down, was rebuilt, again burned and again was rebuilt. Every year we go to this lake as a family, with friends or alone, in spring, summer, fall or in winter when it's iced over. The lake is more precious now, since the Quebec government no longer allows private ownership of lakes. However, our deed on Lac Gravel went back far enough to make ownership legal. When I'm there I still wear my mother's "new" leather jacket from Abercrombie & Fitch, lined in red flannel, from 1922. Her old leather jacket, from 1906, burned up in the last cabin fire. I fish with the rod given to me when I was ten, my "grown-up" rod, still in perfect condition. This beautiful, two-mile lake dwarfs time. When I am there, decades become confused. I almost feel the way I did in 1913.

At the time I was there with the filming crew, I had no idea that Nancy was giving so much importance in the film to the motif of fishing and the life-giving qualities of water. Once the film got underway I never asked about it nor saw the rushes. I was sure they would do a better job with me absent. In fact I was stunned on my first viewing, and questioned if the mermaid tale would confuse viewers. To my knowledge no one has ever been bothered by it. Rather, people have instinctively, if not factually, understood the parallel. The film, which I call a documentary without documents, has had a small but enduring success. Fortunately it seems to have a lasting quality that causes one to recall it after viewing and to make connections between my life, the mermaid's life and the life of art, connections which I'm sure were well thought through when Nancy was creating it. All the risks she took, which were many, had worked out just as she had hoped.

Seven years later, when my Cambridge studio of twenty-five years in the Notre Dame de la Pitié school building was threatened by condominiums, I felt almost as though I were in fact the mermaid taken out of water. I felt I had been deprived of my element and that death was near. All the other artists who had been in the building left. I stayed on, hoping I would still be able to keep my space after reconstruction. Finally I had to give in. The empty, cold building was becoming a shell, its entrails gone. Only shaky stairs were left, with no walls or handrails going up to the third floor. In the final pull-out I felt demented, as though I were cutting my own umbilical cord. I became hysterical at the whole process, throwing out the window into the dumpster below perfectly useable chairs, tables, and shelves that I knew I would need if I were ever to work again. Packages of large prints, too heavy to lift, were dragged across the floor and went out the window along with the racks that held them. I no longer knew what my values were, or if I had any. At this point David Murphy came on to the scene, telling me firmly that I must not destroy any more prints, that he had always liked them and that for the time being he would take them off my hands. What a Godsend! He came with a helper and soon all the prints and all their metal cabinets left the premises, leaving me only the business aspect of the project to deal with which, proved far more complicated and involuted than I could have imagined, and in which now, after eight years, I am still unpleasantly involved.

David took the prints back to his shop. He and I scarcely mentioned them again. They moved out of my thoughts, and with them the studio they had occupied. But all the while David was having one of his associates make an accurate catalogue, recording edition numbers, sizes, etc., and one day he surprised me by saying he was going to have a small show of them. I was not optimistic. For me they were still associated with the nightmarish exit from the studio. On Sunday June 2, 1991, I walked into David's gallery and stopped dead at the entry. I felt I had been swept by a strong wave of refreshing air. All the prints were newly framed. Space surrounded each. Where earlier the frames had suffocated the image, now they breathed differently. I was startled by their impact of vitality, variety, and youthfulness. I was truly thrilled and unbelieving. This little show gave me more professional gratification than any I have ever had, except in the very large shows. It was a glorious affirmation made possible by David's foresight and belief in my work, which was reinforced by an inclusion of one of them in the Museum of Modern Art in New York. What an outcome to a disaster! After the show I came home and lay in the hammock in my little garden, singing, full of gratitude and wondering how I could be so happy.

This show helped me regain some confidence so that I could listen to Vicky's wise advice to look for another studio. With her support I found one where, to my surprise I was able to make collages all that following summer.

~

Slowly as I became accustomed to living with the weight of the real estate nightmare, anger began to replace shame and pushed me to paint again. I decided to attempt to put onto canvas some of the discouraged feelings that had overpowered my life in the lawsuit. The first painting is called "The Ides of March", because it was on the 15th of March that I discovered the extent of my financial embroilment. What I am doing now is unlike what I have done before. The shapes are more definite, the hues denser. On a 42" by 30" canvas I placed in the lower center an image of a stone, a large, rounded, dark magenta-red stone, lying on green grass along with many other stones, one assertive, large, white one and some brown and grey ones. I am that red stone, whose heart has been pierced to allow its blood to flow, spreading through its interior until it pervades and colors its entire outer surface. From the top of the painting come four vivid attacking yellow streaks, a vermilion one, piercing the stone's surface and a black one, powerful and avenging, each streak with its own sharp, vigorous motion and intent to hurt. So far the entire painting is distinctively targeted at the red stone. But in the central right background there came a soft grey, against which five other grey stones are piled, one on top of the other in precarious balance; they may fall but they belong with each other, if one falls they will all go. There is allegiance in this corner. After painting this section I saw that harmony had come into the edge of that turbulent canvas without my knowing it. There was an emotional oasis that I hadn't been conscious of creating. I was surprised, intrigued and excited, eager to get to the next painting to find out what would happen, and conscious that I had embarked on a 'series'. They would all be 42" x 30". They would all spring from the same original emotion, which I would watch working itself out through them. Now I see that the eighth, which I have just finished, will be the last. The distress is ameliorated and this last one, which suggests a balancing act is no longer aggressive, but rather states a "wait-and-see" attitude.

The colors are becoming lighter. The heavy, dark brick-red of the first paintings is replaced by pink in the last picture. The sharp points of pain are turning into circular forms. Again I realize I am painting out my anguish. I feel secure as I work, excited but calm, not knowing what will come next, but not questioning it. At last I have been put back into my element and am sure now I will not have to die like the mermaid.

I thought it was the first time I had painted a "series", but it had happened before, as I found in a review of my first print show at Retina Gallery in Cambridge. Eleanor Kanegis, its director, wrote, "She is a superb and highly intuitive colorist. The shapes that she creates are formed more from an inner order, a feeling of being one with the universe, rather than an intellectual planning of form in space. This approach to the making of art does not always result in each work being an isolated, finished creation. Her art is rather to be viewed and felt in a 'series' of works. This is why in her life she has a need to exhibit often to share with all of us each 'series' of experiences in the visual world she creates."

In February 1993, Jock Reynolds, director of the Addison Gallery of American Art at Andover, Massachusetts, came to my studio to look at these recent paintings. His idea started with a birthday party for March 1, but soon expanded to include an exhibition held at the Addison Gallery. It was to be a small show of only nine paintings, all oils, seven of them from the recent series of abstracts, each 42" x 30". The eighth was a very large representational painting of dismembered stone walls against a dramatic tempestuous sky started six months before the Berlin Wall fell. The ninth painting was a small head, a 14" x 25" profile self-portrait seen through driving snow called "Facing the

Storm". It seemed like an ungainly group but Jock Reynolds knew exactly the space into which each painting would fit to enhance the whole. The work was all painted during my eighty-ninth year except "Walls", which was made the year before.

When I walked into that room I caught my breath, overpowered by the blast of vital energy that swept over me, while at the same time I had a feeling of absolute security in my work that I had never had before. I realized that this was the smallest and the most powerful show of my life. That room of paintings represented a distillation of my very core and I was profoundly grateful at having been given the perseverance and energy to have produced it. Two hundred people were invited to the birthday party. Four hundred came.

Four months after the Andover exhibition another show took place at Barbara Singer's gallery in Cambridge. It was a surprise show, even to me. In January 1994 I had started working in collaboration with Michael Silver, a photographer. We knew each other through John Cage and after his death were drawn together by his memory. I knew nothing about photography, and Michael knew little about painting or collage at which I had been working for twenty years. We both thought of these conditions as advantages. I was ninety-one and Michael forty-six. We thought of that as an advantage too. We decided to call our collaborative work "Transpositions" and to work together in his studio every Monday all day because that was the day he had off from his job. I feared that the work would be too much for me physically, as for two years now I have been on a very powerful medicine which saps my energy, but along with the evolution of our technique came a solution to the health problem. Whenever Michael was performing some strictly photographic work which might take twenty or thirty minutes, I would lie down for a quick nap. This way we managed so that the totally unforced merging of our two psyches fitted with the capabilities of our physiques. Things fell into place with astonishing ease and we made rapid progress. Since our aesthetic approaches harmonized, little time was wasted and soon we were amassing a large number of prints on each of which we had both worked without differentiation as to who did one and who did the other. Each print was unique because we had worked over it until it pleased us both which often meant multiple procedures. We wanted a show. Barbara saw the work, was excited by it, and offered to give us one.

In the stalemate condition of the current art scene, this extremely successful exhibition was a joy. The opening reception buzzed with the curiosity of people questioning how the work had been made, what the images said and how such variety could have come from the wedding of our disparate skills. Only an expert could identify the role that photography had played.

The show had the unmistakable aura of a miracle, of a harbinger for further creativity that has already spawned two more exhibitions for me in the next three months, something that at ninety-two I could not have imagined in my wildest dreams. The first will be at the Art Complex Museum in Duxbury, Massachusetts, organized by Wendy Kaplan, titled "Maud in the Nineties," showing only work made in or after my ninetieth year. The second will be at the Boston Public Library in Copley Square, organized by Sinclair Hitchings, who will show work of mine in several different mediums and periods from 1929 to 1995, work he has privately collected over many years.

There is a gratifying feeling of rightness to all of this, as though it were a blueprint explaining to me why I am having such an extended life. It's a gratification which has been with me from the beginning of writing this book when Lex volunteered to transcribe my work from the handwritten to the printed page. This has rounded things out for me and made writing a less solitary occupation. I like the fact that he is seeing my life as I saw it, as it comes up on the screen of his Macintosh. Only rarely has he expressed an opinion and then more in reference as to how a thing was expressed rather than what was said. Each time I have agreed. To open up your life to your children and to the world brings a strange impersonality. There are no secrets left but there is a gratifying pattern of completion. Despite the roller-coaster of my existence, my children have always shown me patient generosity and together through the years we three have forged a relationship solid enough to live by. My admiration, gratitude, and love for each of them is beyond bounds.

Here I have tried to show the juggling of one woman's attempt at balancing a life of wife/mother/artist as well as sharing the old-age happiness I am presently experiencing in the hopes that it will be catching. Now I end this story of a life like any other, both fragile and tough; the fragility evident from the start, the toughness formed en route. Thanks to the toughness I am still here, writing down my life's experience, which though often painful, has given me a purpose for the last seven years as well as insight.

It becomes clear that the writing resembles my trip to Africa. In both pursuits I entered a new continent where different means of communication were needed. Each essentially started from a place of indecisiveness and was propelled by an adverse experience. In Africa my little black book of names and travel plans, my Baedeker, was stolen at the start; in Cambridge recurring falls on my walks around Fresh Pond forced me to question what I was doing wrong with my life. Each bore the same label: "sink or swim." As an unknown Greek said, "I had perished had I not perished."

Age is a time of passion that fills the gaps emptied by aloneness, gaps from which I have suffered very little, perhaps because from infancy aloneness has been my norm. As Marcus Aurelius wrote, "The greater the individual, the greater the loneness until the point is reached where though the loneness continues, the individual becomes part of the universal revelation." Being old is almost a full-time occupation. There are many small things to bother with, each demanding time. One becomes niggardly, parceling out the use of one's active hours. I usually don't seek or want interruption, but when it comes I enjoy it to the full and try to cope with being overtired when I am alone again. There is so much more to learn now in the time left because in some ways the scope is more demanding, the assumptions more sweeping. Events or persons that I had not acknowledged earlier to be of particular significance now stand out in sharp relief, explaining many things which reshaped my life or put it back in order.

I'm kinder to myself too, less critical of the good or bad things that occur in the present or past. Maybe later I will start to worry about death and dying, but I haven't quite finished living enough yet to forfeit my spare time to apprehension. As Isaak Dineson said of herself, "I am a messenger who has been sent on a long journey to declare that there is hope in the world."

It's summer now, loveable, warm summer. I'm sitting here quietly writing, enjoying my old age, on what I call my porch. The porch is a roofed-over, widened front door step, 5' by 5', 15" off the ground. On it I've put an old wicker armchair that I picked up on the sidewalk on trash collection day. Once pretty, the chair is now crippled with age. Pieces of rattan, defiantly and slightly dangerously stick out here and there.

I'm closely surrounded by greenery and flowering geraniums. Through the many telephone and electrical wires I can see just a small piece of sky. The trunk of a large maple tree opposite the end of my little walkway partially protects me from passing cars. I do not ask how many more summers I will have like this. I am serenely happy. This is my favorite summer resort. This tiny house of mine, which presents a storage problem when I buy a new pair of shoes, as there is no place to put them when they're not on my feet, is home. I can say unequivocally I am here, something Georges Braque claims few people can do, since they are too busy seeking themselves in the past and seeing themselves in the future. I can picture my unusually beautiful, remote place in Canada with space enough to accommodate the contents of several shoe stores, its garden, its studio, its lake and the whole panoply of the sky without a single telephone wire. What is luxury, anyway? For me it is to be able to work at what I enjoy working at, when and where I enjoy doing it. "Nirvana is the capacity to be free moment by moment." It is easier to reach this when you're older, easier to live in the present then. No need to think much about the future. It's too short to bother with, and about the past you can think any way you want, since most people who might check up on you have died. So why not give yourself up to the here and now? Genesis eternal.

Maud Morgan photographed in 1986 with 1976 self portrait.

This book talks about a long life starting in rural Quebec, moving through growing up in New York and proceeding to Paris in the Twenties, where friendships with James Joyce and Ernest Hemingway led to Florida fishing with the latter. After marriage to Patrick Morgan our life moved to Phillips Academy in Andover, Massachusetts where we were surrounded by a remarkable group of students including Frank Stella, Carl Andre and Jack Lemmon. As a single woman in the late fifties, I settled in Cambridge where I became actively involved in the early organization of the Boston Visual Artists Union. I am still living and working in Cambridge where I have two exhibitions scheduled for 1995. One of which will show only work done in my nineties.